Crisis as Catalyst

Crisis as Catalyst

Equity-Oriented School Leadership During Difficult Times

PATRICIA M. VIRELLA

HARVARD EDUCATION PRESS
CAMBRIDGE, MASSACHUSETTS

Paperback ISBN 9781682539736

Library of Congress Cataloging-in-Publication Data is on file.

Published by Harvard Education Press
an imprint of the Harvard Education Publishing Group

Harvard Education Press
8 Story Street
Cambridge, MA 02138

Cover Design: Endpaper Studio
Cover Image: Adrian Olichon via Unsplash

The typefaces in this book are Sabon LT Std and Myriad Pro.

Dedicated to

Hudson and Liv

My naïve, but interested, reader and champion, Derrick

Contents

Foreword

APRIL 20, 2020

Think about where you were on this day. If you recall, it probably felt like the world was frozen in time. We were experiencing a global shutdown due to COVID-19, and personally, I was busy watching the news for my daily updates wondering if the world would ever open up again. Like many other educators, I was also scrambling to put my classes online, figure out how I was going to fulfill my faculty responsibilities, and converting my living room into a childcare center for my eighteen-month-old. However, five years ago at 12:59 p.m., I received an email from Patricia Virella, who was then a doctoral candidate at the University of Connecticut, requesting support to help her generate momentum for her dissertation process.

I was certainly surprised to receive this email. Given that all of us were in the middle of navigating the crisis and reckoning with an uncertain future, I figured no one had any time to consider writing a dissertation. But as soon as we had our meeting, I knew something was different about Dr. Virella. She was determined to use this moment to finish her dissertation, which was a multiarticle project examining the impact of *Ley de Reforma Educativa de Puerto Rico*, an education reform policy legislated in Puerto Rico in 2018.

Over the next year, I was able to witness Dr. Virella transform from student to scholar. We had many discussions about her research agenda, misunderstandings scholars had about Puerto Rico, and how she dreamed of making an impact in schools from her research and not just letting it sit on a shelf. She not only was able to finish her dissertation quickly but also, to my amazement, did it while simultaneously raising two school-age children and developing several side research projects, which would eventually serve as the building blocks for this book. During our initial conversations, Dr. Virella described passionately her interest in studying equity and crisis in schools; however, she learned from her initial work that something was missing. While existing scholarship focused on crises and how leaders responded to them, Dr. Virella quickly saw that how leaders leveraged (or did not leverage) crises to enact equity was missing from that conversation. That gap in the literature is what has positioned *Crisis as Catalyst* as a groundbreaking text in the field of educational leadership.

I recall a conversation we had during the inception of the equity-oriented crisis leadership framework that guides this book. Dr. Virella came to me excited about a revelation she had with her framework. She said to me, "Bro, I got it figured out. The leaders I am studying who are dealing with crisis use hope as a guiding principle." I had no response when she shared this insight. All I could do was nod in agreement at my webcam. Yet, my mind was racing with ideas, and some of my previous thoughts about crisis changed completely after that conversation.

I was amazed at that revelation because before working with Dr. Virella, my initial framing of crisis was that a leader would, of course, prioritize addressing and solving a crisis. I had not considered that they would address a crisis by using hope to frame their decision-making. Now knowing Dr. Virella, however, it makes complete sense that she would address her research from a sense of hope. Even through her own experiences as a doctoral student working on her dissertation at the onset of COVID-19, hope guided her decisions to reach out to me, as she saw opportunity to finish her doctoral program even in the face of crisis.

As Dr. Virella demonstrates masterfully through case studies in each chapter of this book, crises come in all shapes and sizes. The mark of a great leader is not just responding to a crisis, but doing so in an equitable manner so that all constituents in an organization are served through their decision-making. Furthermore, Dr. Virella shows how equity-oriented leadership is not solely a disposition but also a skill that can be developed. This book provides the blueprint to develop that skill set.

Given how accessibly this book is written, it will be helpful to educational leadership programs and in K–12 school district leadership, as crises will continue to happen and morph. This book provides tangible strategies for school leaders to implement into their practice so that they can develop the equity-oriented skill set to help their communities survive as well as thrive through crisis. Like the foundational principle of Dr. Virella's equity-oriented framework, I am hopeful that this book will serve as a catalyst for the development of leaders who lead through crises with care and ensure that all students, and especially students who have been historically marginalized in schools, are supported.

Ramon B. Goings
Associate Professor, Language Literature and Culture
University of Maryland, Baltimore County
Founder, Done Dissertation

> When written in Chinese, the word crisis is composed of two characters—one represents danger, and the other represents opportunity.
>
> —John F. Kennedy[1]

I watched as the young girl ran off camera and down the street, beyond the gaze of the lens. My first week as a new principal started in a state of crisis. Even though I had planned every minute with my leadership team, we appeared to lose one third-grade girl who seemingly ran off after her mom, except that her mom had never left the school building. She was still waiting for her second child, a kindergartner. As we reviewed the cameras and saw her book bag adorned with the latest trendy cartoon run up the busy street, I felt anxiety rise in my chest. I sprang into action, immediately calling the police and then my superintendent.

"Brief me," she stated bluntly.

"Dominique ran up the street, and no one could find her. Her mom was talking to a parent in the school but lost contact with Dominique. Police are here; teachers are walking to her home a few blocks away. Mom is a mess, so I am with her."

Thirty minutes later, the police found Dominique at her home with her stepfather. She explained, "I thought I saw my mom, so I ran after her, but then I realized it wasn't her, so I just went home." The simple answer made sense, yet this was one of the most terrifying experiences I had had as a school leader, and I was only one week into my new job. Once I relayed this message to her mom, she scooped up her kindergartener and headed home, thanking us for our "efficient" and "caring" response.

"I'm just glad she's safe," I said, and then I walked upstairs to my office where my adrenaline dropped and I began to cry.

As a mother, I could not imagine how overwhelming it would feel if my child was lost and there were no leads or ideas about where to find her. As a school leader, I shook. Questions raced through my mind like a buzzsaw cutting through all the skills I thought I had and replacing them with fear and anxiety: Is this the job that I just accepted? Is this type of crisis typical? How do I prevent this from happening again? Was I going to get fired?

Despite feeling guilty because I had put this mother in a terrible position as well as feelings of inadequacy from failing to remind the teachers to keep students with them until the parents were physically present, I also recognized that crises do happen. They happen every day in many unexpected ways.

OUR CURRENT STATE OF POLYCRISIS

In 2016, life felt easier to some degree. Inflation was not as high as it was in 2023.[2] There were only six mass shootings in the year as opposed to seven in the first six months of 2023 alone.[3] The World Meteorological Association explained that the increase in climate change–related disasters would only be exacerbated.[4] Scholars and leaders around the globe agree that we are in an unprecedented state of crisis that has affected various aspects of life, including education and the global economy.[5] *Polycrisis* is a term recently coined by several organizations to describe the simultaneous occurrence of several catastrophic events.[6] In a webinar by UNICEF, a global outlook of polycrises was defined because of the war in Ukraine, the COVID-19 pandemic, inflation, and supply chain issues that have affected worldwide energy and food grain deliveries.[7] The multiple global systems entangled in these ways have significantly degraded humanity's prospects of surviving and thriving. The concept of polycrisis refers to a state in which multiple crises intertwine, as their causes and processes are inextricably bound together to create compounded effects.[8]

In 2022, because of our polycrisis state, several organizations released reports that shed light on the long-term impacts of these crises. The World Economic Forum reported how the COVID-19 pandemic has had an extensive collateral health impact, in part because other diseases were deprioritized.[9] Similarly, in 2022, the United Nations' *Global Humanitarian Overview* reported that the ongoing COVID-19 pandemic and other health crises, natural disasters, and severe resource shortages have had significant impacts on humanitarian needs worldwide.[10] Both reports highlighted that the pandemic, coinciding political strife, and other emergencies have led to a synchronized and multidimensional crisis, demonstrating the need for comprehensive crisis management plans to adapt to evolving situations.

The COVID-19 pandemic has been one of the most significant contributors to the current state of polycrisis. The pandemic not only has caused health and economic upsets but also has disrupted education systems around the world. Education has often been defined as the primary method of increasing human capital, developing an understanding of cultures, and working together as a global society.[11] During a crisis, however, education is often disrupted, leading to a drastic decline in student performance compared with peers across grade levels and around the globe.

Attacks on racially minoritized groups, such as the murders of Black Americans by police officers (often with little recourse), Asian hate spurred by the COVID-19 pandemic,[12] Islamophobia from migration patterns, and anti-Semitism have all been on the rise, undermining the democratic value of schooling. Additionally, the uptick in hate speech and crimes was examined by the European Parliament's Policy Department for Citizens Rights and Constitutional Affairs. Their 2022 report discussed how hate crimes and speech threaten individual dignity and equity and reinforce tension among social groups.[13] The report also acknowledged the lack of adequate means of prevention and response to hate speech and crimes.[14] It is evident that these attacks have significant real-world consequences and require urgent attention and action to ensure the safety and well-being of all individuals and communities.

A recent report published by the National Association of Educational Progress (NAEP) demonstrated how US students perform nationally and globally compared with peers, revealing a drastic decline since the beginning of the COVID-19 pandemic.[15] The Malala Fund found that girls are often the most affected demographic during a crisis, and many do not reach graduation or ever go back to complete their education.[16] According to the Brookings Institute, only 21 percent of teachers in the United States taught a full year's curriculum during the pandemic.[17] Additionally, schools were forced to shut down, and many students were not able to access quality education because of a lack of resources, such as computers and internet connectivity. In addition, the pandemic disproportionately affected marginalized groups, such as girls, students with disabilities, and students from low-income households. As a result, a growing concern is that the pandemic is widening existing educational inequalities and leading to a lost generation of students. To address this issue, it is essential to prioritize education during crises and ensure that all students receive access to quality education. The research and reports cited here demonstrate the fact that the crises we are facing are inextricably intertwined, creating a set of consequences in which individual impacts compound to threaten the environmental and social systems that support our modern civilization.[18] In addition, it is crucial to address the underlying issues that contribute to polycrises, including conflicts, inequalities, and climate change. In so doing, we can create a more resilient and equitable world in which all students have the opportunity to reach their full potential.

(C)risis Versus (c)risis

Between 2019 and 2023, I interviewed fifty principals from across the continental United States and Puerto Rico about crises they experienced as school leaders. Interviews lasted approximately an hour and often referred to crises other than COVID-19, as selected by the principal. The principals ranged in age, experience, ethnicity, race, religion, school level, and school type.

During my interviews, I noticed some distinct characteristics. The principals did not delineate crisis type. All crises were considered to be a priority by the principals, irrespective of whether they lasted three days or three months. To them, a crisis was simply a crisis. How the context of these crises exposed inequities across their schools depended on the individual leaders' strengths, weaknesses, and abilities. School leaders tend to categorize crises such as natural disasters and the COVID-19 pandemic as cataclysmic events from which we cannot imagine recovering—even when we do. The school leaders I interviewed, however, explained that crises affected them differently, depending on the crisis not on its magnitude. In one situation, a principal shared that watching one of her students attempt suicide as her team rushed to assist was the hardest situation she has had to face. Another principal explained that a teacher calling a class of children the N-word was the most challenging crisis, even more so than the longevity and devastating effects of COVID-19.[19] In contrast, several principals described crises as potentially good events to propel equity. For example, Leena shared,

> I agree that crises are certainly something that brings a lot of emotion first and then thought second, if you're not careful. It's definitely an opportunity for growth. We have a lot of good things come out of crisis that we probably wouldn't have gotten to without it. It reminds me to trust my gut a little bit. It's not a business plan. There's no handbook. There's nobody you could call and say, "Hey." Crisis doesn't necessarily have to mean something bad. It can be a crisis that had a lot of good outcomes, too. There are other types of crises in the world that probably are good crisis. That make us as principals think about the possibility of starting anew.

The work on trauma supports the idea that a crisis is a crisis, regardless of its type.[20] Note, however, that different crises can affect individuals and communities differently. For example, the COVID-19 pandemic has exacerbated the mental health crisis among school-age youth, accelerating the need to provide school mental health support on an even larger scale to meet the needs of our nation's youth. Effective leadership during a crisis requires a range of skills and competencies.[21] Leaders must communicate effectively, make decisions under pressure, and manage their own as well as others' emotions. Leaders must also be able to identify and address inequities that are exacerbated by the crisis.[22]

THE NECESSITY OF EQUITY DURING A CRISIS

Equity becomes a fundamental need in a crisis, not just a desire to respond and recover. Considerations about how different groups of people are affected by a crisis should be made according to the characteristics of their context. For example, in the aftermath of Hurricane Katrina, low-income and minoritized communities were disproportionately affected by the disaster because of the lack of resources and access. According to a 2010 study by the National Commission, *Deep Water: The Gulf Oil Disaster and the Future of Offshore Drilling*, the oil spill disproportionately affected low-income and minoritized communities who relied on fishing and tourism for their livelihoods.[23] As a result of this disproportionate impact on these communities, we must bring an equity perspective to support those who are affected by a crisis.

Because of their role, school leaders are positioned to ensure that equity occurs on various levels. For example, current demographic trends have shown an influx in migrant and immigrant patterns[24] The number of international migrants grew to 281 million in 2020, meaning that 3.6 percent of the world's people lived outside their country of birth that year. In the United States, the foreign-born population remained largely flat between 2019 and 2021, with an increase of 337,000 people, or growth of less than 1 percent.[25] The US foreign-born population reached a record 44.8 million in 2018, and as of 2024, immigrants account for 13.7 percent of the US population, nearly triple the share (4.8 percent) in 1970. Assuming current trends continue, the Pew Research Center projects that immigrants and their descendants will account for 88 percent of US population growth through 2065. Immigrants have moved beyond traditional gateway states, and the foreign-born population has extended into other areas of the United States, notably the Southeast and the Pacific Northwest.[26]

Demographic trends have a significant impact on schools, affecting student population, resources, and educational services. Demographic trends can lead to changes in the student population, such as increased students from immigrant or low-income families. The shifting diversity of the student body requires schools to adapt to the specific needs of these students. Demographic trends can also affect the allocation of school resources. For example, schools with a high percentage of low-income students may require more funding to provide additional support services, such as tutoring or counseling. Also, shifting demographic trends can have an impact on the diversity of the teachers. As the student population becomes more diverse, teachers are needed who can relate to and understand their students' cultural backgrounds. Finally, current demographic trends can also influence the school curriculum.

In a school district with a high population of English language learners (ELLs), it is essential to provide these students with resources and support to ensure equal access to education. This could include hiring bilingual teachers, providing translation services, and offering afterschool tutoring for ELLs.

The Shifting Demographics of Our World

Our communities are changing, forcing schools to take stock of how they communicate with the new populations they are meeting. A school leader in northwest Iowa explained, "I'm in a district where probably 25 to 30 percent of our population is Hispanic, and we're seeing a big increase of Micronesia and families. We had a Sudanese population move in before working in the factories we have in our town." Some school leaders take the time to learn about their new student populations, but how leaders communicate is often left out of conversations. For example, Latinos in the United States primarily receive news through the internet.[27] In 2016, the Pew Research Center found that 74 percent of Latinos said that on a typical weekday they used social media or smartphone apps as a news source—a 37 percent increase from 2006. Yet, Latino newspapers neglect political, socioeconomic, and policy information that could contextualize critical issues to empower Latinos to act as informed citizens.[28] Many school leaders may think simply translating communication to Spanish is a way of being inclusive; in a crisis, however, school leaders should use this knowledge of how Latinos obtain news to move their communication to social media or a smartphone app.

Demographic changes and mass migration patterns around the globe require new ways of considering how we communicate during a crisis with inclusivity in mind. Communicating messages through either a robocall or flyers, for example, is more effective than not communicating at all. Both methods have advantages and can be used to reach a broad audience.

Robocalls deliver a spoken message directly to the recipient, while flyers provide a tangible and visual representation of that message. Ultimately, the choice between these two methods depends on the specific content of the message and the target audience. Moreover, it is critical to note that different demographics obtain their information from other sources as well. How leaders negotiate these differences is essential when communicating during a crisis.

During the COVID-19 pandemic, the sudden shutdown of schools astonished everyone. While sitting at dinner with two friends in January 2020 and talking about this mysterious virus called COVID-19, I exclaimed that I hoped it would not come to the United States. I naïvely wondered how devastating it could be. Two months later, during winter break, I was on a call with my department discussing COVID-19 and how it "might" shut down our program and neighboring schools. I will never forget when my colleagues said, "We can make it to Spring Break, and then we will decide if we go remote."

Two weeks later, we were ordered to shut down. Life in the United States had come to a standstill. Initially, communication was a daily data dashboard of deaths, infections, and hospitalizations. As doctors described the virus and expressed feeling overwhelmed, teachers taught remotely. Immediately, schools were expected to cobble together some learning for students. When funds were released, there was a mad dash to purchase Chromebooks, hotspots, and digital platforms, such as Google Classroom. Despite this unprecedented situation, schools were managing. The crisis, however, was already beginning to exacerbate the inequitable toll on marginalized school populations. Archie, a principal from the west coast, shared:

> Before the pandemic, we would host parent coffee meetings to help make sure parents were communicated with daily, understood what an initiative was, or how we supported their kids so they could provide help at home if needed. However, it became about branching out in different ways to connect with families and trying to help ensure we engaged families where they were and provided them with information regarding what they needed. We also thought about our families who could not connect during the day because they were essential workers. But also, those families that need technology and access to the internet. I can't even tell you how many hotspots we bought, and we [paid] the rental for all families. I had to connect with these families differently. I remember spending an entire day with a box full of hotspots in my trunk and driving around some of the most impoverished neighborhoods in Denver. I was knocking on doors

> and trying to find the people that I was looking for who, you know, sometimes didn't live there. One time, I showed up at a student's house, and it turned out to be an autobody shop. Nobody was living there, but they used that address to ensure they could send their children to school. I had to engage with families differently and without judgment. During a crisis was not the time for anything but empathy.

If COVID-19 taught school leaders a lesson they never received in education courses, it was that our communication styles and methods must be flexible and able to adjust according to a school population's needs. In cases in which natural disasters frequently decimate areas, school leaders must use innovative ways to reach their constituents. For example, Galveston, Texas, has experienced an influx of migrant families seeking asylum or new lives in the United States. Dr. Khalid Arar, a professor at Texas State University who has studied children and their sociocultural inclusion at school, claimed in his presentation at the 2023 American Education Research Association Annual Meeting that during one of his visits to a Galveston school, he heard at least twenty languages spoken in one classroom.[29] This type of linguistic diversity underscores the importance of school leaders creating communication strategies that are both multilingual and culturally sensitive. These strategies will ensure that all families, regardless of their background or native language, can access essential information and feel connected to their school community during times of crisis.

Equity Defined

The core principle of equity is to provide students or individuals with what they require to flourish, rather than simply enabling them to succeed. Thus, equity diverges from equality, which provides identical options to everyone at all times, and is tailored to individual needs. It is vital that every child receives personalized support and educational opportunities.

THE SCHOOL LEADER AS THE EQUITY AGENT DURING A CRISIS

School leaders are the captains of their ships. They chart the course, review the goals or plan of their destination, and work with their teachers as a team to reach it. Research has shown that school leaders have the second most significant impact on student learning after teachers.[30] Their role is *that* important. In a crisis, for example, school leaders decide how emergency funding, such as ESSR or McKiney-Vento Homeless Assistance Act funding, should be distributed.

Leadership during a crisis requires a multifaceted approach that prioritizes equity and inclusivity. As the equity agent during a crisis, the school leader plays a crucial role in ensuring that all students, especially those from marginalized communities, have access to the resources and support they need to thrive academically and emotionally. This is particularly important during times of crisis, as vulnerable students may face heightened challenges that require targeted interventions and support.[31] By adopting an equity-centered approach, school leaders can mitigate the impact of the crisis on the most vulnerable students and promote a more inclusive and supportive learning environment. Furthermore, as the equity agent, the school leader should actively engage with the broader community to address the multifaceted needs of students and their families during a crisis. This may involve collaborating with local organizations, government agencies, and community leaders to provide essential services, such as food assistance, mental health support, and technology access. Research has emphasized the importance of community partnerships in supporting students during crises, highlighting the positive impact of collaborative efforts on student well-being and academic success.[32] By leveraging community resources and expertise, school leaders can enhance their capacity to address the diverse needs of students and families, thereby fostering a more resilient and cohesive community during challenging times. Moreover, the role of school leaders as equity agents extends beyond immediate crisis response to long-term systemic change. By advocating for policies and practices that promote equity and social justice within the education system, leaders can address underlying inequities that may exacerbate the impact of crises on marginalized students. This proactive approach aligns with research highlighting the importance of sustained equity-focused leadership in creating more equitable and inclusive learning environments.[33] Through ongoing advocacy and strategic decision-making, school leaders can contribute to creating a more just and equitable educational system that better serves all students.

INTRODUCING A FRAMEWORK FOR AN EQUITY-ORIENTED CRISIS LEADER

During times of crisis, it is essential for leaders to prioritize equity of all types (e.g., racial, gender, religious). To achieve this, I developed the pillars of equity-oriented crisis leadership, a framework that analyzes how leaders handle and recover from crises while also promoting long-term change. From this framework, I detail how these pillars can be used as catalyzers for schools to achieve equity-oriented transformative change. With a focus on marginalized populations and a consideration of multiple perspectives, this framework guides school leaders to establish equitable schools or districts. Crises can be opportunities for change, and my framework is grounded in the belief that equity-oriented leadership is the key to making that change positive and lasting. The framework is iterative and adaptable to the distinct impact of each crisis, consisting of eight elements that support equity-oriented crisis leadership. This framework can ensure that our schools and districts are built on a foundation of equity and fairness. The following eight components make up this framework:

- Hope
- Equity-oriented mindset
- Inclusive decision-making
- Resource allocation, deprivation, and diffusion
- Equitable systems and structures
- Inclusive communication
- Equity-oriented critical self-reflection
- Advocacy for radical change

Figure I.1 illustrates the equity-oriented approach during the postcrisis stabilization phase. The framework is built on hope, providing a stable foundation on which to envision a new future for all. These pillars collectively work to establish a strong foundation for equity in the recovery process. In the following sections, I will outline the components of the equity-oriented crisis leadership framework.

Hope

Hope, according to Snyder, is defined as "the belief that one can find pathways to desired goals and the belief that one can muster the motivation to use those pathways." During times of crisis, cultivating and maintaining hope is essential for advancing equity in education.[34] Rather than embracing simplistic or naive forms of hope, educators and school leaders should prioritize fostering "complex" or "critical" hope.[35] This approach forms the basis of equity-focused crisis leadership, in which case hope acts as a guiding vision for a better future for all students, especially those who are marginalized. Within this framework, hope is regarded as an active and transformative

FIGURE I.1 The equity-oriented crisis leadership framework

force that enables individuals to challenge existing conditions and strive for a more equitable future. By articulating a vision, maintaining optimism, demonstrating perseverance, and fostering creativity, leaders can employ hope as a strategic tool for recovery and as a crucial catalyst for inspiring change.[36] By embracing radical approaches and addressing core issues, hope can contribute to reshaping the future of the school community and advocating for equity for all.

Equity-Oriented Mindset

In this framework, an equity-oriented mindset denotes the cognitive framework that steers leaders in their approach to equity work. This means acknowledging how crises disproportionately affect marginalized groups and recognizing racism's deep roots in all aspects of US life, especially education. Here, students and families from disadvantaged backgrounds often miss out on opportunities and resources. This mindset focuses on tearing down obstacles built by white supremacy in schools to create a truly equal system. It highlights the importance of antiracist leadership and a constant focus on equity as essential parts of being a fair leader. Leaders with this mindset are aware of racial, gender-based, and other inequalities within their school systems. They understand that their decisions during crises might unintentionally maintain the current unfair situation. Because of this, they're encouraged to analyze how their choices affect specific groups by asking questions like, "How will this decision impact [particular student population]?"

Inclusive Decision-Making

Principals face numerous decisions during crises that can rapidly stabilize their environment. The manner in which these decisions are made is critical, as they can have a significant impact on the entire organization. Inclusive decision-making is essential in crisis leadership, involving the establishment of democratic, authentic processes that incorporate diverse perspectives and voices. It is imperative to involve the school community at every level of the decision-making process. How principals assess situations during a crisis, however, depends on their mindset regarding equity issues. Leaders must be deliberate in their decision-making, actively seeking and including input from a diverse range of allies and marginalized populations to make tangible decisions that benefit special populations. By prioritizing inclusive decision-making, equity-focused crisis leaders can ensure that all members of the school community are heard and considered.

Resource Allocation, Deprivation, and Diffusion

In times of crisis, resources may be scarce and limited, underscoring the importance of allocating them through an equity-focused approach. When resources are not distributed equitably, those with greater means may receive priority, resulting in marginalized populations being deprived of essential necessities. In educational leadership, fair resource allocation is vital for equity-driven leadership. Leaders must reallocate financial, material, and human resources to promote teaching and learning for historically underserved students based on factors such as race, ethnicity, socioeconomic status, or language spoken at home. Studies have highlighted unequal funding and unequal access to various school resources, emphasizing the need for principals to ensure that marginalized populations receive the resources they deserve during a crisis.

Resource allocation and deprivation are fundamental components of equity-oriented crisis leadership, demanding careful consideration of how resources are distributed and who is most vulnerable to deprivation. School leaders must also assess how resources are distributed within the community, particularly in marginalized communities that may already face challenges in resource allocation and access. The distribution and deprivation of resources should be guided by inclusive decision-making and an equity-oriented mindset, prioritizing the needs of these vulnerable populations. Furthermore, the equitable distribution of allocated resources is a central aspect of this approach because leaders must decide how marginalized populations will access the resources acquired by the school community. It is not sufficient for leaders to obtain resources; they must also distribute them fairly within the community rather than leave individuals to fend for themselves in resource acquisition.

Equitable Systems and Structures

Schools operate within diverse systems and structures, encompassing aspects such as attendance tracking and homework policies. Even during crises, the hierarchical distribution of power and decision-making responsibility can persist, as noted by Larry Smith and Dan Riley.[37] To support the entire community, however, these systems and structures must be established fairly and consistently aligned with school goals. These systems and structures foster effective integration and equal outcomes for all individuals involved, fostering an environment conducive to student success. Improving a school's structures and systems after a crisis is essential for enhancing student outcomes and family engagement. In New York City, 2.2 million residents lacked broadband internet subscriptions, with individuals from low-income, racial/ethnic minority, or non-English-speaking backgrounds experiencing notable disparities in access to broadband internet.[38] The lack of access has adversely affected student academic achievement.[39] School leaders must approach structures and systems from an equity perspective to ensure equal access for all learners. The policies, procedures, and systems that either promote or discourage the participation of marginalized populations within the school community are pivotal indicators of the fairness of these systems and structures.

Inclusive Communication

Effective management of crises necessitates communication as a pivotal component.[40] Previous studies have demonstrated how bidirectional communication during the Hurricane Maria crisis helped principals make well-informed decisions for students who evacuated Puerto Rico.[41] Smith and Riley stress the importance of "open and credible communication" during a crisis to minimize misinformation and reduce uncertainty among stakeholders.[42] When schools fail to engage in equitable and inclusive communication, marginalized families may feel neglected and underserved.[43] The pandemic introduced new obstacles to communication between schools and families, highlighting the need to employ accessible and consistent communication methods.[44] Inclusive communication encompasses, among other things, translating all school communications for families, utilizing diverse platforms such as social media, and adjusting language that implies white privilege as the norm.

Advocacy for Radical Change

Politicians have capitalized on crises as an opportunity to advocate for reforms. For example, former Secretary of Education Arne Duncan praised Hurricane Katrina as a catalyst for positive change in New Orleans public schools, leading to an educational transformation that resulted in the establishment of the first all-charter school district.[45] Similarly, New York City School Chancellor Richard Carranza emphasized the idea that a crisis should not be wasted but rather used as a platform to advance fairness.[46]

Scholars have urged principals to utilize their influence to effect enduring changes that challenge unjust policies and practices at the school level.[47] Activist and scholar Angela Davis asserted that radical changes are imperative to address the root causes of problems.[48] During a crisis, marginalized communities often bear the brunt of the impact. Black and Brown communities heavily relied on community centers for support during the COVID-19 pandemic.[49] Establishing enduring equity in schools involves scrutinizing cultural and sociopolitical measures that are transparent and mindful of race, with decentralized models of support that prioritize communities as the driving force in addressing crisis-induced challenges.[50]

In the scholarly literature on equity leadership, scholars have recognized advocacy as a catalyst for transformation.[51] Therefore, advocating for radical change places a premium on equity by directly facing institutional racism and xenophobia and advocating against structural oppression that emerges during a crisis. Equity-driven school leaders during a crisis must display courage in their efforts to dismantle systems of oppression. Consequently, this principle is upheld by leaders who seek systemic changes to radically transform their schools or districts on behalf of marginalized groups.

Equity-Oriented Critical Reflection

Engaging in critical self-reflection is essential for the development of equity-centered leaders, as emphasized by Susan R. Madsen.[52] According to research by Laura Hallberg and Louise J. Santiago, leaders need to confront their personal biases and professional challenges to lead with equity.[53] Many leaders, however, struggle to examine how their biases and challenges intersect with their leadership actions. A recent report from the National Center for Education Statistics revealed that the majority of public school principals were white, while the majority of public school students were not.[54] During times of crisis, school leaders must engage in critical reflection and acknowledge their privilege in comparison to the marginalized populations they serve.

Janet Patti et al. have suggested that critical self-reflection is crucial for guiding action and decision-making, particularly during crisis management. They identified three critical areas for critical self-reflection: "1) reflection on what matters, 2) reflection on how we make sense of the world around us, and 3) reflection on our emotions."[55] Critical reflection empowers leaders to recognize oppressive systems and work to dismantling them. Hallberg and Santiago discovered that the childhood experiences of inclusion and exclusion of some 50 participants influenced their approach to equity leadership.[56] School leaders must consider their past experiences and how they influence their decision-making to prevent further marginalization in the US public education system. Leaders must embrace reflection as a crucial tool for driving change to address the explicit and implicit outcomes affecting marginalized populations during a crisis. By critiquing their actions, leaders can enhance future responses and facilitate equitable decision-making in schools and districts.

ABOUT THIS BOOK

In each chapter of this book, I present an exemplary case study of a school principal who led through a crisis and considered one element of the framework more than others to respond to the crisis being experienced. This provides insight into ways leaders can support their schools or districts during a crisis according to each specific pillar. Each chapter includes reflection questions that can be used with leadership teams, faculty, and staff.

The following five premises support this book:

1. All families want the best for their children.
2. Context matters.
3. Trauma is mutually detrimental and debilitating.
4. Equity leadership is an intentional skill and awareness.

ALL FAMILIES WANT THE BEST FOR THEIR CHILDREN

One of the most common phrases I hear about marginalized children is that "their families just don't care." Research shows that this oversimplified view does not hold true; various factors influence parental involvement and engagement. Additionally, the extent of involvement can vary significantly. Namely, the level of parental involvement may manifest differently for different families because of the intricate nature of parental engagement. Parents often feel marginalized by schools and educators for numerous reasons, such as holding hourly jobs, encountering language or cultural barriers, and harboring fear or distrust of the school or its staff. Additionally, disparities in educational opportunities and outcomes can contribute to the disengagement of marginalized families.[57] To address this issue, it is crucial to develop constructive, two-way relationships between schools and marginalized parents.[58] Strategies to improve parent engagement include developing into a "consummate communicator," rethinking family engagement activities, and being straightforward about the challenges and often "inconclusive nature" of education.[59] Furthermore, efforts should be made to create a more family-inclusive atmosphere at all events and meetings and schedule alternative times and ways for parents to engage. Scholarly literature supports the importance of involving marginalized parents in their children's education, such as the book *Home, School, and Community Collaboration:*

Culturally Responsive Family Involvement.[60] Similarly, Jamel Adkins-Sharif, in his work at alternative schools designed to serve marginalized students, highlights the essential aspects of connecting more effectively with families, including being a "consummate communicator" and rethinking family engagement activities.[61] These scholarly works underscore the need for schools to engage actively with marginalized families and address barriers to their involvement in their children's education.[62] Dr. Fernando Naditch, a professor of bilingual education at Montclair State University, explained at a recent university conference that many migrant children's parents have "gone through hell to get into the United States. They have fled undesirable spaces to ensure their children have access to a better life and education."[63] According to John Diamond, a professor of sociology and education policy at Brown University, white supremacy is embedded in education structures through the power to define the purposes of education, curricular content, and discourse around education, which tend to be controlled by white racial actors and steeped in a history in which whiteness is structured as superior to other racialized groups.[64] This embedded structure can lead to the reproduction of racial hierarchies in organizational routines and practices of schools, thus affecting decisions about discipline, grading, and tracking processes. The book is based on the idea that families all want the best for their children, regardless of their makeup, race, religion, or identity. Educators and school leaders should make an effort to understand and support families where they are, recognizing that involvement and engagement can vary widely.

Context Matters

When navigating through a crisis, the surrounding context plays a critical role. Research indicates that school leaders worldwide respond to crises in ways that are heavily influenced by the specific context in which they operate. The distinct challenges and resources present in different locations significantly shape leaders' approaches to crisis management. For instance, school leaders in New York City faced the complex task of admitting and placing students who had arrived from Puerto Rico after Hurricane Maria. They had to address issues such as language barriers, cultural differences, and the potential trauma experienced by these displaced students. This effort required the development of strategies to integrate these students into the urban school system while also providing essential support services.

In contrast, principals in rural areas in the United States faced different challenges during natural disasters and the COVID-19 pandemic. They had to grapple with the logistics of delivering internet hotspots to students and families as well as ensuring that the local infrastructure supported the usage of these hotspots. The key question for them was, "Do these children and families have Wi-Fi access?" This highlights the distinct technological and infrastructure challenges faced by rural communities during crises. The juxtaposition of urban and rural contexts illustrates how the distinct characteristics of each area significantly affect leadership decisions during crises. Urban areas may have more resources and infrastructure but face challenges related to population density and diversity. In contrast, rural areas often struggle with issues of isolation, limited access to technology, and dispersed populations. The context in which students find themselves matters, as crises affect both the living area and the school environment. Therefore, leaders need to make decisions that are specific to the particular context in which they are operating. In urban areas, leaders may focus on coordinating with various agencies and managing large-scale logistics, whereas rural leaders might prioritize innovative solutions to reach geographically dispersed students and families. Furthermore, the financial context varies across districts, and every financial decision made by a leader may be specific to that location. Urban districts might have access to a wider range of funding sources but face higher operational costs. In contrast, rural districts often operate with limited budgets and may need to be particularly resourceful in allocating resources during crises. This financial context significantly influences the options available to leaders and the strategies they can implement.

Effective crisis leadership necessitates a thorough understanding of the specific context in which one operates. Leaders must take into account factors such as geography, demographics, infrastructure, and available resources when devising and implementing crisis management strategies. This context-specific approach enables leaders to deliver more tailored and effective responses to the distinct challenges presented by different environments during times of crisis. According to research by Chen Schechter et al., context can also relate to the internal characteristics of a school.[65] This could be expressed as the level of trust families have for school leaders and staff or as collaborative decision-making.[66] Given the myriad contexts, it is essential to understand that there is no one way to implement this framework. Instead, leaders must apply its fundamental functions to their distinct context to lead through a crisis equitably. It can be argued that a framework, in order to be effective, must be implemented in a unilateral and egalitarian manner, but research has confirmed that this is not true.[67] Leaders must purposefully and progressively redesign their organizational structures and roles while engaging in distributed leadership after a crisis to promote greater staff engagement and ownership. Because of the variable staff and school demographics, leaders should use and adapt this framework to the context in which they lead to facilitate an equitable crisis recovery. Just as every school is different, a crisis can affect areas and locations in many different ways, so all leaders cannot respond in the same way or in only one direction.

Trauma Is Mutually Detrimental and Debilitating

In a recent study I conducted, principals explained that they were "not okay" when crises happen. Many broke down when I asked how they were managing and what overall impact the crisis had on them. The notion that leaders are experiencing burnout has been researched in the educational leadership field, but what has surfaced is the overwhelming impact of secondary trauma and stress. School leaders are hearing tragic stories from students, families, teachers, and district administration. Some directly experience a traumatic event themselves, such as Iris, who had to cope with a student who attempted to take her own life by hanging at the school. Iris raced to bolster the student up, saving her life, while concurrently yelling for students to return to class and radioing for help. The role of a school leader is complex and daunting in ways many individuals cannot imagine, yet they aim to do the job. One leader in New Jersey with whom I worked explained that a student bit, punched, and spat on him. But the leader's response was distinct: "Every day, I greet him with love because I know he needs it." All the leaders in this study expressed the toll that crises had taken on them over the past two years. They are fatigued, but they also appear to work in silos. Therefore, I acknowledge that trauma is mutually debilitating and crippling, even as some leaders manage to marshal onward. With this premise, I believe leaders need to demonstrate an ethic of care when leading through a crisis.

Equity Leadership Is an Intentional Skill and Awareness

Equity leadership is not simply an inherent trait but rather a deliberate skill that necessitates continual development and heightened awareness. School leaders must actively nurture the capacity to identify and rectify inequities, especially during times of crisis when existing disparities may be magnified. Research shows that effective equity-oriented leadership involves a blend of knowledge, skills, and attitudes that leaders must purposefully cultivate and improve. This encompasses the following:

1. Developing a profound understanding of systemic inequities and their repercussions for marginalized populations.

2. Cultivating cultural competence and the ability to collaborate effectively across diverse groups.
3. Sharpening critical self-reflection skills to scrutinize personal biases and privileges.
4. Establishing the capacity for inclusive decision-making and engagement with stakeholders.
5. Acquiring expertise in equitable resource allocation and distribution.

School leaders should actively seek opportunities to enhance these skills through professional development, mentorship, and continuous learning. This may entail participating in equity-focused training programs, engaging in critical discussions with peers, and staying abreast of current research and best practices in equity leadership. Moreover, equity leadership demands a heightened understanding of the distinct challenges confronted by marginalized students and families. Leaders must be attuned to the subtle ways in which inequities manifest in their schools and districts and be prepared to take proactive measures to address them. This awareness extends to comprehending the intersectionality of various forms of marginalization and how they intersect during crises.

By approaching equity leadership as an intentional skill and maintaining a constant awareness of equity issues, school leaders can effectively navigate crises while ensuring that the needs of all students, particularly those from marginalized communities, are addressed. This deliberate approach to equity leadership is essential to effect lasting, systemic change that goes beyond immediate crisis response and fosters more inclusive and equitable educational environments for all students.

CONCLUSION

In this book, I emphasize the critical nature of infusing equity into crisis leadership, particularly within the context of school leadership. I underscore the profound impact of decisions made during a crisis on the entire organization and the diverse populations being served. I highlight the significance of creating inclusive, democratic, and authentic decision-making processes that engage diverse perspectives and voices, including the community, at every level. Moreover, I emphasize that a leader's mindset around equity issues significantly influences assessing and judging specific problems during a crisis. I also stress the importance of intentional inclusivity to prevent adverse impacts on various populations. Furthermore, I outline the characteristics of inclusive decision-making, emphasizing the need for leaders to welcome and include voices from diverse allies and marginalized people, operationalizing decisions with multiple stakeholders involved. School leaders can find time to have necessary conversations, despite crises and the day-to-day work of business administration, by prioritizing clear and consistent communication. Frequent, clear, and concise communication is essential, and school leaders should make themselves available to answer questions and provide details on district, school, and class websites.[68] They can also leverage visual communication methods, including such as short videos, interactive video meetings, and live conversations on social media to engage with the school community.[69] In addition, school leaders should remember the importance of responding empathically during crisis communication.[70] Although the spontaneous nature of crises makes it challenging for school leaders to be fully prepared, cultivating skills relevant to crisis response, such as emotional intelligence and attentiveness to inequities, can reduce some of the burdens they experience while navigating uncertainties. It is essential for school leaders to recognize the need for comprehensive crisis communication plans and to engage in two-way communication with their communities to address ambiguities and confusion. I underscore the imperative for equity-oriented crisis leaders to invite and use diverse perspectives to make tangible choices in the best interests of special populations. This will ultimately aim to make a devastating event and following recovery efforts more equitable and spur long-term change.[71] I hope you will gain a deep understanding of how hope and innovation can drive transformative change toward equity, especially in educational leadership, during times of crisis.

Hope

Hope will never be silent.
—Harvey Milk[1]

I remember when I lived in New York City in 2009. I was about to graduate from Sarah Lawrence College and wanted to teach in an urban school. At the same time, the country was in the midst of the Great Recession. Bills were stacking up, and I wondered how I would meet the needs of my family and make a living. Like many people, I had moments of despair because of the huge financial crisis and not being able to see a way out.[2] Nearby, on January 15, Captain "Sully" Sullenberger saved a US Airways plane from tragedy by landing it on the Hudson River, ensuring the safety of all 155 passengers. Dubbed the "Miracle on the Hudson," hope was inscribed into this event for a nation embroiled in a time of serious debt and despair. "Sully" recalled this crisis: "This event happened during the 2008/2009 financial meltdown. . . . At a time when we needed it, it gave us hope and reaffirmed our faith in humanity."[3]

Hope connects humanity to the notion that there is a brighter future ahead, beyond the daily crises. Many call on hope in a moment of crisis because it simply feels good, feels necessary. Hope is mentioned so frequently during a crisis because to engage in a discourse of despair contradicts the human condition, which is to survive. Dr. John Montgomery wrote that "as a whole, survival is a combination of physical, mental, and emotional challenges, challenges that can change human behavior at such an extent that it can change a person's character."[4] Dr. Montgomery shed light on the notion that to survive, we must work collectively to do so. During a crisis, the notion of survival is often called into question. In the face of difficult economic times, for instance, many people (including myself) reflect practically: "How can we survive if there is a recession? How will we be able to afford food or housing?" Hope is the means by which people can generate creative thinking and courage, improve moods, and achieve proposed goals. School leaders, in particular, must become adept at recognizing, drawing on, and deploying hope whenever a crisis arises in the school setting. In this chapter, I discuss how leaders use hope in tangible ways during times of crisis.

Hope Defined

The confidence in one's leadership ability to shape the future positively or achieve a specific objective through strategic planning and agentic or proactive thinking.

We live in a world in which it is easy to lose hope. In today's climate, crises overlap consistently and seem interminable. Leaders are facing several issues, including recovery from the COVID-19 pandemic, high rates of school shootings, and inequitable policy attacks on marginalized populations.[5] Nevertheless, these leaders are expected to increase student achievement while also deciding if they want to stay in the profession. Because these factors compound daily, hope is often overlooked or even forgotten. The power of hope, however, has the potential to deepen our understanding of crisis leadership in schools.

Hope has been used as an antidote to despair in critical times. It is often described as an anchor to keep everyone grounded, positive, and optimistic in otherwise dismal times. President Obama's ubiquitous image of "Hope" by the artist-activist Shepard Fairey became iconic for these very reasons.

During his 2009 campaign, Obama, like every other candidate, identified the significant problems facing the nation and explained how he would work to resolve them. Not since the Great Depression of the 1930s have Americans experienced such a critical economic crisis; Obama faced a dire financial situation that included a devastating recession and high unemployment. Hopelessness and despair were countered by Obama's appeal to struggling citizens to believe in his vision and mission, which was grounded in hope to turn the country around. In its visual language context, psychological impact, and mass distribution, the "Hope" poster helped transform the candidate's public image and contributed to the presidential campaign's success. Obama has become one of the country's most iconic leaders because of his focus on positivity and optimism coupled with his goal-oriented pathways to success. Obama leaned into the notion that a crisis was occurring and dramatically affecting people's lives. He leaned into the notion that there was a better way, establishing a cabinet that could help him ensure a US recovery. Obama summoned hope to anchor his recovery efforts and move the country forward.[6]

Jochen Kleres and Åsa Wettergren posited that hope propels collective action, manages fear, and generates more hope.[7] Obama gave us an example of how leaders catalyze hope to ensure that their stakeholders will be able to grasp onto a lifeline to move out of the crisis. Moreover, psychology research has proven that hopeful leaders, such as Obama, spur change and continuously engage in cycles of reflection and improvement because they seek better outcomes than the present can offer and arduously fight for change.[8]

As an education practitioner, hope is a powerful tool that can drive change in various disciplines, including economics, activism, and politics. In education, however, hope is often overlooked, and we rely on surface-level acknowledgments of hope that do little to help us navigate through crises. Despite foundational scholars emphasizing hope as a critical factor of change, the literature in education scholarship rarely mentions hope. Instead, education is often framed as a dire system needing transformation or reformation—as if what exists is hopeless. This gap in the literature prevents us from understanding how leaders can lead through crises and liberate the education system from a pervasive sense of despair. Research has shown that leaders must engender hope during a crisis. Hope has the potential to transform schools by helping us view educational leadership through a new lens. How leaders express hope, however, and move within a continuum of hopeful, less hopeful, or even hopeless leadership actions has yet to be studied. Hopeful leadership is built on care, trust, and respect, and it goes beyond interacting with those who are easy to lead or self-sufficient in their classrooms. It must also include those who challenge or resist the organization's forward movement. Hope is crucial to sustained resistance against inequality and allows leaders to tie their vision setting to equity. Hopeful leadership inspires challenges and develops new leadership within the organization. However, with ever-increasing demands placed on leaders, their names, reputations, and careers are continually scrutinized, diverting them away from focusing on their work to inspire students and having to justify their impact on each one. In fact, hopeful leadership and crisis recovery should be (psychological and practical) partners in an interplay for the best possible impact on the organization.

IMPACT OF HOPE ON CRISIS LEADERSHIP

Emotions are reactions to events. A critical incident happens, your brain takes it in to process it, and then your body responds through behavior. The way you behave is a response to your mind's interpretation and your body's reaction (e.g., accelerated heart rate, blood pressure, sweating, dry mouth). Emotions are physiological, cognitive, and behavioral experiences revolving around a cycle that includes the triggering event or crisis; your interpretation of the crisis in physiological, cognitive, or behavioral ways; your awareness of the physical response; and, finally, the urge to act.[9]

Leaders with high levels of hope demonstrate a more deliberate and reflective approach to crisis management. While discussing a student's medical emergency, Charles, a veteran principal in the East, explained: "I've never felt more hopeful in my career. If we can make it through this, we can make it through anything." He continued:

> The crises we have been having, the student medical emergency, COVID-19, school shootings, they have taught us something. It was kind of like when 9/11 happened. Those of us in education remember that time, and it wasn't something we could have possibly prepared for, like what we are going through now. But we reflect on what we've accomplished and were able to do, and it just makes me feel more hopeful that as a team we're able to get through this. We are united, we know what we need to do and despite all the challenges that we faced in the last few years, we look at what we accomplished. So, part of our responsibility is to share that level of hope with our staff. They should feel a sense of community and advocacy because we are united.

Charles's insight shows how hopeful leaders are able to identify their successes and catalyze support from their team to engender more accomplishments. Hopeful leaders tend to slow down their responses, carefully interpret situations, remain mindful of their physical reactions, and act with clear goals in mind.[10] In contrast, leaders with low levels of hope may react impulsively, rely on biased interpretations, overlook their physical responses, and adopt a scattered approach to problem-solving.

Consider, in contrast, Franklin, a male LatinX leader of an elementary school in an urban district. He described his response to facing the challenges of the COVID-19 pandemic and his feelings of hopelessness: "I have no more hope. . . . I rarely do. It's just everything going on, and what do I have to be hopeful for in this school?" Franklin questioned what there was to be hopeful for in his school within the turmoil. This sentiment resonates with C. R. Snyder's hope theory, which emphasizes that hope is a cognitive process resulting from generating multiple actionable pathways toward achieving goals.[11] Franklin's statement reveals his struggle to see viable pathways or reasons for hope within the context of his school and the ongoing pandemic.[12]

In contrast, hopeful leaders are able to look toward goals and opportunities for betterment on behalf of their stakeholders. Hope, for them, is more than an emotion; it is the central value driving what they do. For school leaders in the aftermath of a crisis, hope transcends mere feelings and becomes a fundamental guiding principle influencing all of their actions and decisions. This concept aligns with the idea that hope is not just wishful thinking, but rather is a belief in a brighter future and the possibility of change that is needed to create an overarching perspective of life. School leaders, especially in times of crisis, rely on hope to inspire resilience, drive positive change, and instill confidence in their school communities.[13]

This contrast between Franklin's feelings of hopelessness and the characteristics of hopeful leaders like Charles highlights the significant role of hope in leadership, especially during challenging times. Although Franklin's despair reflects the overwhelming nature of the current circumstances, Charles's hopeful outlook demonstrates resilience and a forward-looking view that goes beyond moments of crisis. This outlook becomes essential for inspiring and guiding others at any time, but especially during crises.

IMPLEMENTING HOPEFUL LEADERSHIP BEFORE, DURING, AND AFTER A CRISIS EVENT

To implement hopeful leadership before, during, and after a crisis, school leaders interviewed for this book described several key strategies they adopted.[14]

Creating a Shared Vision and Moral Purpose

School leaders interviewed for this book emphasized the importance of anchoring their decisions in a shared vision and moral purpose that aligns operations with strategy. As Celine, a veteran principal, responding to the influx of students migrating from Puerto Rico into New York City public schools following Hurricane Maria shared:

> The executive director and I had the same vision. And so, it just seeps down through the organization. Our vision becomes a vehicle, a leadership tool, in terms of being able to discuss knowledge, not necessarily give opinions on things, but let staff and students develop and form their own opinions through this big bucket of empathy and hope. That's deep in my own leadership style, and also, through the school's vision, of seeing different perspectives, and taking on what it's like to be in someone else's shoes.

Celine's insight highlights a few key considerations for school leaders when developing and examining their shared vision and moral purpose:

1. Alignment at the Top: Celine emphasizes the importance of the executive leadership team being aligned on the vision. This ensures a cohesive message and approach that can then permeate the entire organization.
2. Vision as a Vehicle for Dialogue: Celine sees the school's vision as a tool to facilitate open discussion and the exploration of different perspectives, rather than as a rigid directive. This allows staff and students to engage with the vision in a meaningful way.
3. Grounding in Empathy and Hope: Notably, Celine roots the school's vision in empathy and hope. This suggests that an effective shared vision should inspire compassion for others' experiences and a sense of optimism about the future.
4. Personal Leadership Style: Celine indicates that this approach to vision and purpose is deeply aligned with her leadership style, underscoring the importance of leaders modeling the behaviors and mindsets they wish to cultivate.

By anchoring decisions in a shared vision and moral purpose imbued with empathy and hope, school leaders can guide their teams toward achieving common goals, even in the face of a crisis. This approach inspires optimism, fosters dialogue, and aligns the organization around a compelling, values-driven purpose.

Empowering Middle Management

Introducing new leadership styles that empower middle managers in schools, such as vice principals, coaches, and supervisors, can enhance decision-making processes and promote a sense of ownership among staff members. As Felicity, a novice principal, explained in response to the influx of students migrating from Puerto Rico to New York City public schools after Hurricane Maria: "I think that the team approach that we have at the school helps us build collaboration and shared responsibility. We know that we cannot do this by ourselves, that our students need us to be together and to use each person's expertise." Felicity's insight highlights a few key ways that empowering middle management can foster hopeful leadership during a crisis:

1. Collaborative Culture: By embracing a "team approach," Felicity has cultivated a culture of collaboration and shared responsibility among her staff. This helps ensure that the burden of crisis response does not fall solely on the principal's shoulders.

2. Leveraging Expertise: Felicity recognizes that her middle managers, such as those involved in the student intake process, have valuable expertise that should inform decision-making. Empowering them to share their knowledge promotes a sense of ownership.
3. Responsive Problem-Solving: When Felicity's team identified a parent in need of additional support, they were able to quickly mobilize the school counselor and parent coordinator to provide resources. This nimble, distributed problem-solving is enabled by an empowered middle-management structure.
4. Shared Leadership: Felicity does not position herself as the sole leader, but rather sees her role as facilitating a collaborative, team-based approach. This shared leadership model builds resilience and a sense of collective responsibility during a crisis.

By empowering middle managers and fostering a culture of collaboration, Felicity has created an organizational structure that can more effectively navigate the challenges of a crisis like the influx of students from Puerto Rico. This approach distributes decision-making, leverages diverse expertise, and promotes a sense of shared purpose—all of which are hallmarks of hopeful leadership.

Involving Students in Decision-Making

Involving students in leadership roles and decision-making processes can foster a sense of community, empowerment, and engagement within the school environment. This involvement helps students feel valued and invested in the school's success, which can lead to increased motivation and hope. As Millie, a principal with more than twenty years of experience, described the impact of the migrant student influx from Puerto Rico following Hurricane Maria: "With all of the work that we're doing around equity, it makes me think about things that I could have done. Thinking about our student council that we now have; it makes me think about what we could do. We could have rallied together to put together a collection of donations or what have you." Millie's insight highlights a few key ways that involving students in decision-making can support hopeful leadership during a crisis:

1. Empowering Students: By involving students in leadership roles and decision-making processes, Millie recognizes the opportunity to empower them to take an active role in the school's response to the crisis. This fosters a sense of community, ownership, and engagement among the student body.

2. Mobilizing for Action: Millie specifically mentions the student council as a vehicle for rallying students to take concrete action, such as organizing donation drives. This demonstrates how student involvement can translate into tangible, hopeful outcomes during a time of crisis.
3. Equity-Focused Approach: Millie notes that her reflections on student involvement are tied to the school's work around equity. This suggests that empowering marginalized students to lead can be a powerful strategy for promoting hope and justice in the face of crises that disproportionately affect certain communities.
4. Missed Opportunities: By acknowledging the things she "could have done" to involve students, Millie demonstrates a reflective, growth-oriented mindset. This indicates an understanding that more could have been done to harness student leadership and agency, which is a key insight for strengthening hopeful crisis response in the future.

Overall, Millie's comments underscore the transformative potential of involving students as active partners in the school's decision-making and crisis response efforts. By empowering young people and mobilizing their energy and ideas, school leaders can cultivate a profound sense of community, purpose, and hope—essential ingredients for navigating challenging times.

Establishing Regular Check-Ins and Communication

Establishing regular check-ins with the team and community can help leaders understand concerns, fears, and priorities while also fostering open communication channels. As Abraham, a veteran principal from Northern California, explained:

> I was purposeful in saying, "The only new thing we're launching is this advisory thing," and that's really just very loosely structured around the idea of "here's twenty kids you're going to check in on once a week just to make sure that they're alive and they do okay and the Chromebook works," and we'll do some college and career stuff as we go along, but we're not pushing a lot of new initiatives.

Abraham's approach highlights a few key ways that regular check-ins and communication can support hopeful leadership during a crisis:

1. Prioritizing Connection: By instituting a simple "advisory" program in which teachers check in with small groups of students weekly, Abraham has made student well-being and basic needs the top priority. This conveys care and concern.

2. Pacing Change: Rather than overwhelming his staff with numerous new initiatives, Abraham is intentionally limiting the scope of change. This helps maintain stability and manage stress during the crisis.
3. Modeling the Process: As Abraham notes, he made sure to "model the one on ones with my teachers and staff to ensure they had a model and space to articulate their concerns." This demonstrates the importance of the check-in process and provides a template for others to follow.
4. Acknowledging Unique Challenges: Abraham recognizes that his school community is facing technological "growing pains" that may not be as acute in other districts. By being attuned to his local context, he can tailor the check-in process accordingly.
5. Creating Open Communication: Through these regular check-ins, Abraham is fostering an environment in which staff and students feel empowered to share their fears, needs, and priorities. This open dialogue is crucial for maintaining hope and stability.

By instituting a system of regular, structured check-ins, Abraham has created a communication framework that keeps his entire school community informed, aligned, and supported during the crisis. This helps cultivate a sense of stability and hope, even amid significant uncertainty.

Creating Structure and Stability

Clear, consistent, and accurate communication with the school community helps establish stability during uncertain times, providing reassurance and guidance to all stakeholders. As Abraham explained:

> So a lot of my communication was done through cellphones, because that was before we even knew what Zoom was, let alone used it as our predominant means of communication. So, we did have a couple of staff meetings to talk about, "All right, what are we doing here? What is our goal? Where are we in the school year?" Over half our students take advanced placement classes, so part of the conversation was, "Where are you at on your AP curriculum pendulum?" Most people, at that point, were either almost done or were in heavy-duty review, which made it a little bit easier on our older students in terms of the workload, and a lot of the conversation was, again, "How do we get from here to spring break?" So, we kind of set a three-week mark of, "What does this look like?" We didn't have a learning schedule or anything like that. We didn't start with anything like that. That was probably, if I reflect back on that experience, probably my greatest mistake was not coming out of the gate with a hard schedule, like

> a bell schedule that kids followed when they were at home because a lot of our kids just took those couple weeks off, quite carelessly, and it was a little bit of a struggle.

Abraham's reflections highlight a few key ways that creating structure and stability can support hopeful leadership during a crisis:

1. Clear Communication: Abraham emphasizes the importance of clear, consistent communication with staff and the broader school community. This helps ensure that everyone is informed and aligned.
2. Goal-Setting: By having conversations about the school's goals and where they are in the academic year, Abraham is providing a sense of direction and purpose amid the uncertainty.
3. Realistic Planning: Abraham and his team engaged in pragmatic planning for the next three weeks, rather than trying to map out the entire crisis response. This allowed them to adapt as the situation evolved.
4. Structured Schedules: In retrospect, Abraham believes his "greatest mistake" was not immediately implementing a structured schedule for students learning from home. This lack of routine led to many students disengaging.
5. Lessons Learned: Abraham is reflecting on his experience to identify areas for improvement. This iterative approach will help him lead more effectively if faced with a similar crisis in the future.

Although Abraham acknowledges that there was no perfect playbook for responding to the sudden shift to remote learning, his insight underscores the importance of proactively establishing clear structures, schedules, and communication channels. This provides stability and reassurance to students, staff, and families during an inherently destabilizing time. By learning from this experience, Abraham can strengthen his ability to create structure and stability when leading through future crises.

Maintaining Hopeful Realism

Leaders should communicate hope while being aware of the reality of the crisis. As Emilia, a veteran principal from upstate New York, explained:

> I always struggle with the phrase "learning loss." Conceptually I understand it, but what I struggled with coming off of the pandemic, or even the three months, we were closed is you can't lose what you never had. They were never exposed because they weren't in school, they were online and they barely were online. They didn't lose that learning, but there appears

that came back to school and did everything they're supposed to have that learning. So in a way, yes, it's learning loss, but I just inherently struggle with that phrase.

Emilia's insight highlights the importance of maintaining hopeful realism as a school leader during a crisis:

1. Reframing Challenges: Emilia pushes back against the deficit-based language of "learning loss," recognizing that many students simply did not have the opportunity to learn certain content because of disruptions during the pandemic. This reframing avoids demoralizing students and staff.
2. Acknowledging Realities: At the same time, Emilia acknowledges the very real learning gaps that emerged, noting that "in a way, yes, it's learning loss." She does not shy away from the difficulties, but rather seeks to address them constructively.
3. Focusing on Progress: Despite the challenges, Emilia reports that her school still saw a 6 percent increase in end-of-year grades. This demonstrates a hopeful outlook, highlighting what was accomplished rather than solely dwelling on setbacks.
4. Adaptability: Emilia indicates that her school had to find "a new way to do it" in terms of teaching and learning. This adaptability and willingness to innovate, even in the face of crisis, reflects a hopeful mindset.

By maintaining this balance of realism and hope, Emilia is able to lead her school community through the pandemic in a constructive manner. She does not ignore the very real difficulties, but rather she frames them in a way that inspires confidence and resilience, instead of despair. This hopeful realism is essential for school leaders navigating complex crises. Emilia's approach stands in contrast to leaders who may become mired in hopelessness or unrealistic optimism. By acknowledging challenges while still believing in the ability to progress, Emilia models the kind of balanced, solution-focused leadership that can help schools weather storms and emerge stronger. This hopeful realism is a crucial skill for educational leaders to cultivate, especially in times of crisis and uncertainty.

Deploying Hope During a Crisis: Practical Strategies

Educational leaders play a crucial role in guiding their schools through times of crisis and uncertainty. Hope theory can provide valuable insight into how leaders can support their staff and navigate the challenges of a crisis. By understanding hope theory and providing emotional and practical support, educational leaders can help their staff envision a better future and work toward achieving their goals.

- **Understand Hope Theory:** Educate yourself and your team about hope theory, which can help leaders understand ways to support their staff during times of crisis and uncertainty. By providing emotional and practical support, educational leaders can help their staff envision a better future and work toward achieving goals.
- **Show Emotions:** During a crisis, leaders are often afraid to show emotions. Instead of fluctuating on a spectrum spanning anxiety and enthusiasm, leaders can focus primarily on hopeful ways to spur change and recovery. Emotions are physiological, cognitive, and behavioral experiences that revolve around a six-part cycle, and leaders who have high levels of hope can often engage in mindful strategies to center themselves and act with a sense of direction toward achieving a goal.
- **Provide Vision and Direction:** Hopeful leaders can look toward goals and betterment on behalf of their stakeholders. Hope for them is more than emotion; it is the central value driving what they do. By providing a clear vision and direction, leaders can inspire hope and optimism in their team, even in the face of a crisis.
- **Reflect and Assess:** Hopeful leaders engage in reflection and assessment of the crisis before taking action. They are aware of their body's response and act with intention and provide direction. Taking time to reflect on and assess the situation before acting can help leaders make more informed and hopeful decisions.
- **Provide Support and Encouragement:** Leaders can provide emotional and practical support to their team during a crisis, including making resources available, offering encouragement, and listening carefully and consciously to team members to help them navigate through their challenges. By providing support and encouragement, leaders can help their team members remain optimistic about the future.

As leaders navigate the complexities of crisis management, understanding and deploying hope becomes paramount. Hope theory offers valuable insight into how leaders can support their teams, inspire resilience, and drive positive change. By embracing hope as a guiding principle, leaders can cultivate optimism, provide vision and direction, and foster a sense of purpose within their organizations.

In the face of challenges like the COVID-19 pandemic, educational leaders must not shy away from showing emotions but, instead, should focus on hopeful strategies to lead their teams through turbulent times. By educating themselves and their teams on hope theory, providing support and encouragement, and engaging in reflective practices, leaders can harness the power of hope whenever it is needed.

Reflection Questions

- How has hope been a driving force in historical events, similar to the "Miracle on the Hudson" or President Obama's campaign?
- In what ways can educational leaders cultivate hope within their organizations during times of crisis?
- How does understanding hope theory contribute to effective crisis leadership in schools?
- Reflect on a time when you or a leader you know demonstrated hopeful leadership qualities during a crisis. What impact did this have on the outcome?
- What practical strategies can you implement to deploy hope in your leadership approach during challenging times?

Case Study

KIARA

School Administrator, Northeast United States

> There's always hope and there's always a positive way to do everything, and there's always a teachable moment.

Kiara, a dedicated Black and LatinX school administrator, has been serving in an urban elementary school for more than a decade. She faces the ongoing challenge of gang violence, which poses a constant crisis affecting the safety and well-being of her students.

EQUITY-CRISIS DILEMMA

Kiara's school faces socioeconomic challenges, including issues exacerbated by the presence of gangs in the community. According to data gathered by her district, her school has a substantial number of students eligible for free or reduced-price lunch, indicating a high level of need within the student population. Recently, Kiara has noticed an uptick in her grade 3–8 students being recruited for local gangs. After a few conversations with parents, Kiara realized she has to create a more urgent process to stop these recruiting efforts. She explained, "I've had several children die before due to gang violence and gunshot wounds, but it is really bad out there now." She continued:

> Last year, I went to a mom and I said, "Mom, I don't like who your son hangs out with. We got to get this together or you're going to cry." I tell parents that meaning—their child may die . . . will probably die if they get involved in the gang. A year later, it was devastating to have to show up after her son was murdered. And so, I just hugged her, and I didn't say anything because we'd already talked about it, it happened.

Kiara further explained: "I've told several Mommies get it together or you're gonna cry. Then we meet over the casket and we both cry. So, I needed to do something." Gang violence in the community surrounding the school has had a profound impact on students, creating an atmosphere of fear and instability. Kiara recognized the urgent need to address this issue to ensure a safe learning environment. She implements proactive measures such as increased security presence, conflict resolution programs, and trauma-informed support for affected students.

EQUITY-ORIENTED CRISIS SOLUTION BASED IN HOPE

Central to Kiara's leadership approach is fostering hope as a guiding principle amid the challenges of gang violence. She explained: "People would probably describe me as the most positive person. There is always something positive. There's always hope every time, and that's not Pollyana, that's real hope. It causes me to say 'Kiara! Step up! Shake it off, find a way and move forward.' " She emphasizes pathways thinking (the cognitive process of identifying and generating multiple viable routes or pathways to achieve a desired goal) by developing targeted intervention programs, mentorship initiatives, and extracurricular activities that offer students constructive pathways away from gangs. By setting clear goals for student success and well-being, Kiara instills a sense of purpose and direction in the school community. Also, understanding the crucial role parents play in steering their children away from gang involvement, Kiara collaborates closely with families.

She organizes workshops on recognizing signs of gang affiliation, provides resources for intervention and support, and fosters open communication channels to address concerns promptly. By empowering parents with knowledge and tools, she helps them guide their children toward positive alternatives.

Drawing from Snyder's hope theory, Kiara employs pathways thinking to create diverse opportunities for students to explore their potential beyond the influence of gangs. She encourages goal-directed energy by setting academic and personal development goals for each student, nurturing in them a sense of agency and empowerment. Through consistent reinforcement of hope as a transformative force, Kiara inspires resilience, optimism, and determination among students and staff alike.

In navigating the complex landscape of gang violence, Kiara's unwavering commitment to nurturing hope as a central tenet of her leadership not only mitigates the immediate crisis but also cultivates a culture of positivity, growth, and empowerment within her urban elementary school community. As she stated: "If I lose hope, it's time to throw in the towel, but I don't. I will continue to think about how we can stop having Mommies crying. If we're in a bad place, hope feeds me. We set goals, programs, and we meet them. We will make this a safer environment for our students. There is always hope."

CASE STUDY ANALYSIS

Individual and Small-Group Questions and Activities

- How does Kiara's approach to fostering hope and addressing gang violence resonate with your leadership style?
- Reflect on a challenging situation you have faced in your role as a school leader. How did you maintain hope and positivity during that time?
- In what ways do you currently collaborate with parents to address issues affecting students' well-being and safety in your school community?
- How can pathways thinking and goal-setting be integrated into your leadership practices to empower students and staff in times of crisis?

- Role-play scenarios in which school leaders engage with parents about gang recruitment concerns.
- Discuss effective communication strategies and support mechanisms.
- Brainstorm proactive measures and intervention programs that can be implemented to address gang violence in a school setting. Share ideas for creating safe, hopeful learning environments in which students are empowered to choose positive paths.
- Analyze case studies of schools that have successfully reduced gang activity by strategically deploying hope. Identify key strategies and best practices that can be adapted to your school context.

Whole-Group Activities

- Conduct a workshop on fostering hope and resilience in the face of adversity, inspired by Kiara's leadership approach. Discuss the importance of maintaining a positive outlook and setting clear goals for student success.
- Organize a panel discussion with community members, law enforcement officials, and mental health professionals to explore collaborative approaches to addressing gang violence in schools. Encourage dialogue on building partnerships for safer communities.
- Develop a schoolwide initiative focused on promoting hope as a central value in leadership. Create visual displays, inspirational messages, and activities that reinforce the importance of hope in overcoming challenges and fostering a supportive school environment.

Equity-Oriented Mindset

> To live is to choose. But to choose well, you must know who you are and what you stand for, where you want to go and why you want to get there.
>
> —Kofi Annan[1]

As the sun rose over the bustling city, a young Ursula Burns gazed out of her modest apartment window, her mother's words echoing in her mind: "This is where you're going to grow up, but this is not what defines you." Little did she know that those words would shape her remarkable journey. "If you have an opinion, you should make it be known," Ursula later recounted, a testament to her unwavering determination. She pursued a path in engineering, eventually joining Xerox, where her tenacity and leadership propelled her to the helm of the company. "All of us now are pioneers. Every one of us," she remarked, reflecting on her historic appointment as the first Black woman to lead a Fortune 500 company. Throughout her career, Ursula remained a steadfast advocate for equity and inclusion, emphasizing, "You have to give more than you take away from the world." Her extraordinary rise not only made history but also inspired a generation, proving that where one comes from does not determine where one can go.[2]

In the context of crisis leadership, Ursula Burns's journey exemplifies the significance of an equity-oriented mindset in guiding leaders to address the specific challenges posed by a crisis while centering equity. Her approach underscores the vital role of equity and inclusion in effective crisis management. Burns's conscious efforts to understand how crises disproportionately affect marginalized groups, along with her proactive work to dismantle institutional inequities and level the playing field, highlight the essential equity-oriented mindset that leaders must adopt during turbulent times. Burns's leadership philosophy aligns closely with the principles of an equity-oriented mindset, which emphasizes the need to actively engage in equity work, even amid crises. By aligning her values and practices with diversity and inclusion principles, she demonstrates that effective leadership requires a deliberate consideration of the needs and challenges faced by marginalized populations. This commitment ensures that their voices are heard and their distinct circumstances are addressed, preventing further marginalization. An equity lens allows leaders to navigate crises while also upholding principles of fairness, justice, and equal opportunities for all. As Burns stated, "You have to give more than you take away from the world," reflecting her belief in the importance of serving others and prioritizing their needs. This mindset is crucial for leaders, as it empowers them to make decisions that prioritize equitable outcomes, particularly for special populations disproportionately affected by crises.

An equity-oriented mindset, as defined within the framework of equity-oriented crisis leadership, encompasses a set of values and practices that are essential for leaders to engage in equity work during times of crisis.[3] It involves a conscious and deliberate consideration of how the crisis affects marginalized populations, thereby emphasizing the need to dismantle barriers and address systemic inequities, particularly in domains such as education.[4] When I interviewed educational leaders across the country, they identified ways that mindset showed up in their schools. For example, Eliza, a midcareer principal in North Carolina, shared:

> There was a change in mindset, especially as it pertains to academics. Pre-pandemic, teachers would say, 'Well, the kids come low to us. They're low, they're down a grade level and look to our Spanish immersion students as high performers.' Well, even with our Spanish immersion kids, we saw that once we returned back into the building during the pandemic, even those kids had experienced a learning loss.

Charles, a veteran principal, shared a different perspective about how his mindset affected his leadership:

> It's my job to not wear any nerves or concerns on my sleeve. I have to be very calm; I have to show that I've got everything in control and that everybody's okay. In order for them to come down and bring that mindset back to focusing on, we're here, everybody's safe, let's get back to what we normally do.

These perspectives highlight how some school leaders described their mindset and the mindsets of others during a crisis. Eliza's quote demonstrates a shift in mindset, especially concerning academics, as the pandemic revealed that even high-performing students, such as those in Spanish immersion programs, experienced learning loss. This suggests that the crisis prompted a reevaluation of preconceived notions about student performance and the need for a more adaptive mindset to address the challenges facing all students. In contrast, Charles's quote emphasizes the importance of maintaining a calm and composed demeanor as a leader, with a focus on managing emotions and projecting stability to support the school community's well-being. This insight reflects the evolving mindset of school leaders in the midst of crises, which encompasses reexamining academic expectations and adopting a composed and supportive leadership approach. Moreover, both leaders explained how equity-oriented mindsets are deployed during a crisis. Eliza's change in mindset demonstrates an awareness of the diverse experiences and challenges students face and emphasizes the need for an equitable approach to education—especially in times of crisis. Charles's perspective on leadership regarding demeanor is an example of confronting bias with a growth mindset. By acknowledging the need to remain composed and focused on ensuring everyone's well-being, Charles's approach aligns with principles of equity-oriented leadership, especially in times of uncertainty and chaos. The importance of an equity-oriented mindset lies in its ability to provide leaders with the awareness and perspective necessary to make decisions that prioritize equitable outcomes, especially for special populations disproportionately affected by crises. An equity-oriented mindset and its application in uncertain times enable leaders to continue navigating the turbulence while upholding principles of equity and inclusion.[5]

Leaders can apply an equity-oriented mindset in crisis management by embracing a set of values and practices that prioritize equity and inclusion. This equity-oriented approach necessitates a purposeful examination of how crises exacerbate existing disparities and disproportionately burden marginalized communities. It requires focused efforts to tear down institutional obstacles and rectify deep-rooted, systemic injustices that perpetuate inequalities during times of upheaval. Leaders can also demonstrate inclusive decision-making, allocate resources equitably, and advocate for radical change to ensure that their crisis management efforts prioritize equitable outcomes, especially for special populations affected by the crisis.[6] By managing individuals at work and focusing on equity, leaders can create a more inclusive environment and drive strategy and growth, reaping ample rewards in the process.[7]

In this chapter, I hope to help school leaders gain a comprehensive understanding of an equity-oriented mindset and its application in crisis management. I elucidate an equity-oriented mindset as the essential mental schema for leaders to engage in equity work, based on the explicit consideration of how crises affect marginalized populations. Furthermore, I highlight how given the pervasive nature of systemic racism in the education system, an equity-oriented mindset is instrumental in breaking down existing barriers and addressing inequities. By recognizing the key factors of equity-oriented leadership and identifying how it applies in crisis management, school leaders can become better equipped with the awareness and perspective necessary to navigate unanticipated challenges while prioritizing equitable outcomes, especially for special populations. The insight I present in this chapter underscore the significance of leaders embracing an equity-oriented mindset in order to manage crises more effectively, particularly with steadfast commitment to promoting equity and inclusion.[8]

UNDERSTANDING THE EQUITY-ORIENTED MINDSET

An equity-oriented mindset, as articulated by Estela Bensimon, is the fundamental mental framework necessary for leaders to engage effectively in equity work.[9] It requires leaders to move beyond mere representation and interpersonal relationship-building, urging them either to reshape or dismantle inequitable structures and systems. This mindset acknowledges that inequity can be challenging to name and even harder to change. It also necessitates a long-term commitment to fostering equity, even when the results may not be immediately tangible. By embracing an equity-oriented mindset, leaders can create an environment that is always inclusive of others, driven by conscious strategies to help it grow, and derive benefits that come from prioritizing what is equitable for all.

Bensimon coined the concept of "equity-mindedness" to describe the cognitive schema that administrators, faculty, and staff must develop to address racial inequity in educational institutions. According to Bensimon, an equity-oriented mindset involves several key attributes, including understanding the accountability and critical reframing of race-based inequities as a problem of practice, encouraging critical race consciousness, reflecting on organizational practices to make them more culturally relevant, and strategically navigating resistance to equity efforts.[10] With an equity-mindedness, individuals are expected to become conscious of racialized patterns embedded in policies, practices, and norms; use disaggregated data to identify racial equity gaps; and take responsibility for changing policies, practices, and norms that perpetuate racial inequity.

The Center for Creative Leadership illustrates the concept of an equity-oriented mindset in action by emphasizing the integration of equity as a fundamental leadership principle. In the realm of education, an equity-minded teacher is accountable for scrutinizing practices and policies, recognizing and addressing inequities through inquiry, and adeptly handling resistance to equity endeavors. In a professional setting, implementing equity involves providing equal opportunities for all employees based on their individual requirements, ensuring job descriptions are accessible, and transitioning to skills-based recruitment to cultivate fair working environments.

In the realm of education, an equity-oriented mindset encompasses various facets that are essential to foster an inclusive and equitable learning environment. One prominent example is the concept of equity-minded teachers, who recognize their responsibility to scrutinize the practices and policies perpetuating inequities. These educators employ inquiry to identify and address equity issues while also strategically navigating resistance to equity efforts. Furthermore, equity-focused teaching transcends mere inclusion by acknowledging the influence of systemic inequities on students' experiences. It involves purposefully cultivating a learning environment in which all students have equal access to learning, feel valued and supported, and enjoy an equitable chance of achieving positive outcomes.[11] Additionally, the concept of equity-minded organizations in K–12 education extends to administrators, faculty, and staff, necessitating a conscious awareness of racialized patterns embedded in school policies and the commitment to using disaggregated data to identify and rectify racial equity gaps. Patrice, a novice principal from the Midwest, explained how she used data to support students' social-emotional learning as they returned to in-person learning post-COVID.

> We immediately began diving into the zones of regulation and talking about how to regulate ourselves. We did that as an entire school, and that became a common language; we talked to everybody and everybody had a toolbox of strategies. The data showed that nothing was happening until students and even some faculty could get regulated. The adults were finding ways and tools that would help them regulate, so then they can deal with disregulated students to get them regulated. In the beginning, it was a whole shift of the mindset. It was a very real statistic, particularly about the African American boys in our population and how they were viewed by faculty and staff. We saw so many in-school suspensions (ISS) post-pandemic, and I remember thinking this is a lack of skill. So, I named it for teachers. The data was inequitable. So, I had my teachers teach those toolbox skills intensively. We pulled the kids and named what was going on for them or what we saw. They were not ready to learn, so we were

> practicing both the teachers and the students at getting better at regulating. I can say that in the last two and half years, given COVID, we had no students in the ISS room. The focus now is on supporting the students, understand how they perceive academics and the classroom environment. I did not want the mindset to be we put them in a room because they're a "problem" and walk away.

An equity-oriented mindset offers real-life solutions or strategies to mitigate inequities. For example, Patrice's quote emphasizes implementing strategies such as the "zones of regulation" and providing students and faculty with a "toolbox of strategies," which reflect a commitment to fostering an inclusive and supportive learning environment. This approach acknowledges the importance of regulating emotions and creating a common language for emotional well-being, which is essential for addressing the diverse needs of students, especially those from marginalized backgrounds. Furthermore, Patrice highlights the significance of confronting bias with a growth mindset by recognizing and addressing inequitable disciplinary practices, particularly concerning African American boys. The intentional focus on providing students and faculty with the necessary skills and support to regulate their emotions and behaviors demonstrates a proactive effort to create a more equitable and inclusive educational environment. Additionally, this example underscores the importance of shifting the mindset from punitive disciplinary measures to a more supportive and empathetic approach, ultimately leading to a significant reduction in in-school suspensions. This exemplifies an equity-oriented mindset that prioritizes understanding and addressing the diverse needs of all students.

An equity-oriented mindset is crucial for school leaders when navigating crises because it enables them to prioritize the needs of all students, particularly those from special populations. This approach involves being cognizant of the disparities that may be exacerbated during a crisis and making intentional efforts to address them.[12] For instance, during the COVID-19 pandemic, school leaders with an equity-oriented mindset ensured that students from low-income families had access to necessary technology for remote learning, such as laptops and internet hotspots. By recognizing the uneven impact of the crisis on different student groups, these leaders were able to allocate resources more fairly and support the academic continuity of all learners.[13]

To center equity during crises, school leaders can adopt various strategies that stem from an equity-oriented mindset.[14] For example, they can proactively gather data on the specific challenges faced by special populations, such as students with disabilities or English language learners, and use this information to tailor support measures. Additionally, leaders can involve representatives from these groups in decision-making processes to ensure that their voices are heard and their needs are considered. By doing so, school leaders will be better equipped to make decisions that are truly equitable and beneficial for all students.

Furthermore, an equity-oriented mindset empowers school leaders to reevaluate existing policies and practices through an equity lens during a crisis. For instance, in the aftermath of a natural disaster, leaders can reassess attendance policies to account for the disproportionate impact on students from marginalized communities. By being attuned to the potential inequities exacerbated by the crisis, leaders can adapt policies to be more flexible and responsive to the diverse circumstances of their student body, mitigating further marginalization and promoting a more just and inclusive educational environment.

An equity-oriented mindset, however, may be difficult to engage in during a crisis. Some challenges leaders may face when trying to implement an equity-oriented mindset during a crisis include the following:

1. **Limited Resources:** During a crisis, leaders may face resource constraints, challenging their ability to address the diverse needs of special student populations. For example, providing technology for remote learning to all students, especially those from low-income families, can be resource-intensive.[15]
2. **Resistance to Change:** Implementing an equity-oriented mindset may be met with resistance from those accustomed to the status quo. This resistance can hinder the adoption of new policies and practices that are essential for promoting equity during a crisis.
3. **Lack of Training and Support:** Leaders and staff may lack the necessary training and support to understand and address equity issues effectively. This can impede the implementation of equity-focused strategies and activities.[16]
4. **Organizational Culture:** The existing organizational culture may not be conducive to fostering an equity-oriented mindset. Overcoming ingrained biases and promoting inclusivity within the organizational culture can be a significant challenge for leaders.[17]

Dealing with the difficulties of integrating an equity-focused mindset during a crisis demands a multidimensional strategy. This is how the foundational elements merge, enabling a holistic framework for recovery.

Application of Equity-Oriented Mindset During a Crisis

During a crisis, leaders can implement various strategies to foster an equity-oriented mindset. Research indicates that leaders can utilize a crisis to address long-term equity issues by actively listening for ways to address inequities. One effective approach is to proactively gather data on the distinct challenges faced by specific student populations and use this information to tailor support initiatives. For instance, Victoria, a midcareer principal in Washington, D.C., shared her data-collection efforts based on lessons learned from the COVID-19 pandemic. She explained that she will be more proactive in the future:

> I learned over the years of the pandemic that basic needs weren't being met. Some kids weren't eating. They didn't have food and we'd have parents say we don't have any more money we don't have food, especially our undocumented families. They're not eligible for snap benefits and so I'm really trying to get them food, making sure that nobody was going hungry. Luckily, D.C. put out a provision that you couldn't kick people out for not paying rent but also with that was a concern as to where are people going. Families had been separated at shelters. So I had to begin to develop data collection dashboards so we knew as much as possible where our families were from and how we could support them based on their needs. . . . We had some partnerships with food delivery services that were successful, such as the Capital Area Food Bank Project, where we were able to distribute food weekly to students and families. I'm so proud of the communities, my teachers maintained and the love virtually that they maintained. I think the things they also tried to do outside of regular school for our kids that don't hear any English at home, like hangouts where you could just come and play Minecraft or whatever, and we would try to do the hangouts in half English, so they could hear English because that's something that also like another equity issue, right? Like if you're never hearing it but you're supposed to be in school learning it, you know that immersion is gone. The teachers, that would hold morning breakfast club or they've just sit on the computer and eat breakfast with kids but like that Community was, I think a big success.

Victoria emphasized the importance of addressing basic needs, such as providing food to underserved families and creating opportunities for non-English-speaking students to hear and engage in the language. Victoria also highlighted the success of partnering with food delivery services to distribute food to students and families and the teachers' efforts to maintain a sense of community and support for their students outside of regular school hours.

Involving representatives from these groups in decision-making processes ensures that their perspectives are valued and that their specific needs can be met.

Leaders can establish standard procedures for collaborating with historically marginalized communities to comprehend their needs and set priorities accordingly. By embracing the following strategies, leaders can work to establish a sustainable equity-oriented mindset.[18] Following are practical tactics that leaders can utilize, accompanied by reflective questions to assist them in effectively implementing such strategies.

1. **Proactively Gather Data**
   Leaders should actively collect data on the specific challenges faced by special student populations. This involves conducting surveys, interviews, and focus groups to understand their unique needs and circumstances. By analyzing this data, leaders can tailor support measures effectively, ensuring that resources are allocated where they are most needed.[19] Leaders should consider the following:
   - What specific data can we collect to better understand the challenges faced by our special student populations?
   - How can we ensure that the data-collection process is inclusive and representative of all voices?
2. **Use Inclusive and Appropriate Communication Channels**
   Effective communication is vital during a crisis. Leaders should utilize various communication channels to keep stakeholders informed and maintain transparency. This may involve using emails, newsletters, social media, and community meetings to disseminate information. Ensuring that communication is accessible and inclusive helps build trust and keeps everyone engaged in the decision-making process.[20] Leaders should consider the following:
   - What communication channels are most effective for reaching our diverse stakeholders?
   - How can we ensure that our communication is clear, accessible, and inclusive for all audiences?
3. **Equitable Systems and Structures—Reevaluate Policies**
   Leaders must regularly reevaluate existing policies and practices through an equity lens. This involves assessing how current policies may disproportionately affect marginalized groups and making necessary adjustments. For instance, attendance policies may need to be adapted to account for the challenges faced by students from low-income families during a crisis.[21]

Leaders should consider the following:

- Which current policies may be perpetuating inequities, and how can we adapt them to be more inclusive?
- What processes can we implement to ensure ongoing evaluation of our policies through an equity lens?

4. **Seek Credible Information**

   During a crisis, it is essential for leaders to seek credible information from trustworthy sources. This includes consulting experts and staying updated on best practices related to crisis management and equity. By grounding decisions in reliable data and expert advice, leaders can navigate challenges more effectively and implement strategies that promote equity.[22] Leaders should consider the following:

   - What are the most reliable sources of information we can consult during this crisis?
   - How can we verify the credibility of the information we receive to ensure informed decision-making?

5. **Involve Representatives for Inclusive Decision-Making**

   Incorporating representatives from diverse groups in decision-making processes is crucial for ensuring that all voices are heard. Leaders should establish committees or advisory boards that include students, parents, and community members from various backgrounds. This inclusive approach enriches the decision-making process and ensures that the distinct needs of different populations are considered. Leaders should consider the following:

   - Who are the key representatives from diverse groups that we can involve in our decision-making processes?
   - How can we create a safe space for these representatives to share their perspectives and needs?

6. **Lean on Hope—Be Positive and Maintain Perspective**

   Maintaining a positive attitude and perspective is essential for leaders navigating crises. While acknowledging the challenges, leaders should focus on solutions and opportunities for growth. By fostering an environment of hope and resilience, leaders can inspire their teams and communities to remain committed to equity and inclusion, even in difficult times.[23]

   Leaders should consider the following:

   - How can we cultivate a culture of hope and resilience within our organization during this crisis?
   - What specific actions can we take to maintain a positive outlook while addressing the challenges we face?

7. **Confront Bias with a Growth Mindset**
   Leaders should approach bias with a growth mindset, believing in the capacity for change within individuals and organizations. This involves recognizing biases that may exist within the team and actively working to address them. By cultivating a culture of learning and development, leaders can empower their teams to engage in equity work and challenge inequitable practices.[24] Leaders should consider the following:
   - How can we foster a growth mindset within our team to address bias and promote equity?
   - What training or resources can we provide to support our team in recognizing and confronting bias?

During a crisis, it is crucial for effective leadership to adopt a mindset that prioritizes equity and inclusivity. By actively gathering data, involving a diverse range of representatives in decision-making, and evaluating policies from an equity perspective, leaders can ensure that the specific challenges faced by marginalized groups are acknowledged and addressed. Additionally, seeking reliable information and maintaining transparent communication fosters trust and engagement among all stakeholders. As leaders navigate the complexities of crisis management, cultivating a culture of hope and resilience and addressing biases with a growth mindset will empower teams to embrace change and advocate for equity. By incorporating these approaches into their leadership practices, leaders can establish sustainable pathways toward equity that extend beyond the immediate crisis, providing opportunities for all individuals to thrive.

CONCLUSION

Recent crises, including the COVID-19 pandemic, have presented school leaders with unprecedented challenges, emphasizing the need for an equity-oriented mindset in navigating such difficult times. The extended nature of the COVID crisis, coupled with its distinct characteristics, has made it clear that promoting equitable outcomes is essential to effectively address all the compounded crises facing school systems. School leaders have been called to take focused and deliberate action that addresses the well-being of all individuals in their communities, especially those disproportionately affected by crisis. The importance of leadership at all levels of the system, particularly in times of crisis, has highlighted the need for school leaders to examine and address the emotional needs of teachers and students. Therefore, when leading during a crisis, school leaders must adopt an equity-oriented mindset to ensure that their actions promote equitable outcomes and address the needs of all members of the school community.

Chapter Discussion Questions

- How do you prioritize equity and inclusion in your daily operations as a school leader, especially in addressing the needs of marginalized student populations during a crisis?
- What strategies might you employ to ensure that your school's decision-making processes and resource allocation prioritize equitable outcomes, particularly for special student populations affected by a crisis?
- How do you proactively gather and utilize data on the specific challenges faced by special student populations to tailor support measures and address inequities, especially during times of crisis?
- What steps could you (or do you) take to involve representatives from diverse student groups in decision-making processes to ensure that their voices are heard and their needs are considered, particularly when navigating crises that affect the student body unequally?
- How might you reevaluate existing policies and practices through an equity lens during a crisis, and what adaptations could you make to ensure that they are more flexible and responsive to the diverse circumstances of your student body?
- What challenges have you encountered in implementing an equity-oriented mindset during a crisis, and what strategies have you employed to address these challenges effectively?
- How do you confront bias with a growth mindset and create a culture that fosters inclusion and belonging for all individuals, especially during times of crisis, within your school community?
- What guidance, materials, professional learning opportunities, and time do you need to ensure that your equity-oriented mindset remains sustainable in the long term, particularly as you work toward recovery and beyond in the aftermath of a crisis?
- How do you engage families from diverse cultural, socioeconomic, and linguistic backgrounds to build effective family-school partnerships, especially when working to promote equitable outcomes for all students during and after a crisis?
- What are the most important contributors to a positive working relationship with your superintendent, and how do you facilitate such a relationship to ensure that your efforts to achieve equity and inclusion are supported at the district level, particularly during times of crisis?

Case Study

LEENA

Principal, East United States

Leena has been the principal of a large urban school for seventeen years. The school serves a diverse student population, with 80 percent of the children being of Latino descent. Within this group, 29 percent are English language learners, 25 percent are students with disabilities, and 30 percent are in temporary housing. The school has been a hub for the community, providing stability and support for many families. The recent influx of migrant students, however, has brought to light existing educational inequities within the school. The arrival of these students has highlighted disparities in access to quality education and resources, disproportionately affecting the migrant student population. Leena is deeply concerned about the widening achievement gap and the emotional well-being of these students. She realizes that the crisis has brought to the forefront the urgent need to address equity issues within her school.

Equity-Crisis Dilemma

The manifestation of the problem became evident as Leena observed that a significant number of migrant students were unable to engage fully in the educational process because of a lack of access to necessary resources and support. For instance, she noticed that some migrant students lacked access to appropriate language support services, specialized instruction for their disabilities, and stable housing, which significantly affected their ability to thrive in the school environment. Furthermore, Leena also observed the impact of the migrant crisis on some of her staff, many of whom had family members who also were migrants. This personal connection to the crisis added an extra layer of emotional strain and urgency for Leena and her staff. It became clear that the crisis was not only affecting the students but also taking a toll on the emotional well-being of her staff, who were grappling with the challenges faced by their families and communities. In response to these observations, Leena realized that the crisis had brought to the forefront the urgent need to address equity issues within her school. She understood that an equity-oriented mindset was crucial in guiding her to address the specific challenges posed by the crisis while centering equity. By recognizing these challenges and their impact on both students and staff, Leena was motivated to take conscious steps to address these issues using an equity-oriented mindset. She understood that it was essential to gather data on the specific challenges faced by migrant students and involve representatives from diverse student groups in decision-making processes to ensure that their voices were heard and their unique needs were considered. Additionally, she was committed to reevaluating existing policies and practices through an equity lens and investing in effective communication and learning communities to foster inclusion and belonging for all individuals during this challenging time.

Equity-Oriented Crisis Solution

The arrival of these students has highlighted disparities in access to quality education and resources, disproportionately affecting the migrant student population. Leena's concerns prompted her to consider a more comprehensive and equitable approach to addressing these challenges. In response to this pressing issue, Leena has begun to explore a multifaceted strategy that embraces an equity-oriented mindset to ensure that all students, especially those from marginalized backgrounds, have equal access to quality education and support. This approach involves conscious data gathering, inclusive decision-making, reevaluation of policies and practices, confronting bias with a growth mindset, investing in effective communication and learning communities, and providing peer support and technical assistance. Leena shared:

> The first thing we did was we met about it. We talked about the impact. Because we are a school that has 30 percent of our students in temporary housing, we have already set up a team, like we have clothes here by the nurse's room, we have utilities, we have a social worker in-house, and we also have a social worker from the district that coordinates our outside resources. Our parent coordinator is really good too in finding out resources and walking parents through the process like getting Medicaid, getting healthcare, getting additional supports.

Leena engaged in an equity-oriented mindset by including inclusive decision-making. For example, Leena involved representatives from her leadership team, including migrant faculty members and the parent coordinator. In inclusive decision-making processes, leaders must ensure various voices are heard and their unique needs are considered. This ensures that the strategies implemented are truly equitable and beneficial for all students. Leena then shared how she reevaluated policies and practices through an equity-oriented mindset:

> We have a lot of students that come throughout the year from the Dominican Republic. So, for us, we knew that the emotional toll would be great, and although we were welcoming a different migrant population, thinking about the resources, it was going to be the same in some respects, but honestly, we had to consider what this population needed.

Leena reevaluated existing policies and practices through an equity lens to ensure that this particular group of students and families had what they needed. She adapted these policies to be more flexible and responsive to the diverse circumstances of her student body, ensuring that they did not perpetuate or exacerbate existing inequities.

Finally, Leena shared how providing peer support and technical assistance to her students, families, and faculty provided an equity-oriented support for them:

> Like one case was in the middle of last year, we tried to have different people involved in the intake process and they're really good, like they have been working in the school for more than fifteen years, so anything that they notice, they are to tell us right away. There was one case where we noticed that the mom wasn't looking up, the child looked fine, but the mom did not look fine. So, we immediately . . . what we did was . . . like we go and we talk a little bit more, like, "Hi, how are you? We're here for you. Is there anything that we need? We see that your student is fine, he came from Long Island. You were in Long Island. Is everything okay? We just want to make sure that we have the right setting, that we're supporting him in the best way."
>
> And the mom immediately said, "I would like to . . . do you have a guidance counselor? I would like to talk to the school counselor." So, I said, "Okay." We set that up right away, and mom was trying, I think . . . there was a family dispute because after the hurricane, she didn't even want her child to be in Puerto Rico because she saw

that everything was very challenging, and she decided to bring him to the United States. And I think the father didn't want that. The father stayed behind. So, I had my parent coordinator also help her with setting up Medicaid and a shelter. We wanted to provide her with the necessary support to get them off the ground.

Leena ensures that individuals and organizations engaged in changing their practices benefit from ongoing support, an opportunity to share experiences, and the feedback and critique of their peers. She also provides technical support and assistance such as training, coaching, or process improvement. Additionally, Leena confronts bias with a growth mindset, believing that people can change, and she fosters that belief in her team.

Leena's leadership actions, guided by an equity-oriented mindset, have the potential to yield significant long-term gains in equity within her school. By consciously gathering data on the challenges faced by migrant students and involving representatives from diverse student groups in decision-making processes, Leena is laying the foundation for a more inclusive and equitable educational environment. Additionally, her reevaluation of policies and practices through an equity lens and her commitment to confronting bias with a growth mindset are essential steps toward dismantling systemic inequities and fostering a culture of diversity, equity, and inclusion. These actions align with the pillars of equity-oriented crisis leadership, as they prioritize equitable outcomes and address the specific challenges posed by the crisis while centering equity.[25] Furthermore, Leena's approach resonates with the concept of shared equity leadership, which emphasizes the leaders' collective embodiment of equity values and practices.[26] By leveraging these strategies for long-term gains in equity, Leena's school can become a model for fostering an inclusive and supportive educational environment in which all students have equal access to quality education and support.

CASE STUDY ANALYSIS

Individual and Small-Group Discussion Questions

- **Highlighting Disparities:** How did the recent influx of migrant students reveal existing disparities in access to quality education and resources within Leena's school? Consider how these disparities reflect systemic inequities that need to be addressed through an equity-oriented mindset.

- **Challenges Faced by Migrant Students:** What specific challenges did migrant students encounter that hindered their full engagement in the educational process? Discuss how these challenges not only affected their academic success but also their emotional well-being, emphasizing the need for tailored support.
- **Impact on School Staff:** In what ways did the crisis affect the emotional well-being of the school staff? Analyze how their emotional state influenced their ability to effectively support students, highlighting the importance of staff well-being in fostering an equitable learning environment.
- **Recognizing Equity Issues:** How did Leena's observations during the crisis lead her to recognize the urgent need to address equity issues within her school? Reflect on the significance of awareness in driving equity-focused actions.
- **Components of an Equity-Oriented Mindset:** What are the key components of an equity-oriented mindset, and how did Leena apply these components to tackle the challenges posed by the crisis? Discuss how her approach exemplifies the principles of equity-oriented leadership.

Whole-Group Activities

- **Group Discussion on Migrant Student Challenges:** Conduct a discussion focusing on the specific challenges faced by migrant students, such as access to necessary resources, language support services, and emotional well-being. Encourage participants to share their observations and insight, fostering a deeper understanding of these issues through an equity lens.
- **Brainstorming Strategies for Equity:** Facilitate a brainstorming session on potential strategies to address disparities in access to quality education and resources for migrant students. Encourage participants to consider inclusive decision-making, policy reevaluation, and confronting bias as essential elements of these strategies.
- **Role-Playing Inclusive Decision-Making:** Organize a role-playing activity in which participants take on the roles of school leaders,

teachers, and support staff to simulate inclusive decision-making processes. Emphasize the importance of involving diverse voices and ensuring that unique needs are considered in addressing the challenges faced by migrant students.

- **Reflective Dialogue on Growth Mindset:** Engage in a reflective dialogue about the concept of a growth mindset and its application in confronting bias within the school community. Encourage participants to share examples of how they have applied a growth mindset to promote inclusion during times of crisis.
- **Action Steps for Equity:** Collaboratively develop a set of action steps based on Leena's approach to addressing equity issues within her school. Encourage participants to identify specific measures that can be implemented to ensure equal access to quality education and support for all students, particularly those from marginalized backgrounds.

Critical Reflection

> Human beings are not built in silence, but in word, in work, in action-reflection.
>
> —Paulo Freire[1]

Philosophers such as Max van Manen, Daniel Liston, Kenneth Zeichner, and Todd Dinkelman define critical reflection as deliberation about broader social, historical, political, and cultural contexts of education and about relationships between educational practice and the construction of a more equitable, justice, and democratic society.[2] In education, scholars such as John Dewey have described critical reflection as a habit of "critical examination and inquiry."[3] In my teacher preparation program, my professors taught me to reflect—after school ended and the children went home—on how the day proceeded, and what key events and elements I needed to remember and unpack. As a school leader, the hustle and bustle of every day, week, and month caused time to pass too quickly, but I always deliberately thought about my day as I drove home. This reflection, initially, was not intentional, but gradually it became a natural and welcome habit of practice.

For many leaders, reflection is an inherent part of the job. We think about what we must do, what problems are arising, what needs fixing. The list has no end. Reflection is integral to school leadership because it allows leaders to engage in an assessment and a reassessment cycle about their assumptions, presuppositions, thinking processes, and meaning-making. School leaders who practice self-reflection can readily recall events and have preexisting tools at hand to apply when a crisis arises. Self-reflection and knowledge application also promote emotional intelligence to ensure leaders meet the needs of their school staff, faculty, and families during stressful times. The practice of reflecting during a crisis is also critical, however, as it can provide leaders with new insight into making programmatic changes to their schools after the crisis. In a 2011 *Washington Post* piece on the role of reflection in leadership, Colonel Eric Kail, a battalion leader, explained,

"Gaining wisdom from an experience requires reflection."[4] For school leaders who have experienced atypical levels of crisis, reflection—critical reflection specifically—can provide wisdom that may fundamentally change the school environment and catalyze change for marginalized students.[5] Critical reflection becomes more about examining the prevalent issues a leader faces with a critical eye, instead of just checking off a task list or solving simple problems.

Defining Equity-Oriented Critical Reflection

Equity-oriented critical reflection involves deeply examining one's assumptions, beliefs, and decision-making to align practices with values of equity and inclusivity, especially during crises.

In a crisis, critical reflection allows leaders to think deeply about the systems and structures that need to be solidified or changed. This is important to understand what needs to be done for the school's trajectory. Case in point: Charles, who works in the east, explained his school had no nurse. Although some states require schools to employ nurses, many do not have such mandates or provide adequate funding to support school nursing positions. The Centers for Disease Control and Prevention (CDC) recommends at least one full-time nurse for every 750 students, but most states fall short of this guideline.[6] Charles had to think dynamically about this significant shortage after facing a situation with a student who was experiencing a low pulse rate. He explained:

> I know that in Detroit, it is tough to get an ambulance, and we don't have a nurse, so when this kid's pulse was barely there, we had to call an ambulance, but we also had to use a defibrillator. Well, the ambulance showed up, and they helped us get the student stabilized and transported. When I reflected on that experience, I thought about the long-term effects and what short-term items had to be taken care of. In the long term, we needed a much more comprehensive plan to support kids in medical emergencies, so I lobbied for an additional defibrillator and training for our staff. I also thought about the mental impact on our staff who witnessed the literal lifesaving efforts of this child. At one point, I thought I was going to have to take this child in my car and rush to the ER. So, I wanted to create spaces where we regularly checked in on the mental health of our staff. The experiences leaders have can be life-altering and scary. And they are also responsible for setting a healthy work environment.

Clearly, the process of analyzing and making meaning of this experience for Charles was multipronged once he began to reflect on all aspects of this crisis.

To be self-reflecting in the midst of a crisis can be daunting, but Charles demonstrated that critical reflection is required to step back and explain what happened, what could have been done better, and what needs to happen in the long term to provide students with an equitable environment that meets their needs.

Research conducted by Susa Madsen highlighted that developing equity-oriented leaders requires critical reflection, while researcher Christa Boske emphasized that leading for equity demands confronting personal biases and professional challenges.[7] Laura Hallberg and Louise J. Santiago, however, found that although most leaders are willing to engage in equity leadership, they need help to reflect on how their biases and professional challenges intersect with their leadership actions.[8] The National Center for Education Statistics recently revealed that 78 percent of public-school principals were white, whereas only 48 percent of public-school students were white, making it crucial for school leaders to reflect critically during times of crisis and acknowledge their privilege.[9] Janet Patti et al. emphasized the importance of critical self-reflection in decision-making, especially in crisis management.[10] Leaders need to reflect on what matters and how to make sense of the world and their emotions. In reflection during a crisis, leaders must dismantle oppressive systems that negatively affect marginalized populations. Hallberg and Santiago found that critical reflection helped some leaders recognize how their past experiences influenced the decisions they made and how those decisions affect others.[11] As racism continues to permeate the US public education system, leaders who critically reflect during crises can stem further marginalization through detracking and other inequitable policies. Thus, critical self-reflection involves leaders adopting this practice as a means of changing outcomes for marginalized populations and critiquing their actions to secure more equitable responses to future crises within their school or district.

Several leaders I interviewed engaged in reflection during a crisis as a way to adjust their responses when considering marginalized students. For example, Samuel, a veteran principal from the Northeast shared:

> To go back to my point on reflection, I keep talking to my staff about [the fact] that it's not going to be pretty [recovery from crisis]. We need to understand what happens in the first couple of weeks of school, we need to reflect on that and build from there. And maybe we have to back up a second, take a breath, and say, "Okay, this isn't working. What do we do

> next?" And that's going to be feedback from our students. It's going to be feedback from our families. It's going to be feedback from our teachers, and we have to try to put that all together and come up with the next best thing to do.

Similarly, Leena, a novice principal in upstate New York, shared that being in the midst of a crisis moved her to reflect more quickly:

> Crisis brings me to reflection much faster. If something is just in place and working, you're not questioning it, you're not working through it. But after a crisis, you're always like, "Man, well, this has to change. This was a good thing to put into place." So, I do think crises sometimes force you to think and reflect, while other opportunities don't.

Some of the leaders I interviewed felt it necessary to model and encourage reflection for students. For example, Deborah, a midcareer principal in New York City explained, "As a leader, I think it's important for me to teach my kids about empathy, reflection, having a heart, being a good citizen. These are little nuggets that I always try and drop in my children's spirit." Critical reflection is a valuable approach that involves self-awareness, careful observation, and flexible responses. In this example, Deborah practices reflective leadership continuously on her own personal beliefs and decisions, encouraging self-improvement and growth. This approach allows leaders to model reflection and empathy for their teams while they also developing their own skills in awareness, judgment, and action. By being reflective, leaders can create a relationship-based organization, support the personal and professional development of their team, and make better decisions to improve team performance. Therefore, a leader also listens to students' reflective thoughts, because doing so fosters a culture of self-improvement, empathy, and personal growth—all of which are essential for effective leadership and team development.[12] To enable transformation, Devita Bishundat et al. explained that leaders must reflect on their practices first before providing opportunities for others to be reflective.[13]

By contrast, some principals discussed how the lack of reflection impedes their work. Angela, an early career principal in the Southwest, explained:

> I was actually part of what we called the COVID response team . . . a group of administrators that planned all the rollouts for all those changes and all the pivots that we had to make during all of this. . . . It was more action, not more reflection. There wasn't enough reflection. We didn't really have a lot of that, and that's something that I think, looking back, would have been very beneficial for leaders.

By reflecting during and after a crisis, principals could ensure a safe space in which they could make decisions that secured processes toward recovery and consistent assessment and reassessment of their actions. Overall, these findings suggest that critical reflection allows leaders a way to find the space to step back from the urgency and examine their responses. Although this is essential at all times, it is particularly significant when crises distinctly affect marginalized populations.[14] In short, a leader's awareness of making decisions during a crisis should lead to understanding the impact of those decisions on *all* stakeholders.

THE SIGNIFICANCE OF EQUITY-ORIENTED CRITICAL REFLECTION DURING A CRISIS

Engaging in critical reflection allows leaders to identify experiences that affect their response to equity issues, understand the importance of deep ongoing learning, and purposefully decide how presuppositions constrain their understanding of the world. Specifically in the context of school leadership, effective leaders plan and prepare for various crisis events; once past a crisis, they reflect on what worked, which elements need to be corrected, and what other parts of their school need evaluation. In this way, leaders help everyone recover and return to a typical learning environment as soon as possible.[15]

Additionally, critical self-reflection has been found to affect the actions of culturally responsive school leaders and their ability to overcome barriers in promoting equity and inclusivity.[16] The significance of critical reflection in crisis leadership is further emphasized by the reflections of district leaders in the education sector, particularly in response to the COVID-19 pandemic. Clearly, critical reflection, which always offers a crucial view of managing any emergency, is particularly important for navigating the series of unprecedented crises that leaders have faced in the twenty-first century.

The Elements of Equity-Oriented Critical Reflection

Leaders tend to spring into action when a crisis occurs. Depending on their skills, dispositions, experiences, and biases, the decisions leaders make based on their knowledge may spur new actions that yield hoped-for results or resolutions. But the decisions and the actions must be rational to address the situation effectively. This involves understanding the stages of a crisis and implementing a well-defined crisis management plan. Crisis response encompasses planning and actions to address natural and human-made disasters, critical incidents, and tragic events. When responding, the leaders should reflect critically within the specific social, political, or cultural context—having a "when, not if" mentality regarding crisis management planning, being proactive and not reactive, and defining specific crisis scenarios and contingency plans is essential. By understanding the nature of crises and having a well-prepared crisis management plan, leaders can make more informed and effective decisions to mitigate the impact of the crisis.

Critical reflection is a robust process that involves identifying, questioning, and assessing deeply held assumptions about knowledge, perceptions, beliefs, feelings, and actions. It goes beyond a mere reading assignment or summary of an activity. The aim is to change one's thinking about a subject and, consequently, one's behavior. This process is essential in all disciplines and can take various forms, such as formal essays, blog entries, or short-paragraph answers to questions. According to Dr. Barbara Jacoby, critical reflection adds depth and breadth to meaning by challenging simplistic conclusions, comparing varying perspectives, examining causality, and raising more challenging questions. It is the process of analyzing, reconsidering, and questioning one's experiences within a broad context of issues and content knowledge.[17] Similar to Jacoby's view on critical reflection, Dewey's relational view of transformative learning emphasizes the importance of critical reflection. Dewey defined critical reflection as the active, persistent, and careful consideration of any belief or supposed form of knowledge.[18] This definition highlights the nuanced and essential nature of critical reflection in challenging and reevaluating one's beliefs and knowledge. Critical reflection is a personal and self-learning process that contributes to leaders becoming more conscious about their motivations and the concept of "doing no harm" to the communities and partners with whom they interact. When practiced through a critical lens, reflection becomes a tool that creates more engaged students and more meaningful experiences. The ultimate outcome of a leader's critical reflection during any event is to generate, deepen, and document student learning.[19]

THE ROLE OF EQUITY-ORIENTED CRITICAL REFLECTION IN CRISIS SCHOOL LEADERSHIP

Understanding a crisis requires understanding its defining features, including profound uncertainty coupled with a sense of urgency to minimize or avoid potential negative outcomes. Acting in a crisis entails addressing the situation and minimizing its negative impact.[20] This can involve crisis action planning, creating a crisis communications team, identifying points of contact for various teams, and training an emergency response team. In a crisis, people process information differently and may revert to more fundamental or instinctive fight-or-flight reasoning, making it necessary to simplify and communicate messages clearly.[21] We've discussed some of these key concepts and features in prior chapters, but the key point to emphasize is the importance of learning the lessons of past emergencies. Knowledgably acting on a crisis involves understanding its nature, planning, communication, and previous learning.[22] As highlighted in a recent interview, DreamBox Learning CEO Jessie Woolley-Wilson's approach to critical reflection holds valuable insight for school leaders leading through crises, especially when it comes to being vulnerable and using reflection to make substantial changes for the future. For example, during the COVID-19 pandemic, DreamBox Learning provided free w-fi access through the end of the 2020 school year, committing the company to equitable dissemination of its materials. As part of their efforts to provide equitable access to educational resources during the COVID-19 pandemic, DreamBox Learning conducted a review of their platform, which unexpectedly revealed hidden biases, such as gender biases. According to CEO Jessie Woolley-Wilson, this crisis presented an opportunity to embrace critical reflection to address these biases. Similarly, school leaders facing crises must embrace critical reflection to ensure that their actions align with their values and commitment to inclusivity. By critically examining their decisions and practices during a crisis, school leaders can identify potential biases and ensure their actions align with their school's values and goals. This reflective approach is particularly important in times of crisis, when leaders may feel pressure to act quickly without considering the broader implications of their decisions. For example, a school leader, such as Charles, facing a medical emergency because of the lack of a school nurse could engage in critical reflection to identify systemic issues and develop long-term solutions. By reflecting on the incident, the leader, in this case Charles, recognized the need for additional medical equipment, staff training, and mental health support for staff who witnessed the event. This critical reflection allowed Charles to move beyond a quick fix and work to create a more equitable and supportive environment for students and staff. In times of crisis, leaders must be willing to confront their biases and the ways in which systemic inequities may be perpetuated through their actions. By embracing critical reflection, leaders can transform crises into opportunities for growth and positive change, building stronger, more inclusive school communities. School leaders facing crises must similarly embrace critical reflection to ensure that their actions align with their values and commitment to inclusivity. By critically examining their decisions and practices, school leaders can identify potential biases and ensure that their actions align with their school's values and goals. This reflective approach can help school leaders lead effectively and build a stronger, more inclusive school community, even (and especially) in times of crisis.

Critical reflection, then, is a transformational tool for leaders leading through a crisis. Woolley-Wilson's proactive stance in scrutinizing and amending the company's software to eliminate biases during the COVID-19 pandemic exemplifies this process, aligning operations with core values of inclusivity and fairness. This process also mirrors the theoretical framework proposed by Jürgen Habermas, who emphasized the role of reflection in understanding and utilizing knowledge. For school leaders, this means engaging in a similar process of introspection and critique, not just to navigate the immediate challenges of a crisis but also to uncover and dismantle underlying systemic issues that may perpetuate inequality or hinder effective crisis management. In so doing, leaders can ensure that their responses are not only immediate and practical but also ethically grounded and socially responsible. This will pave the path for long-term positive change within their institutions.

Habermas's theory of communicative action provides a framework for understanding the process of critical reflection, which is central to transformative learning. Habermas posited that knowledge is gained through self-emancipation, which is facilitated by reflection leading to a transformed consciousness or "perspective transformation."[23] This process of knowing or reflecting, then acting based on the information gained from reflection, is a key component of Habermas's critical theory. Through this process, individuals become self-consciously aware of knowledge, enabling them to critique ideology and distorted knowledge.[24] This framework becomes particularly relevant to the context of school leadership, especially during a crisis. School leaders are often challenged by managing diverse groups of people, making decisions under uncertainty, and promoting innovative strategies.[25] Critical reflection can help school leaders navigate these challenges. For instance, during the COVID-19 crisis, school leaders needed to reflect on directives from the district and fully understand their implications before implementing any action that ensured the continuity of education.[26] This process of reflection followed by action, as informed by Habermas's theory, leads to increased strategic crisis management and leadership in schools. Leaders become more necessarily responsive and adaptive, strengthening their ability to lead through challenging times.[27]

INCORPORATING CRITICAL REFLECTION INTO LEADERSHIP PRACTICE

Like many routines that should be part of a leader's day, critical reflection is a vital exercise for helping leaders continue to lead throughout a crisis. Leaders may wonder how to deploy or utilize critical reflection during a crisis: initiating a mindful approach, engaging in self-care, and devoting time across the school to foster collective critical reflection. Leaders describe how they reflect in many disciplines to marshal change and recovery. The practical use of critical reflection must be continuously embedded in both each school's organizational routine and each leader's practice and style. Within the framework of action versus knowing = new action (see figure 3.1), I describe how leaders can incorporate reflection into their daily agendas.

Starting with a Mindful Approach to Critical Reflection

Mindfulness can significantly affect and support school leaders during a crisis. By integrating mindfulness into their routines, leaders can engage in critical reflection by asking specific questions about the day's events and how they connect to a crisis. This approach enables leaders to delve into the more profound nature of how crises affect them and their schools, fostering a more just and equitable school environment. As part of critical reflection, mindfulness allows leaders to engage in an assessment and reassessment cycle about their assumptions, presuppositions, thought processes, and meaning-making, which are essential in crisis leadership. This approach also enables leaders to gain wisdom from their experiences, make informed and effective decisions, and dismantle oppressive systems that harm marginalized populations. Furthermore, the transformative power of critical reflection when supported by mindfulness is underscored by the need for leaders to use this process to understand and address dangerous systemic issues, such as unequal funding and disparate outcomes based on a demographic or zip code that perpetuate inequality. This process involves leaders adopting a practice of reflection to change outcomes for marginalized populations and to critique their actions to improve future responses to crises. By critically reflecting on their decisions and practices, school leaders can identify

FIGURE 3.1 Knowing Leads to New Action for Leaders

Knowing → Acting —Informs→ Leader engages in new actions to solve crisis, equitably potential biases and align their actions with their school's values and goals, leading to a stronger, more inclusive school community.[28]

Practical Strategies for Mindful Critical Reflection

School leaders can enact several strategies when starting with a mindful approach to critical reflection during a crisis.

Practice Awareness and Reflection

Identify problems regularly to prevent them from becoming crises and avoid oversimplifying events. This involves focusing on teaching and learning, showing resilience, and deferring to experts when necessary.[29]

To regularly identify problems before they become crises, school leaders can employ the following:

1. Schedule regular check-ins with teachers, staff, and students to proactively identify emerging issues.
2. Analyze data trends over time to spot potential problems early, rather than reacting to individual data points.
3. Avoid oversimplifying complex situations by seeking diverse perspectives from experts and stakeholders.
4. Maintain a relentless focus on teaching and learning, even amid other demands, to ensure that staff stay on track with the core mission.
5. Demonstrate resilience in the face of setbacks by modeling a positive, solution-oriented mindset for the school community.

Cultivate Mindful Leadership Dispositions

Setting intentions, investing in others, and building self-regulation skills are all practices that help school leaders remain nonjudgmental, patient, present, aware, and calm—qualities that are essential during a crisis.[30]

To cultivate essential mindful leadership qualities, school leaders can purse the following:

1. Set clear intentions for leadership and regularly revisit them to stay grounded.
2. Invest time and energy in developing their team, empowering others, and building trusting relationships.
3. Develop self-regulation skills through practices like meditation, journaling, or exercise to manage stress and emotions.
4. Strive to remain nonjudgmental, patient, present, aware, and calm, especially during challenging situations.

Adopt Mindfulness Practices

Breaking ruminative loops in thinking allows leaders to leave work at work, be present with students and teachers, and promote self-care throughout the school day.[31]

To integrate mindfulness into their daily work, school leaders can support the following:

1. Build in regular breaks to disengage from work and avoid rumination.
2. Practice being fully present when interacting with students, teachers, and staff.
3. Encourage and model self-care practices like taking breaks, getting enough sleep, and maintaining work-life balance.

Reflect and Inquire

Engaging in reflection and inquiry helps understand one's relationship to ambiguity, loss of control, and threat. The goal is to ask reflective questions and make decisions that have a meaningful impact on students, staff, and community.[32] To engage in reflective practice, school leaders can consider the following:

1. Regularly ask questions like: What assumptions am I making? What am I learning? How can I grow?
2. Seek feedback from trusted colleagues, mentors, or coaches to gain new perspectives.
3. Carve out dedicated time for reflection, either individually or with their leadership team.
4. Use reflective practices to meaningfully examine how they are affecting students, staff, and the broader community.

School administrators can develop the self-awareness, emotional intelligence, and adaptive skills necessary to successfully address intricate challenges and promote a fair and inclusive school environment by consistently applying these practical techniques.

Enacting Critical Reflection

Leaders can model critical reflection while leading through a crisis by practicing self-reflection to recall and apply existing knowledge. This task requires significant emotional intelligence to benefit individual team members.[33] Self-awareness, learning from experience, and improvement of decision-making are all advantages of reflection.[34] Overthinking and analysis paralysis, however, are also very real drawbacks that may interfere, given that leaders need to act quickly and decisively in a crisis. Leaders must balance reflection and reaction, adapting their approach to specific circumstances. The irony of a disruptive event like a crisis is that it actually heightens the need for outstanding leadership and underscores valuable leadership competencies, through success in their presence and failure in their absence.[35] By balancing reflection and action, leaders can tactically navigate a crisis while also fostering self-awareness, learning from experience, and making informed decisions. Angela, a principal in the Southwest, explained how this works:

> It was peaks and valleys. But within my school, I feel like our staff really came together. I think we all support each other and love each other, and I think we all had an opportunity as a staff to reflect. We were able to come together and like reflect and celebrate. We reflected on what we did and how we adapted. And I think we were able to model reflection and its importance post-crisis to our community and to our families. I think that's really important because it provided more in-depth information and understanding about what we all just went through. The reflection showed our community and families to pause which is what you need when you want to make changes after a crisis.

Making Time Across the School

Time is probably the most sought-after commodity in a school. Finding time is essential to provide learning opportunities, offer professional development, and meet other needs to bolster the equitable environment of a school. But time is limited. Students attend a limited number of school days; teachers have finite hours of professional learning. How we plan our routines into our precious time schedule—including the use of critical reflection—need not be exhaustive (or exhausting), but it should be consistent. Leaders can find ways to embed critical reflection once a day for ten to fifteen minutes to ask themselves, "What happened today that matters most? How do I connect what matters the most to the crisis I led through? How am I feeling about what is happening? What did I learn (knowledge I gleaned?) How did this make me act? What new actions do I need to take? Who do I need to inform/collaborate with?" These questions tap into the profound nature of how crises affect us. I used to go to the gym weekly to run off steam and energy and reflect on these questions. I used my voice memo app to capture any random ideas or thoughts. Sometimes, I knew that my reflections required a thought partner. I needed to unpack what I was feeling and thinking with someone who was listening as a sounding-board. Walking is also a stimulating exercise to help leaders free their mind to think about their day through a more critical lens. In essence, leaders can use myriad ways to tuck into these key questions to reflect on how they navigate through their days—during times of crisis or periods of relative calm—to prepare them for future crises and the steps they need to take to support the school's recovery.

To ensure that school leaders guide their institutions through crises with equity at the forefront, leaders can deliver professional development (PD) sessions around critical reflection. School leaders can begin these sessions with a case study or a period of free reflection that employs critical questions and encourages reflective practice. Charlotte Danielson has emphasized the importance of reflection in teaching for professional advancement, which necessitates more than mere acknowledgment; it demands active demonstration by leaders.[36] School leaders should demonstrate critical reflection to vividly illustrate these practices. In the process, they should examine their underlying beliefs and assumptions to inform future actions. This practice is about introspection and leading by example, showing colleagues ways to analyze their teaching methods critically and to assess the impact of these methods on students. Leaders can encourage educators to embrace continuous learning and improvement by incorporating reflective practices into PD and daily routines. This approach can bridge the gap between theoretical knowledge and practical application. In so doing, a culture of professional inquiry and collaboration that is essential for navigating crises and promoting educational equity can be continually fostered.[37]

THE TRANSFORMATIVE POWER OF CRITICAL REFLECTION IN CRISIS LEADERSHIP

Although hard to undergo, professional learning inevitably occurs after a crisis and, at times, even during the event. For example, several leaders I spoke with discussed the professional learning sessions they facilitated during the COVID-19 pandemic and following the 2020 summer Black Lives Matter protests. One leader explained that she thought teachers were using a deficit mindset during the COVID-19 pandemic to describe the behaviors of students submitting work: "I could not move forward with other learning sessions that did not directly address this mindset. I was angry and disappointed, but I also knew that it would still be pervasive even after the pandemic if we did not address this issue now." Darla, a novice principal in New York City, critically reflected on what she knew, how she acted, and how she felt during that same time:

> We started building our schoolwide vision in June and then revised [it] again during the summer break. We reflected on what our vision for blended learning [was] and [asked] how does it change from the vision

> that existed pre-COVID? And in their reflections, they were able to share what they learned from the end-of-the-year professional learning about equity and reflect on where do they think we should go next year. So, we took those reflections and developed a vision, and one of the key statements in there is including equity in our work for all. So, it's not just one particular group that needs an equity perspective, but we all need to be a part of the equity work in our building and becoming more culturally responsive.

In this excerpt, Darla demonstrated how critical reflection provided a guide to make substantive changes—in this case, a schoolwide vision postcrisis. In particular, by providing a collective opportunity to reflect, her faculty and staff became part of the recovery process instead of merely responding to the new vision. This sparked further transformations and changes, such as curricular enhancements and modifications to respond to crisis events. Darla continued:

> The reflection and vision work also has led to the idea of switching curriculums. So, we are switching our ELA curriculums for the whole building. We're going with more culture responsive texts which aligns to this new vision we have all developed. So again, it's just one step in the right direction, although I know that is not going to be the be-all and end-all. Switching the curriculum is not going to fix all the equity needs in the building, but at least now it's much better than where we were.

This knowledge provided Darla with a new plan of action to chart a new course that would have long-term impacts. Research conducted by Lasater et al. showed that, when it came to data-driven practices, teachers who exhibit a deficit mindset or thinking fostered an unsafe professional work environment, moving from instruction to accountability measures and seeing students as numbers, not as people.[38] Darla's critical reflection connected her to a new plan of action, which will fundamentally disrupt the organizational practices and make her work environment healthier. She concluded:

> I learned how important it is to listen. You have to listen to everything that's being said but also [to] the things that aren't being said. And while listening, also being courageous enough to take certain challenges, even if those challenges are messy. When I just think about this whole thing and where we started in March and going into it with one mindset and then having to shift gears and make those shifts quickly. In thinking about instruction alone, going into the crisis, and we were thinking that we were going to do the same type of instruction that we did pre-COVID in the

school building, and then after listening and reflecting, making adjustments. When I think about the work around equity that I started doing with the staff, just thinking about realizing that the work needed to happen, being worried about jumping into it because it was such a messy time, but knowing that it was important anyway and that change needed to happen. Though there was going to be a challenge with it, . . . it still needed to happen anyway. So, just knowing that trusting that gut instinct, that it's okay for it to be messy, but it still has to happen. I would say that was the big learning from the reflections in this whole process.

CONCLUSION

Critical reflection is essential for school leaders during crises. It allows them to reassess their decision-making process, gain new knowledge, and take practical actions to resolve any crisis and promote stability and security among students, teachers, and parents through an equity lens. In a crisis, critical reflection allows leaders to think about the systems and structures that need to be solidified or changed. More important, it challenges leaders to articulate why those changes are needed for the school's trajectory.

When I was a principal, our school's enrollment would fluctuate, but I could not understand why this happened so often. When I had worked with several schools previously, this issue never arose. I began to reflect on what I was seeing. The students left frequently and would never show up in our local afterschool programs. When I inquired about this problem, I received no answer except that "families just leave." I met with my school culture team, who explained that five or more homeless shelters in the area directly fed into our school. Given that the aim of homeless shelters is to support families until they found a permanent home, it made sense that students would not stay at school for long periods of time: they were in temporary housing, and so, our school was also temporary. I then created a plan to support these families by notifying the teachers if they were in transient housing, providing supplies for students and families, and confirming regular communication with any new school they attended if we learned where they were headed. Although the new process was not foolproof, it did establish a new perspective of seeing students and supporting families who were seeking both schooling and housing.

Critical reflection allows you not only to consider the past, but also to question it. "What can we do differently in support of the teachers AND students?" By knowing more about our student population, we were able to provide our teachers with different types of supports while we also tried some innovations like changing schedules (with varying success). The key takeaway is that critical reflection is a safe avenue to make relevant changes. It empowers leaders to engage in assessment-and-reassessment cycles about their assumptions, presuppositions, thought processes, and meaning-making. Critical reflection becomes more about discerning and examining the prevalent issues with a critical eye, and not simply creating a task list or following a problem-solving approach. It involves understanding the defining features of a crisis, acting on them, and relying on critical reflection to guide leadership. By critically reflecting on their decisions and practices, school leaders recognize potential biases and misalignment with school values and goals. Habermas's theory of communicative action provides a framework for understanding the process of critical reflection as a vehicle for transformative learning. With a daily practice of critical reflection in action, leaders will become more responsive, especially in crisis situations.

Chapter Discussion Questions

- How do broader social, historical, political, and cultural contexts affect crisis in your school?
- What assumptions and presuppositions guide your decision-making during a crisis?
- How do you reflect on the impact of a crisis on marginalized students and their families?
- What new knowledge have you gained from a past or current crisis, and how have you applied it to promote stability and security among students, teachers, and parents?
- In what ways do you reassess your leadership decisions through an equity lens during a crisis?
- How might you identify and address potential biases in your leadership actions during a given crisis?
- What systems and structures need to be solidified or changed in response to specific crises, and why?
- How could you (or do you) foster a more just and equitable school environment through your leadership actions during a crisis situation?
- What are the long-term implications of a past or current crisis for your school, and how do you plan to address them?
- How could you (or do you) model and encourage critical reflection for your staff and students during a crisis?

Case Study

GRACE

Principal, Western United States

> They didn't want to come back because they were scared. Now we're more aware of what's going on. We're not taking any chances. We're not cutting any corners.

Grace, a dedicated principal with ten years of experience, faced a profoundly distressing situation in a rural school district on the West Coast. A substitute teacher entrusted with the care of her students used racist language, directing the N-word at a class of young learners. She explained, "Some of the students ran out of the classroom to find me and other admin. They told us that he called the students the N-word and told them that he was going to kill them. He told the kids he had bombs in his backpack, that he was going to kill them, and he chased one of the students around the classroom."

Equity-Crisis Dilemma

Grace explained that she immediately escorted the substitute out of the building while security accompanied her and took down the teacher's license plate. She called the police immediately and had them patrol the parking lot for days after the incident. During the day, although the school touts being a "cell-phone free campus," she explained, "230 of my students were calling their parents and telling them what happened. Parents are calling, wanting to know what's going on. What happened? Is there an active shooter, or if there's a bomb, has it been found?" That evening, Grace sent a communication to parents and held office hours to discuss the traumatic event. This abhorrent behavior created an immediate equity-oriented crisis leadership dilemma for Grace, requiring her to embrace a thoughtful and proactive response.

In the midst of the crisis, Grace had to navigate the complex intersection of ensuring the safety and well-being of her students, addressing the trauma experienced by the school community, and upholding principles of equity and justice. The incident not only posed a direct threat to the students' physical safety but also inflicted emotional harm, highlighting the pervasive nature of systemic racism and its impact on educational environments. Grace's swift and decisive actions in removing the substitute with the assistance of law enforcement, followed by communicating with parents, were essential for managing the immediate aftermath of the crisis. She also recognized, however, the need for long-term measures to address underlying issues of equity and inclusion within the school, specifically emphasizing the importance of proactive and sustained efforts to create a safe and supportive learning environment for all students.

Equity-Oriented Crisis Solution

Grace's response to the substitute teacher's behavior exemplified the transformative power of critical reflection in crisis leadership. By critically reflecting on the incident, she identified potential biases (cultural, or the tendency to judge other cultures by the standards of one's own culture, often leading to the assumption of superiority of one's own culture and contextual, or refer to biases that arise from the circumstances surrounding the transmission of cultural information, such as copying the traits of particular models or under particular social contexts) and ensured that her actions aligned with the school's values and goals.[39] After the incident, Grace met with her school team to assess what its impact on the staff was. She considered the various demographics of her staff and encouraged them to share. She then initiated a substitute-buddy program using a small stipend form the Elementary and Secondary School Emergency Relief funds she was given. Teachers would volunteer at their grade level and check in with the substitute teachers at least three times a day while also providing feedback or support as needed. At the end of the day, the principal and the teachers would connect to discuss the substitutes and evaluate whether to have them return. Moreover, Grace considered adding student thoughts and feedback at the end of each substitute's tenure, but first wanted to assess how the substitute-buddy program was working.

Grace's reflective approach helped her lead appropriately and build a stronger, more inclusive school community postcrisis. Providing a buddy at the grade level for substitute teachers created leadership opportunities for the teachers, mutual accountability across the school, and a degree of relief for the principal to attend events or meetings out of school without fear of hearing about another similar incident. Incorporating critical reflection into her leadership practice was essential for Grace, especially during this crisis. Her proactive stance in scrutinizing and amending the school's policies and practices to eliminate biases and to promote inclusivity demonstrated the significance of critical reflection in crisis leadership. This reflective approach addressed the immediate challenges of the crisis while also uncovering and dismantling latent-systemic issues that were potentially perpetuating inequality. As a result, it was possible to create long-term positive change within the school.

Grace's case study is a compelling example of how critical reflection can be a powerful tool for school leaders to navigate crises, promote equity, and foster a more just and inclusive school environment. Her thoughtful and deliberate approach to crisis leadership, grounded in critical reflection, set a high standard for addressing and preventing similar incidents in educational settings.

Grace's Strategies for Critical Reflection

When incorporating critical reflection into her leadership practice, Grace employed several strategies to ascertain that her actions aligned with the school's values and goals. First, she engaged in regular self-assessment and self-questioning to identify and challenge her biases and assumptions. This involved consciously examining her thoughts, decisions, and actions to uncover any underlying prejudices that could affect her leadership during the crisis. As part of her critical reflection during the crisis, Grace closely examined her own decision-making process and the actions she took. She realized that in the initial response to the crisis, she had prioritized the needs of the majority student population over the specific challenges faced by marginalized groups, such as students with disabilities or English language learners. Through deeper reflection, Grace recognized that this was influenced by her own biases and assumptions about which students were most "deserving" of immediate support. She had unconsciously fallen into the trap of making decisions based on her lived experiences and perspectives, rather than truly centering the needs of the entire school community. Grace also reflected on how her past experiences as a teacher had shaped her leadership style. She realized that she tended to make unilateral decisions without fully consulting her staff, which could reinforce top-down power structures and stifle the voices of those closest to students. This realization prompted Grace to commit to a more collaborative, inclusive approach going forward. By engaging in this critical self-reflection, Grace was able to identify blind spots in her leadership that could have perpetuated inequities, even unintentionally, during the crisis. Armed with this newfound awareness, she was able to adjust her actions and decision-making processes to better align with the school's values of equity and inclusivity. This reflective practice allowed Grace to transform the crisis into an opportunity for growth and positive change within her school community.

Second, Grace actively sought feedback from diverse stakeholders, including students, parents, teachers, and community members. By listening to and considering different perspectives, she gained a more comprehensive understanding of the crisis and its implications. These strategies enabled Grace to lead confidently during the crisis, demonstrating the transformative power of critical reflection in addressing immediate challenges and fostering long-term positive change within the school community.

CASE STUDY ANALYSIS

Individual Reflection Questions

- How did Grace's actions during the crisis align with the school's values and goals?
- What biases and assumptions might have influenced the substitute teacher's behavior, and how can we address them?
- How did the incident affect the school community, and what measures can be taken to address the trauma experienced?
- How can school leaders proactively promote inclusivity and equity to prevent similar incidents in the future?

Small-Group Activities

- **Case Analysis:** Divide the group into smaller teams to analyze specific aspects of the case, such as the immediate response, the long-term measures, and the impact on the school community. Each team can then present its findings to the whole group.

- **Scenario Planning:** In small groups, develop potential scenarios for similar crises and discuss proactive measures that can be implemented to address them while upholding principles of equity and justice.

Whole-Group Activities

- **Critical Reflection Workshop:** Facilitate a workshop on critical reflection using Grace's strategies as a framework. Encourage participants to engage in self-assessment and seek feedback from diverse stakeholders to identify and challenge biases.
- **Equity-Oriented Crisis Leadership Simulation:** Conduct a simulation exercise in which participants assume the role of school leaders facing an equity-oriented crisis. This will allow them to apply critical reflection and decision-making in a realistic scenario.

CHAPTER 4

Inclusive Decision-Making

Peace requires everyone to be in the circle—wholeness, inclusion.
—Isabel Allende

Making decisions as a leader is a huge part of the job. As a school leader, I found myself making a never-ending number of decisions, from the bell schedule to vacation time to what lunches students hated. In fact, an article written for the School Superintendent Association by McDaniel and Gruenert found that principals make an average of three hundred decisions a day and nine thousand decisions a month.[1] These decisions range from the significant to the trivial, but they all involve a principal saying yes or no. Given the nature of all these decisions to be made, leaders must make choices about when to include multiple stakeholders and when not to do so. Although some decisions have to be made in the moment and at the leader level, at other times, leaders should make decisions in conjunction with multiple stakeholders. A crisis is one such time when leaders should include multiple perspectives so that collaborators can work through the complexity of the problem together.

In times of crisis, the ability to make effective decisions is paramount for leaders across various sectors. The way decisions are made during a crisis can have a profound impact on the overall organization, its stakeholders, and the community at large. Inclusive decision-making plays a crucial role in guiding leaders through challenging times by engaging diverse perspectives and voices to inform strategic choices.[2] I define inclusive decision-making as the process by which leaders engage multiple stakeholders, particularly those from marginalized populations. Leaders who embrace inclusive decision-making develop consensus on pressing issues when a crisis is involved.

Natural disasters are a type of crisis that is typically unexpected or that allow only for a small window of preparation. Leaders often identify challenges, destruction, and other factors in the aftermath by assessing the incurred damage within the school or community. One early morning in

2022 a leader walked into a school, distressed by what she saw after Tropical Storm Ida. Her school, located in Northern New Jersey, was flooded, resulting in a necessary and immediate closure. The building was more than one hundred years old and required substantial maintenance to fix this unexpected disaster. Students were given laptops, and remote learning commenced. Principal Grace explained, "The water flooded our entire school after unprecedented rains, and I could do nothing else but close until we got support." The state had already designated the school with Targeted status, which meant they were tasked with raising academic scores even in the face of such a significant disaster. Feeling pressure, Grace began to make decisions without considering her impact on, or the inclusion of, various community members. After three weeks of the school's closure, the turnout for remote learning was low, teachers felt disengaged, and academic scores stalled. After eventually returning to school for in-person learning, Grace reflected on what she had learned from the experience:

> I find that I have to have a sense of buy-in from the teachers. I think that's one of the lessons I learned. First, I have to get buy-in, and I think one of the things that I will use to get the teacher buy-in is showing them that I'm genuinely here for them, and I care about them. And now more than ever, it's not just caring about what they're doing in the classroom. Of course, that's the main focus, but I think as an administrator, it is important for us to care about the teachers. I should have taken a minute and asked, "How are you guys doing?"

When experiencing a crisis, leaders may often take a top-down approach because of the overwhelming nature of the crisis and how quickly crises evolve. During and after the critical moments of a crisis, however, a leader can, and should, reflect on and establish protocols for inclusive decision-making.

DEFINING INCLUSIVE LEADERSHIP

The decisions leaders make during a crisis can determine the organization's ability to navigate challenges, mitigate risks, and seize opportunities for growth. Effective decision-making is essential for maintaining stability, building resilience, and ensuring continuity in times of uncertainty. Leaders must make timely and well-informed decisions that align with their organization's values, goals, and priorities to steer it successfully through turbulent times.

The decisions made during a crisis can have far-reaching consequences that affect the overall organization in profound ways. From financial implications to reputational risks and operational changes, every decision shapes the organization's trajectory and influences its stakeholders' experience. Leaders must consider the long-term effects of their decisions on organizational culture, employee morale, customer relationships, and community trust to uphold the organization's integrity and sustainability. Following are some of the chief consequences of noninclusive decision-making during crises:[3]

1. **Financial Implications**
   Noninclusive decision-making can lead to poor resource allocation, inefficient use of funds, and missed opportunities for cost savings. Decisions made without input from diverse stakeholders may fail to identify creative solutions or anticipate unintended financial impacts. This can result in budget deficits, depletion of reserves, and long-term financial instability for the organization.
2. **Reputational Damage**
   Decisions that do not reflect the needs and concerns of all stakeholders can erode trust and damage the organization's reputation within the community. Stakeholders may perceive the organization as insensitive, biased, or unresponsive, which can have a negative impact on public perception, media coverage, and relationships with key partners.
3. **Operational Disruptions**
   Siloed decision-making during crises can result in operational challenges, such as low employee morale, resistance to change, and lack of buy-in from frontline staff. This can lead to breakdowns in communication, coordination, and service delivery, ultimately hindering the organization's ability to effectively respond to the crisis.
4. **Erosion of Organizational Culture**
   Exclusive decision-making processes can foster a culture of mistrust, resentment, and disengagement among employees. When individuals feel their voices are not heard or their needs are not prioritized, it can undermine the organization's values, morale, and sense of community, making it more difficult to navigate crises and maintain resilience.

By considering these potential consequences, leaders can recognize the importance of embracing inclusive decision-making practices during times of crisis. Engaging in diverse perspectives, building trust, and prioritizing the needs of all stakeholders can help organizations weather storms, emerge stronger, and maintain their integrity and sustainability in the long run.

Inclusive decision-making, as defined by Mollie Galloway and Ann Ishimaru, involves creating democratic, authentic processes that engage diverse perspectives and voices in decision-making.[4] This approach emphasizes inclusivity, equity, and collaboration to ensure that decisions reflect the needs and values of all stakeholders. By involving a wide range of voices in the decision-making process, leaders can harness collective wisdom, foster innovation, and promote social responsibility within their organizations.

In short, inclusive decision-making is a critical component of effective leadership during crises, enabling leaders to navigate challenges with empathy, equity, and integrity. By embracing inclusivity in decision-making processes, leaders can build trust, foster resilience, and drive positive change within their organizations and communities. By understanding and implementing three key principles—that is, creating authentic, democratic processes; engaging diverse perspectives; and involving the community at every level—leaders can make more informed decisions that consider a wide range of viewpoints and ultimately lead to better outcomes.

Defining Inclusive Decision-Making

Inclusive decision-making is a critical leadership practice that involves engaging a diverse range of stakeholders to inform strategic choices, particularly during times of crisis. This approach emphasizes equity, collaboration, and the incorporation of multiple perspectives to ensure that decisions reflect the needs and values of all affected parties.

Creating an Inclusive, Democratic, Authentic Decision-Making Process

Creating inclusive decision-making processes involves establishing frameworks that promote fairness, transparency, and participation among all stakeholders. Inclusivity ensures that decisions are not made in isolation or based on limited perspectives, but rather take into account the needs and concerns of a diverse range of individuals. By incorporating democratic principles, such as open communication, collaboration, and consensus-building, leaders can foster a sense of ownership and accountability among those involved in the decision-making process. According to research conducted by Karen Bell and Mark Reed, having an inclusive decision-making process empowers marginalized individuals and engages a democratic process.[5]

Engaging Diverse Perspectives and Voices

Engaging diverse perspectives and voices is a cornerstone of inclusive decision-making. It involves actively seeking input from individuals with varying backgrounds, experiences, and viewpoints to ensure that decisions reflect the complexity and diversity of the organization and community. By valuing different perspectives, leaders can gain valuable insight, challenge assumptions, and identify innovative solutions to complex problems. Diversity in decision-making promotes creativity, critical thinking, and adaptability. When leaders embrace diverse perspectives, they create an environment in which individuals feel empowered to contribute their distinct insight and expertise. This collaborative approach not only enhances the quality of decisions but also fosters a culture of inclusivity and belonging within the organization.

Involving the Community at Every Process Level

Involving the community at every process level is essential for ensuring that decisions are informed by the needs and priorities of those directly affected by them. Community engagement goes beyond mere consultation or token representation; it requires active participation, collaboration, and partnership with stakeholders throughout the decision-making process. By involving the community at every level, leaders can build trust, foster relationships, and promote shared ownership of decisions. Community members bring valuable knowledge, perspectives, and lived experiences that can enrich discussions and lead to more effective outcomes. Involving the community also builds social capital, strengthens networks, and enhances resilience in times of crisis.

FACTORS INFLUENCING DECISION-MAKING IN CRISIS LEADERSHIP

In times of crisis, effective and inclusive decision-making is crucial for navigating challenges and ensuring organizational resilience. But when it comes time to act, several key factors often influence how decisions are made in the moment, ultimately shaping outcomes and responses to crises. These factors include a leader's existing mindset on equity issues, gender differences in decision-making, and the tendency to rely on others' opinions.

Factor 1: The Importance of an Equity Mindset—and the Risks of a Noninclusive Mindset

Leaders with an equity mindset recognize that crises often exacerbate existing inequities and disproportionately affect marginalized groups. They understand that decisions made during a crisis must actively address systemic barriers and disparities, rather than perpetuating them. An equity-focused mindset leads leaders to pursue the following:

- Seek out and center the voices and experiences of those most affected by the crisis.
- Analyze decisions through an equity lens to identify potential unintended consequences.
- Allocate resources and support in ways that prioritize the needs of vulnerable populations.
- Collaborate with community stakeholders to cocreate equitable solutions.
- Monitor outcomes to ensure decisions are having the intended equitable impact.

In contrast, leaders without an equity-focused mindset may make crisis decisions that inadvertently reinforce existing power structures and marginalization. This can manifest in the following ways:

- Relying on business-as-usual approaches that overlook the distinct needs of underserved groups.
- Making unilateral decisions without receiving meaningful input from diverse stakeholders.
- Allocating resources in ways that widen, rather than close, disparities.
- Failing to proactively address systemic barriers that create unequal access and outcomes.
- Neglecting to monitor the differential impact of decisions on marginalized populations.

In the end, a leader's approach, whether or not it is focused on fairness, influences the inclusiveness and impartiality of their response to crises. It is essential for leaders to cultivate a mindset that prioritizes fairness to make choices that promote social justice and aid the most vulnerable in times of turmoil.

Factor 2: Gender Differences in Decision-Making During Crises

Gender differences can also influence decision-making processes during crises, as highlighted by research that suggests men and women may approach decision-making differently in crisis situations. Factors that affect these different approaches include risk assessment, communication styles, and leadership approaches.[6] Understanding these gender differences can provide greater insight into how to leverage diverse perspectives and decision-making strategies effectively during crises.

Research has indicated that female educational leaders are more risk-averse than their male counterparts in crises. Studies also have shown that women in leadership often approach decision-making with greater caution, carefully weighing potential negative consequences before taking action. This tendency can manifest in various educational contexts, in which female leaders may prioritize their students' and staff's stability and well-being, opting for strategies that minimize risk. In contrast, male educational leaders may be more willing to embrace risks to resolve crises more quickly. This difference in risk perception can influence decisions made during critical moments, such as school closures, budget cuts, or emergency responses to safety threats. For example, during the COVID-19 pandemic, research found that female educational leaders were more likely to adopt cautious approaches in their decision-making processes.[7] These leaders often emphasized thorough planning and stakeholder consultation, reflecting a heightened sensitivity to the potential impacts of their decisions on the school community. This cautiousness can lead to more deliberate and inclusive decision-making, ultimately benefiting the educational environment. Even while noting these tendencies, however, the gender gap in risk-taking may vary depending on the context and the specific challenges educational leaders face. In high-stakes situations, for example, female leaders may adapt their strategies, balancing risk aversion with the need for decisive action to support their institutions effectively. Overall, the evidence suggests that female educational leaders typically exhibit more risk-averse behavior than their male counterparts, particularly in crisis situations in which the implications of decisions are significant. Understanding these dynamics can help inform leadership training and support initiatives to foster effective decision-making in educational settings.[8]

Factor 3: Reliance on Others' Opinions in Decision-Making

Reliance on others' opinions in decision-making is a pivotal aspect for leaders, particularly during crises, as highlighted by research conducted by Joseph Scanlon, Ira Helsloot, and Jelle Groenendaal.[9] Factors, such as organizational culture, leadership style, and past experiences, however, also can influence a leader's inclination to depend on others' perspectives. For example, a leader in a traditionally hierarchical organization might feel compelled to adhere to established norms, leading to an overreliance on senior staff opinions while also neglecting input from junior employees or marginalized groups. This can result in an echo chamber effect, in which only certain voices are heard, ultimately hindering innovation and inclusivity. Conversely, leaders who have experienced the benefits of diverse input may be more likely to seek varied opinions. Although seeking input is crucial, there is a risk of becoming too reliant on others' opinions, which can lead to decision paralysis or a lack of accountability. Leaders must find a balance between valuing input and maintaining their judgment and vision. To address these factors, leaders should take an active role in fostering a culture of inclusivity that encourages all voices to be heard while also creating an environment in which they can confidently make decisions. They should be mindful of their teams' dynamics, recognizing when certain voices dominate discussions or when others are marginalized. This awareness can manifest in the form of disengagement from less vocal team members or a need for more innovative ideas. Leaders can mitigate these risks by implementing structured decision-making processes that ensure diverse perspectives are included while also allowing for decisive action when needed.[10]

CONSEQUENCES OF NONINCLUSIVE DECISION-MAKING

Regardless of which factors contribute to siloed or leader-driven decisions, noninclusive decision-making practices can have significant consequences, particularly in crisis leadership contexts. These consequences can affect organizational effectiveness, community relations, and overall outcomes. Two key consequences of noninclusive decision-making include white cultural hegemony within public schools and adverse effects on various populations because of a lack of inclusivity.

White cultural hegemony can be both a driver of and a consequence of noninclusive decision-making in public schools. The dominance of white cultural norms and values may shape decision-making processes in ways that marginalize diverse voices and perspectives, leading to biases, inequities, and exclusionary practices. This can result in decisions that fail to adequately address the needs of all students, families, and staff members, perpetuating systemic inequalities.[11] Additionally, the lack of inclusive decision-making can also reinforce and maintain white cultural hegemony within educational institutions. When decisions are made without meaningfully incorporating diverse viewpoints, the status quo of white dominance is preserved, making it difficult to challenge and dismantle. The literature suggests that white cultural hegemony in schools often manifests through curriculum content that predominantly reflects white, Eurocentric perspectives; disciplinary policies that disproportionately affect students of color; and hiring practices that lack diversity among teachers and administrators.[12] In crisis situations, such as the COVID-19 pandemic, the maintenance of white cultural hegemony can lead to decisions that exacerbate existing inequities, such as unequal access to remote learning resources or inadequate support for marginalized communities.[13] To address the consequences of white cultural hegemony in decision-making, schools must implement inclusive practices that center the voices and experiences of people of color.[14] This may involve diversifying leadership teams, providing antiracism training for staff, and collaborating with families and community members to develop culturally responsive policies and programs. By prioritizing inclusive decision-making, schools can challenge white supremacy and work to achieve more equitable and just educational outcomes for all students.

Noninclusive decision-making practices can have also adverse effects on various populations within organizations and communities, particularly marginalized groups, such as people of color, individuals with disabilities, LGBTQ+ individuals, and low-income families. For example, decisions regarding curriculum changes or disciplinary policies may be made in school settings without input from these groups, leading to outcomes that do not reflect their needs or perspectives. This can result in a curriculum that overlooks the contributions and histories of diverse cultures or disciplinary measures that disproportionately affect students of color, contributing to a school-to-prison pipeline. The actual outcomes of such exclusion can include feelings of alienation, decreased academic performance, and heightened tensions within the school community, ultimately perpetuating cycles of inequity and disenfranchisement. As Selim highlights, the lack of inclusivity in decision-making can significantly affect those whose voices are not heard, reinforcing the importance of actively seeking diverse perspectives to foster a more equitable environment.[15]

In short, the consequences of noninclusive decision-making in crisis leadership extend beyond immediate outcomes to long-term implications for equity, diversity, and organizational resilience. By recognizing the possibility of these consequences and embracing more inclusive decision-making practices, leaders can foster a culture of inclusivity, promote social justice, and enhance their ability to navigate crises effectively while prioritizing the needs of all stakeholders.

CHARACTERISTICS OF INCLUSIVE DECISION-MAKING

With a new understanding of the importance of inclusive decision-making, we now turn to several key characteristics that define inclusivity in the decision-making process: welcoming and including voices from diverse allies and marginalized populations, seeking diverse perspectives to operationalize decisions, and forming tangible decisions in the best interest of special populations. I'll explore each of these characteristics in turn.

1. **Welcoming and Including Voices from Diverse Allies and Marginalized Populations**
   Inclusive decision-making involves actively seeking input from a wide range of stakeholders, including marginalized populations and diverse allies, or individuals or groups who actively support and advocate for the needs and rights of marginalized communities, leveraging their privilege and influence to foster inclusivity and equity. Diverse allies play a crucial role in decision-making by bringing different perspectives to the table, challenging assumptions, and ensuring that the voices of underrepresented groups are heard and considered. This collaborative approach enhances the quality of decisions, strengthens community ties, and promotes a culture of mutual support and understanding.

   Frazer, a veteran principal from New Jersey, explained how, during crises, he brokers the inclusion of allies into his decision-making:

   > I consider how do I understand the culture and the climate in this building and how do I begin to develop plans to shift the culture post-crisis. The saboteurs [in the building] had much influence; they were the ones that would create the wind, and you had a significant number of teachers over the fence sitters who were just willing to go in whichever direction. So, I worked with my assistant superintendent, Maxine, who became a vital member in helping me understand the history of the building and develop an understanding of these different individuals. Understand them contextually and historically, to be able to come up with better plans to minimize their impact, to be able to identify the potential allies that we had in the building, and to begin to leverage opportunities to bring these allies kind of closer and help create that momentum we needed to shift the culture of the school.

   Frazer's comments illustrate the vital role of diverse allies in fostering inclusive decision-making, particularly during times of crisis. By actively engaging with his assistant superintendent and understanding the historical context of his school community, he demonstrates how leaders can broker the inclusion of various voices to develop more effective plans. This approach aligns with welcoming and including diverse allies and marginalized populations, as it emphasizes the importance of collaboration and the need to leverage the unique perspectives of those who may have been previously overlooked. By identifying potential allies and creating opportunities for their involvement, leaders like Frazer can enhance the decision-making process, ensuring that it is informed by a comprehensive understanding of the community's needs and challenges. By welcoming voices from different backgrounds, experiences, and viewpoints, leaders can ensure that a comprehensive understanding of the issues informs decisions.

Leaders can identify and seek out the voices of diverse allies and marginalized populations through several practical strategies, particularly in time-sensitive situations. First, establishing clear channels for input, such as surveys or suggestion boxes, allows community members to share their thoughts and concerns quickly. Leveraging existing relationships with community organizations can facilitate quick outreach, ensuring that the voices of those who may be harder to reach are included. Additionally, using technology for rapid feedback—such as polls or virtual meetings—can help gather input efficiently, especially when anonymity is encouraged. When time is tight, prioritizing key stakeholders, including representatives from affected communities and student leaders, becomes crucial for obtaining critical insights. Leaders should also create a sense of urgency by framing discussions around the immediate impact of decisions on the community, motivating stakeholders to engage quickly. Organizing brief, focused discussions or roundtable meetings can further streamline the collection of diverse perspectives. Finally, following up with stakeholders to acknowledge their contributions and explain how their feedback influenced decision-making builds trust and encourages future participation. By implementing these strategies, leaders can effectively incorporate the voices of diverse allies and marginalized populations, enhancing the inclusivity and quality of their decision-making processes.[16]

2. **Diversifying Perspectives to Operationalize Decisions**
Effective inclusive decision-making requires leaders to seek diverse perspectives actively to inform their decision-making processes. This may involve engaging with individuals from different departments and levels of hierarchy or including external stakeholders to gain insight that may not be immediately apparent. For instance, in health-care settings, hospitals like the Mayo Clinic involve multidisciplinary teams made up of health-care professionals with diverse expertise to make collaborative decisions regarding patient care, thereby ensuring a holistic

approach that considers various perspectives for optimal outcomes. To effectively operationalize inclusive decision-making in a school setting, leaders must ensure that follow-through includes all of the relevant populations. This approach involves not only seeking diverse input during the decision-making process but also ensuring that the resulting plans and policies are implemented equitably across the school community.

Practical strategies include conducting impact assessments to evaluate the potential effects of decisions on different student populations and staff, creating implementation teams that consist of diverse representatives to ensure that all voices are heard, and providing targeted support to help various groups adapt to new policies. Additionally, leaders should monitor progress and outcomes by regularly collecting and analyzing data to identify any disparities in implementation. Establishing feedback loops will allow for ongoing input from the community, ensuring that adjustments can be made in real time. By celebrating successes and sharing lessons learned, school leaders can reinforce the importance of inclusive decision-making and encourage continued participation from all stakeholders. This comprehensive approach not only enhances the decision-making process but also fosters a more inclusive and effective educational environment.[17]

3. **Forming Tangible Decisions (and Outcomes) in the Best Interest of Special Populations**
   Inclusive decision-making aims to create tangible outcomes that prioritize the best interests of special populations within an organization or a community. This may involve developing targeted strategies, policies, or interventions that address the specific needs and concerns of marginalized or vulnerable groups. For example, nonprofit organizations like the United Nations Children's Fund (UNICEF) focus on inclusive decision-making processes to develop programs and initiatives that benefit children in underserved communities worldwide, ensuring that decisions are made with the well-being of special populations as a primary consideration. This becomes particularly important when working with individuals who have experienced a crisis. By adopting a structured, organizationwide approach postcrisis, organizations can ensure sustainability over time.[18]

   During a crisis, school leaders can draw valuable insight from nonprofit organizations like UNICEF that prioritize inclusive decision-making processes to benefit underserved communities. Inclusive decision-making is essential for fostering a sense of belonging, collaboration, and resilience among school staff and students during challenging times. School leaders can emulate nonprofit practices by implementing structured approaches to inclusion, such as promoting meritocracy, integrating diverse ideas, providing connection opportunities, and recognizing contributions formally. By embedding inclusive practices into their leadership strategies, school leaders can enhance engagement, trust, and performance within their educational communities. Leena, a novice principal from Upstate New York, explained how she kept a keen eye on the younger grades in her K–21 school. She shared:

> The classrooms we still struggle with are those very young grades. We have the K through 21 autism program. If the parents were overwhelmed (during the COVID lockdown) or the parents were essential workers or whatever the reason was, it's not like you could go to that house and set up a five-year-old on the Chromebook and set them up with a preferred adult that would help that kid get on the laptop. They really need hand-over-hand assistance, and that's a huge, if you want to talk equity piece just in general for the educational climate, [it's] the students who are severely, severely disabled, unfortunately, don't get the same benefits as they would with in-person instruction with their physical therapy, occupational therapy, speech therapy or a special education licensed teacher. We did start home visits over the summer 2021 for the extended school year program and at least have an adult physically go to the homes. It's certainly not because the parents don't value education. It's just such an overwhelming situation to have a child so severely disabled, plus other children in the home, plus a pandemic. It's really a hard balance trying to get the family to engage in work that you know isn't exactly going to do what you want it to do anyway. That's been really tough.

School leaders like Leena demonstrate the vital significance of inclusive decision-making, especially when facing crises that affect vulnerable student groups disproportionately. By adopting the approaches of organizations such as UNICEF and giving priority to the requirements of marginalized communities, school leaders can promote a stronger sense of unity, cooperation, and adaptability within their educational institutions. Ultimately, inclusive decision-making is not only a moral obligation but also a strategic requirement for school leaders who aim to steer their institutions through difficult times and ensure fair results for all students, irrespective of their backgrounds or situations.

Strategic decision criteria are equally crucial for school leaders navigating crises, enabling them to prioritize actions that align with their core objectives and have the most significant impact on student well-being and academic success. These criteria help school leaders maintain transparency, equity, and accountability in decision-making processes while also safeguarding against oversight and ensuring fair comparisons between available choices. The following strategic decision criteria are crucial for school leaders navigating crises.

Before moving on from these three key characteristics of inclusive decision-making, I'd like to offer three more cross-cutting considerations for leaders when embarking on the decision-making process: focusing on equity and transparency, aligning with core objectives, and ensuring accountability and oversight.

Focusing on Equity and Transparency

In all circumstances, decision-making criteria should prioritize equity, ensuring that the needs of all students, especially marginalized populations, are considered. Additionally, the criteria should promote transparency in the decision-making process, allowing stakeholders to understand the rationale behind the choices made. Leaders should reflect on whether their decision-making processes prioritize equity and transparency. For instance, are the needs of all students, especially marginalized populations, being considered, and are the decisions made transparent enough for stakeholders to understand the rationale behind them?

Aligning with Core Objectives

The decision criteria should also be closely aligned with the school's core mission, values, and objectives. This ensures that decisions made during a crisis support the overarching goals of the institution and have the greatest positive impact on student well-being and academic success. Leaders should reflect on whether their decisions align with their core objectives. For example, are the decisions made during a crisis supporting the overarching equity goals of the institution and having the greatest positive impact on student well-being and academic success?

Ensuring Accountability and Oversight

Finally, the decision criteria should incorporate mechanisms for accountability and oversight, safeguarding against oversight and bias. This could involve establishing clear metrics, feedback loops, and review processes to ensure that decisions are made fairly and with the best interests of the school community in mind. Leaders should reflect on whether their decision-making processes include mechanisms for accountability and oversight.

Comparative Analysis of Options

Ideally, the decision criteria should enable school leaders to conduct fair comparisons among available choices, weighing the potential impacts and trade-offs of each option. This allows for more informed and well-rounded decision-making during times of crisis.

These strategic decision criteria build on the key characteristics of inclusive decision-making outlined earlier, such as welcoming diverse voices, seeking multiple perspectives, and prioritizing the needs of special populations. By aligning decision-making processes with these criteria, school leaders can navigate crises more effectively, maintain the trust and engagement of their stakeholders, and ensure that their decisions have the greatest positive impact on student outcomes and overall school success.

STRATEGIES TO FOSTER INCLUSIVE-DECISION MAKING

During a crisis, leaders may not feel as though they have an opportunity to build an inclusive decision-making process. Even under stress, however, leaders can use a variety of strategies to support more inclusive decision-making and increase their chances of successfully weathering the storm. Depending on the type of crisis that is underway, leaders may have an opportunity or even a requirement to wait and gain consensus from significant stakeholders; in other situations, they may be able to take a smaller, more localized community of voices into account. For example, Flora, a novice principal in New Jersey, had to pause and consider district-level conditions and stakeholders during the shift to remote learning as a result of the COVID-19 pandemic. During a different crisis—as her school struggled with gang activity—she felt that she had to move more quickly to prioritize the interests of her school community. She explained:

> When we had to immediately shut down because of COVID, I had to defer to the district's way of doing things. However, I learned that they were speaking from a global point of view. I needed my people—my staff, faculty, and families most importantly—to help me decide what the initial lockdown time would look like. But when we had gangs in our school, I didn't have to wait for the district. Instead, I really wanted it to be my school solution. I had to consider how the gangs were affecting my school

> and what we were going to do as a result of their activity. This was a more local issue to our school, so I gathered my leaders and we created plans and we made decisions. We had to consider do we limit parents who were gang members? Was that equitable for the child? We had to consider the safety measures and protocols. I mean, I wanted to go talk to the gang members but I didn't. We began by shifting the culture with families and renaming expectations and we spoke with one voice so the school leadership team was consistent. It definitely minimized the problems we had [with] the gang activity in the school.

Leaders can and should generally identify and gauge when they need to work with their wider community stakeholders immediately, or when they can wait. Based on the interviews I conducted, leaders shared how they fostered inclusive decision-making and the strategies they used that helped them to do this work. I next present strategies that can be used before, during, and after a crisis event.

Before a Crisis

Crisis will occur, and leaders have to be equipped to respond to them; however, they also should consider ways to be proactive. Reflecting on her leadership following the COVID-19 pandemic, Leena, a novice principal from Upstate New York, explained the lessons she learned and how those lessons would inform her inclusive decision-making when encountering the next crisis:

> I think the more you can be explicit as to your "why?" the more people are willing to listen and follow you. I did it when it was convenient or popped in my head, but now I try to make sure all of my communication and decision-making as to why what we're doing. And even if people don't agree or they're uncomfortable with some of the directions, they at least understand where it's coming from.

Working in groups to develop contingency plans for various crisis scenarios, including active-shooter situations, allows for opportunities to apply inclusive decision-making principles. Engaging a diverse set of stakeholders in the planning process ensures that multiple perspectives are considered and that the resulting plans are responsive to the needs of the entire school community. Discussing how inclusive decision-making can be applied in developing and implementing these plans emphasizes the importance of collaboration, communication, and transparency in crisis preparedness. By involving stakeholders in the planning stages, schools can build trust, foster a sense of shared responsibility, and create crisis response strategies that are more likely effective and widely supported. By integrating these elements into the proposed activities, the focus on inclusive decision-making is strengthened, ultimately leading to more effective and equitable school safety measures that address the concerns and needs of all community members. Building on Leena's insight about the importance of clear communication and inclusive decision-making, the following strategies can further enhance community engagement and collaboration in crisis response efforts.

- **Foster Transparent Communication:** Maintain open and transparent communication channels to ensure that all community members have access to information regarding recovery plans and progress.
- **Engage the Community from the Start:** Involve community members in decision-making processes early on to establish trust and collaboration.
- **Establish Collaborative Partnerships:** Foster collaboration between stakeholders like local organizations, government agencies, and community leaders to ensure comprehensive decision-making.

During a Crisis

During a crisis, leaders are expected to have all the answers, but that's just not possible. Crises are unpredictable, and because of their novel nature, they don't present in the same ways. Therefore, during a crisis, leaders must consider who they can bring forward to be part of the inclusive decision-making. In some cases, in which tensions might arise from unions or other organizations, leaders should instead coalesce, coming together to work through the crisis. Dan, a novice principal in rural Connecticut, explained that during the COVID-19 pandemic,

> I was worried. I had staff members that were afraid to come back to school, and I don't know how to help that. I don't know how to make them feel safe. There's nothing I can do to make anyone feel 100 percent safe, and that's what I'm communicating to my union rep. My saving grace is my union rep is in my building. She's the president of my union in this district, and she is one of my team leaders and one of my teacher leaders. She is one of the people on that team, so she's both somebody that I rely on and can trust and she's my confidant, but at the same time she also wears that union hat role. That has been a saving grace for me, and a lot of this is like, I'll bounce some just initial ideas off her and say, "What do you think?" She's bluntly honest but in a good way, not in a, "No way! We're going to make this a contract issue." It's more like, "I think if you take it

> in this direction a little bit more, it'll be more palatable and we'll get more people to rally around it." That has been so exceptionally helpful for me.

Dan exemplifies how fostering inclusive decision-making during a crisis can lead to more effective leadership and stronger community ties. He builds trust by actively involving his union representative in discussions and valuing her input. He ensures that diverse perspectives are considered, ultimately enhancing the overall response to challenges faced within the school environment. Dan's experience underscores the importance of equipping novice leaders with the support and resources necessary for effective decision-making during crises while also highlighting the need to role-model inclusive behaviors and to embrace diverse perspectives to foster collaboration and innovation in problem-solving.

- **Set up New Decision-Makers for Success:** Ensure that novice leaders are equipped with the necessary support and resources to make effective decisions during crises.
- **Model Inclusive Behaviors Consistently:** Lead by example by demonstrating inclusive behaviors and holding leaders accountable for the same.[19]
- **Utilize Diverse Perspectives:** Embrace diverse viewpoints within decision-making processes to challenge assumptions, uncover blind spots, and generate innovative solutions.

After a Crisis

After a crisis occurs, critical reflection is an integral part of the process, and it is essential to consider how your inclusive decision-making looks and what you want it to look like in the future. Many leaders are keenly aware of how their faculty and staff view the student body and community postcrisis. For example, Victoria, a midcareer principal from Washington, D.C., explained how she now considers the community needs when hiring teachers:

> When I interview teachers, I always ask what are the causes of the achievement gap one to see if someone calls it out, not as an achievement gap, but an opportunity to gap and to root out saviors . . . like I am not a savior. I do not need saviors on my staff, that is not what we're here for; we're here to be part of and work alongside our community members. I'm very aware of not getting on a high horse and thinking I have all the answers, and we have to be really careful with that, and that can be hard, I think, in stressful times like a crisis.

In reflecting on her approach to hiring and community engagement post-crisis, Victoria demonstrates her commitment to inclusive decision-making by actively considering the diverse needs of her community and recognizing the importance of collaboration rather than adopting a savior mentality. This thoughtful consideration informs her future practices and emphasizes the need for leaders to engage with their communities meaningfully to address systemic challenges and foster a more equitable educational environment. Victoria's reflective approach also highlights the necessity of investing in capacity building and providing training for community members to actively participate in decision-making processes while emphasizing the importance of seeking authentic input from stakeholders to ensure that decisions are informed by a diverse array of perspectives and experiences, ultimately driving more equitable progress in the aftermath of a crisis.

- **Invest in Capacity Building:** Provide training sessions and workshops to empower community members to participate actively in decision-making processes postcrisis.
- **Up Your Game on Authentic Input:** Encourage authentic input from stakeholders to ensure decisions reflect a broad range of perspectives and experiences.
- **Explicitly Consider Equity Implications:** Deliberately consider the equity implications of decisions made after a crisis to drive more equitable progress toward organizational missions.

CONCLUSION

Inclusive decision-making is a cornerstone of effective leadership, especially during times of crisis. Leaders who prioritize engaging diverse perspectives and voices in their decision-making processes can navigate challenges with empathy, equity, and integrity. By embracing inclusivity, leaders can build trust, foster resilience, and drive positive change within their organizations and communities.

Chapter Discussion Questions

- How do the decisions made by leaders during a crisis affect the overall organization and its stakeholders?
- What is the significance of inclusive decision-making in guiding leaders through challenging times?
- Can you provide examples from your own context of how noninclusive decision-making practices have, or could have, adverse effects on various populations?

- How can you, as a current or future leader, foster inclusive decision-making before, during, and after a crisis event?
- From your personal perspective, why is it important for leaders to engage diverse voices in decision-making processes, especially during crises?
- What are some strategies that you as a leader might employ to promote inclusivity in your decision-making processes during times of crisis?
- How can leaders ensure that decisions made postcrisis consider equity implications and drive more equitable progress within their organizations?

Case Study

LARRY

Principal, Eastern United States

In the wake of the tragic Uvalde, Texas, school shooting, Larry, a principal from a racially diverse and affluent district, found himself at a critical juncture. Faced with the urgent need to revamp the school's active-shooter process, Larry embarked on a journey to enhance school safety while fostering inclusive decision-making within his community. The Uvalde school shooting, which occurred on May 24, 2022, shook the nation as a devastating reminder of the threats that schools face.

Equity-Crisis Dilemma

For Larry, this incident underscored the importance of enacting proactive measures to ensure the safety and well-being of students, faculty, and staff. As it did for many school leaders, May 25 brought concerns from parents directly to Larry about what his school was doing to protect their students further. Larry explained:

> After Texas, there's definitely more arousal of parent concern about what we're doing proactively. I think they understand what we have done, what the district has always done, but I think there's a curiosity as far as what's next, right? That's the kind of theme I've been hearing, like, okay now, now what? Also, what are we doing in addition to what we're already doing? I've met with a father, very nice guy, but understandably, you know, like everyone else, he is concerned. He asked me do all the doors have the sensors on them, so

> does an alarm go off if the doors are propped open, things like that. So, you know, there's definitely specific inquiries about the future.

As principal, Larry recognized the pressing need to reassess their active-shooter protocols in light of the Uvalde tragedy. He also understood, however, that implementing changes unilaterally could lead to resistance and overlook valuable perspectives within the school community. To address these challenges, Larry adopted inclusive decision-making strategies that engaged faculty, staff, families, and the board in the process. First, he began by evaluating his communication to parents:

> Since I do the bulk of the writing of the communication with the community as the principal, I want to be transparent, but I also don't want to overshare. I want to be very judicious in what I let out in the public, and in that statement we put out after Texas. I put a line in there that's like, basically, we do stuff that the public, that you guys don't know about, and you won't know about, because we want to maintain a level of privacy of our protocols. However, there's a balance, and I have to welcome in our community so they also have a sense of safety.

Equity-Oriented Crisis Solution

To ensure that all voices were being heard before any new decisions or policies were made, Larry organized town hall meetings, focus groups, and surveys to gather diverse perspectives on enhancing school safety measures.

- **Town Hall Meetings:** Larry hosted Town Hall meetings during which stakeholders could voice their concerns, suggestions, and feedback regarding school safety. This open forum allowed for transparent communication and built trust among community members.
- **Focus Groups:** Small focus groups were formed to delve more deeply into specific aspects of the process to response to active-shooter situations. These sessions facilitated in-depth discussions and brainstorming sessions to generate innovative ideas for improving school safety.
- **Surveys:** Surveys were distributed to gather input from a wider audience within the school community. By collecting anonymous feedback, Larry ensured that all voices were heard, regardless of rank or position.

Through these inclusive decision-making strategies, Larry gained valuable insight into the diverse perspectives within his community. As a result of his inclusive decision-making process, Larry felt more parent support than angst. He explained:

> The support, you know, we received from parents after Texas, it's very much what can we do, what can we fundraise, what do you guys need? I also realized that one part of the Texas shooting that wasn't a large focus of our school but came out of our surveys was the need for more wellness and mental health supports for our students. So, we are bringing on a psychologist in training, and we have increased the hours our current school psychologists have.

Collaboratively, Larry along with his leadership team, and a cadre of parents in the parent association developed a comprehensive plan to revamp the active-shooter process, incorporating best practices and tailored solutions to address specific concerns raised by stakeholders.

Active-shooter drills are generally organized in the same manner across schools, but with some variations. Although Larry's school did not have an active shooter, the collective trauma of the Uvalde shooting worried many parents. Thus, Larry had to find a way to include parents so that he could not only establish safety and security but also hear what the families, faculty, and staff were thinking to enhance their measures as necessary. By leveraging inclusive decision-making strategies in response to the Uvalde school shooting, Larry successfully enhanced school safety while also fostering a sense of unity and collaboration within his community. Larry's approach serves as a testament to the power of collective action in creating safer learning environments for all.

CASE STUDY ANALYSIS

Individual Reflection Questions

- How did Larry's approach to communication with parents demonstrate a balance between transparency and maintaining the privacy of school protocols?
- Reflect on the specific inquiries from parents after the Uvalde school shooting. How did these inquiries influence Larry's decision-making process?

- In what ways did Larry's inclusive decision-making strategies, such as town hall meetings and focus groups, contribute to a sense of trust and collaboration within the school community?
- How did Larry's response to the need for more wellness and mental health supports for students showcase his adaptability and responsiveness to community feedback?
- Reflect on the impact of Larry's actions to enhance school safety and foster a sense of unity within the school community.

Small-Group Activities

- **Role-Playing Exercise:** Divide into groups and role-play scenarios in which different stakeholders (parents, teachers, students) express their concerns and suggestions regarding school safety measures. Discuss how these perspectives can be integrated into decision-making. Dividing into groups and role-playing scenarios in which different stakeholders express their concerns and suggestions regarding school safety measures can help foster inclusive decision-making. By giving voice to parents, teachers, students, and other community members, this exercise acknowledges the value of diverse perspectives in addressing complex issues like school safety. The role-playing format allows participants to step into the shoes of those who may be affected by safety decisions, encouraging empathy and a more holistic understanding of the challenges faced by various groups. Discussing how these perspectives can be integrated into the decision-making process emphasizes the importance of inclusive practices in developing effective and equitable safety measures.
- **SWOT (Strengths, Weaknesses, Opportunities, and Threats) Analysis:** Conduct a SWOT analysis focusing on the school's current safety protocols since the Uvalde shooting. Identify strengths, weaknesses, opportunities, and threats to enhancing school safety. Conducting a SWOT analysis focused on the school's current safety protocols since the Uvalde shooting can provide valuable insight for enhancing school safety through inclusive decision-making. A SWOT analysis can pinpoint areas where inclusive practices can be implemented or improved. For example, a strength might be the existence of a diverse safety committee that includes representatives from various stakeholder groups.

A weakness could be the lack of student input in the development of safety protocols. Opportunities may arise from collaborating with community organizations that specialize in crisis response and trauma-informed practices. Threats could include budget constraints or resistance to change from certain groups. By considering these factors through an inclusive lens, the SWOT analysis can inform decision-making that prioritizes the needs and concerns of all community members.

- **Scenario Planning:** Work in groups to develop contingency plans for various crisis scenarios, including active-shooter situations. Discuss how inclusive decision-making can be applied in developing and implementing these plans. Working in groups to develop contingency plans for various crisis scenarios, including active-shooter situations, allows for the application of inclusive decision-making principles. Engaging a diverse set of stakeholders in the planning process ensures that multiple perspectives are considered and that the resulting plans are responsive to the needs of the entire school community. Emphasize the importance of collaboration, communication, and transparency in crisis preparedness. By involving stakeholders in the planning stages, schools can build trust, foster a sense of shared responsibility, and create crisis response strategies that are more likely to be effective and widely supported.

Whole-Group Activities

- **Panel Discussion:** Organize a panel discussion with a guest speaker to share their experiences of and insight into inclusive decision-making during a crisis. This discussion can provide valuable insight and real-world examples. Encourage open dialogue and questions from participants and allow them to ask questions and share their experiences. By emphasizing the importance of diverse perspectives, the discussion can highlight how inclusive practices lead to more effective crisis management. Research shows that embracing diverse viewpoints enriches decision-making, helping to uncover blind spots and generate innovative solutions.
- **Community Safety Forum:** Host a community safety forum in which stakeholders can come together to discuss school safety concerns, share ideas, and collaborate on initiatives to enhance

safety measures. This forum should prioritize inclusivity by ensuring all voices are heard, particularly those from marginalized communities who may be disproportionately affected by safety issues. Facilitating collaborative discussions can help stakeholders share ideas and cocreate initiatives that enhance safety measures. Inclusive decision-making is crucial in these contexts, because it allows for a more comprehensive understanding of the challenges faced by diverse groups within the community.

- **Collaborative Action Planning:** Facilitate a workshop in which participants work together to create an action plan for implementing inclusive decision-making strategies in their own schools during crisis situations. This is not just a workshop—it's a platform for taking ownership. By working together to create action plans, participants can share best practices and lessons learned, particularly from examples like Larry's. This collaborative approach not only fosters a sense of ownership among stakeholders but also reinforces the idea that effective crisis response requires contributions from a diverse range of individuals. Encouraging participants to reflect on the role of inclusivity in their decision-making processes can lead to more equitable outcomes and a stronger commitment to addressing the needs of all community members.

CHAPTER 5

Inclusive Communication

Nothing in life is more important than the ability to communicate effectively.
—Gerald R. Ford, former United States president[1]

Every fall, I look forward to the letters from my children's new teachers. The bright colors and unbridled enthusiasm to begin the new year always feel nostalgic and are a welcome tradition to close the summer. Like so many others, my children eagerly await these notes, finding out who their teacher is and what some of their expectations are. I start talking to my kids about the letter and see their excitement (or dread) that the summer is over. As a school leader, I recognize that these carefully crafted letters were part of a teacher's diligent practice to welcome families to another school year. This practice, however, is not isolated to teachers alone. Most principals prepare for the new school year during the summer by communicating with families and community stakeholders. Dexter, a principal in his third year who participated in my study, shared, "I send a 'Welcome Back' letter every year! I reintroduce myself and discuss any new policies the district passed. I also add things I learned from last year or problem areas such as attendance policies. A few weeks before the school year starts, I have the teachers send notes home introducing themselves." Dexter's communication routine for a new year is typical for most school leaders. Dexter pays close attention to his communication and what he will and will *not* say. He checks the links in any email communication to ensure they work, eliminating the possibility of broken communication. Leaders and teachers are expected to communicate with their families throughout the year. The detail-oriented nature of Dexter's approach shows the importance of getting communication right—a skill that is particularly important during a crisis.

Communication is a way of exchanging information with students, families, faculty, and staff. Leaders model communication by providing their staff and faculty with weekly updates, memos, and emails. Communication also initiates the yearlong relationship with families and teachers during the school year. Frequent and consistent communication engenders trust and support for the students. Teachers begin to communicate how their students are doing, what resources can be accessed, and which upcoming events are happening at the school. Communication is especially essential in a crisis because it must occur in ways that allow all school community members to feel they belong and will receive the information, regardless of their race, ethnicity, experiences, or other parts of their background.

In this chapter, I share aspects and components of communication that leaders should keep in mind while communicating with their school community. First, I discuss the overall important role of and necessity for communication in a school. Next, I define inclusive communication, elaborating on elements of inclusive communication such as reflecting, supporting differences, promoting participation, being context-aware, connecting through storytelling, and centering marginalized voices. I provide leaders with an understanding of what they should consider when communicating with their school communities during a crisis. Then, I discuss the inclusive communication framework, sharing how leaders included framework elements to assist crisis recovery at their schools. I highlight a case study of Eliza, who revitalized her communication plan during the onset of the COVID-19 pandemic. I close with guiding questions to reflect on the chapter.

Every day, schools send out information to various stakeholders in the school community. Principals send weekly update memos to their staff and faculty, while teachers send home notices or emails to families, communicating about their class or a student issue or celebration. Schools are expected to communicate regularly with families and staff while also maintaining a balance between navigating too much or too little information. Communication is vital to maintaining healthy and productive relationships between students, faculty, and families.[2] By definition, communication is the transmission of information from one source to a particular audience. Thus, leaders must be skilled at delivering this information to communicate effectively in verbal and nonverbal ways.

Today's educational landscape is different from ever before and it is changing in unprecedented ways. School leaders are tasked with a continually changing context, requiring them to hone their communication skills to build a strong and positive school culture while engaging in change. For instance, the shift toward online learning and hybrid models has been a significant change that leaders are contending with. Some other major changes include rising rates of chronic absenteeism among students, integrating new technologies like artificial intelligence to transform learning, addressing teacher shortages and cultivating diverse talent pipelines, and responding to divisive political issues that have increasingly disrupted classroom discussions and school board meetings from 2021/2022 – present.[3]

Leaders are also tasked with engaging in challenging discussions that require them to communicate effectively. Staff and families need to be heard and valued to welcome their input. Some of these stakeholders, particularly those from marginalized populations, feel that their voices disappear from the discussion. Researcher Tracey Salamondra explains that regardless of the challenges or success principals and other school leaders face, their communication should include three key elements: trust, transparency, and active listening.[4] These critical components engender effective communication by building a relationship that can navigate challenges. Salamondra argues that trust encourages mutual respect and collaboration, creating a safe space in which teachers, students, or families relay their concerns openly and leaders respond to them. Eliza, a principal from Midwest, shared:

> I understand that it's important to be able to communicate what's happening and explain why I was making decisions I was. I understand that I had to communicate the "Why?" behind my decisions. That's the main thing that helps me to be an effective leader amid a crisis because I had teachers looking at me, asking, "What do we do now?" They would ask me, "What will virtual learning look like? You know, what does our scheduling look like? Who's going to teach these classes?" I was learning as I was going. I let the team know that I don't have the answers, but we can brainstorm some potential ideas and propose them to the county, and then we'll go from there.

Eliza's comments show how collaboration requires a level of humility and transparency as well. Transparency is critical because it demonstrates the school leaders' purpose, goals, and values, which are both implicitly and explicitly stated during communication. Finally, Salamondra argues that active listening allows individuals to process and clarify what they are hearing. Unlike other types of listening, active listening is strategic because it requires the listener to ask relevant questions and explain the message.[5] All of these components—trust, transparency, and active listening—apply to crisis situations and equity. The benefits derived from how school leaders effectively navigate challenging conversations can serve them well during a crisis, mainly when inequities arise. Communication cannot be trusted without acknowledging the challenges a particular community or demographic faces. Communication cannot be transparent without identifying who is benefiting from or being harmed by the school community's expectations, resource access, and recovery efforts. Finally, school leaders cannot actively listen to their stakeholders without examining their implicit biases and communicating with equity at the center. Inclusive communication allows school leaders to develop their equity-mindedness and embrace feedback that will spur potential long-term changes for their school postcrisis.

DEFINING INCLUSIVE COMMUNICATION

Communication provides critical information to a school community about the impact of a crisis on the community, access to resources, and school openings and closings depending on current conditions. A quick online search of the terms "crisis" and "communication" populates with numerous articles about what to do and how to communicate with multiple stakeholders when experiencing a crisis or in the aftermath of a crisis. It is not enough for school or district leaders to send out information without considering the context in which they lead, who the recipients (families) are, and if they are even receiving clear information in full. Perhaps one of the most harmful events that compounds the impact of a crisis is a leader's lack of communication. For example, during the COVID-19 pandemic, some leaders felt bootstrapped by how their district communicated. Dan, who led a middle school as a first-year principal in March 2020, shared: "I wanted to tell kids right away [that we were closing the school], and my superintendent said, 'No, you can't tell kids we're closing for two weeks. We're not going to tell them till the end of the school day. We just want to tell them to clean their lockers out. Then we'll tell them at the end of the day it's going to be for two weeks.' "

Dan further explained that he felt he did the students and staff a disservice because they "never really had a chance to really say bye to each other and that was a choice that my boss had made. As a new principal, I didn't feel confident saying, 'Well, screw that. We're going to say bye to kids.' " Dan's concerns echo those of many of the leaders I interviewed who followed the district's lead about communication (or lack thereof) during a crisis. The leaders also shared that they had to follow a few parameters and district announcements as they wrote their communication to their school. Very few leaders, however, considered the inclusivity of their messages and how families were engaging in the communication. But inclusivity is a very important component of communication. When leaders consider inclusive communication, they become responsive to the needs of their school community by being flexible, evaluating how school community members respond to their communication, and making the necessary adjustments to ensure equity. Inclusive communication requires leaders to share where everyone feels they belong, they have access to resources and information, and they are still part of the community, whether online or in person.

Inclusive Communication Defined

Inclusive communication is flexible. Evaluate how school community members are responding to the communication and make necessary adjustments. The goal is to create communication in which everyone feels they belong and everyone has access to the necessary resources and information.

THE ELEMENTS OF INCLUSIVE COMMUNICATION

This exploration of inclusive communication highlights two crucial elements of communicating during a crisis: mindful reflection and inclusive participation.

Element 1: Mindful Reflection

Reflection is a cornerstone of the field of education. Several texts from foundational scholars, such as John Dewey and Paulo Freire, explain that for educators to engage actively as pedagogues and leaders, they must reflect. Freire writes, "Within the word, we find two dimensions—reflection and action. If one is sacrificed even in part, the other immediately suffers."[6] Freire's *word* connects to school leaders' communication during a crisis because their reflection of the state of the crisis and their decision-making (action) require a paired process to ensure that the intended audience of the communication is receiving it and that the intended message is responding to their needs. Reflection in this sense also requires being mindful, slowing down, and thinking deeply about what is happening, why, and which ideas support a return to normal through an inclusive environment.

Research has also shown that implicit biases—a prejudice or negative attitude toward a specific social or racial group[7]—are exacerbated by crisis. For example, researchers from the Department of Pediatrics at the Connecticut Children's Medical Center found in their examination of literature that pediatric providers' implicit bias could negatively influence clinical decision-making and outcomes for marginalized youth and their families.[8] Findings from this research team suggest that individuals must recognize their implicit biases to reduce the impact on marginalized youth and families. One way to do this is through mindful reflection. Research has shown that mindful reflection can mitigate bias.[9] Mindfulness has a positive impact on individuals by providing techniques to rely on previously established associations, such as stereotypes. A study conducted in 2015 by Lueke and Gibson found that mindful meditation reduced implicit age and racial bias in a sample of 72 individuals from a large Midwestern university. This research and other studies have contributed to the knowledge that implicit biases are omnipresent, despite educators' commitment to best intentions. It is essential for leaders experiencing a crisis to recognize that their implicit biases may be amplified and affect their decisions. To practice mindful reflection, school leaders can engage in three techniques: (1) mindful breathing—taking a breath, focusing on what happens, and moving to action; (2) journaling—writing in a stream of consciousness, and then reading the notes to clarify thinking; and (3) walking—taking a stroll or brisk walk to reconnect with the outside and get a sense of what one is feeling. Mindful reflection is an active process, requiring school leaders to monitor their thoughts (crises can be scary and may contribute to panicked ideas); grapple with ambiguity and the unknown (an answer might not always be possible); consider the multitude of different stakeholder perspectives (some who think a leader is doing too much and some who think a leader is not doing enough); and examine the crisis closely to consider how responses are communicated through overarching principles and the school's mission or vision. Applying mindful reflection has several benefits, such as deep learning and critical thinking, which are necessary during a crisis, as well as reducing anxiety to function more clearly. Mindful reflection also improves social skills and regulates emotions, which is critical when communicating about critical issues and solutions.

Element 2: Inclusive Participation

Including multiple voices from various populations within the communities served by the school is an integral part of inclusive communication. When leaders welcome and promote participation from various stakeholders, they learn the best way to support the school community. School leaders can use a variety of approaches to encourage participation, including developing community agreements or adopting protocols to ensure that voices are heard equally. Because marginalized communities are often silenced, leaders need to make concerted efforts to include them. Talk protocols can provide community members with a way to share the mic. Leaders can prepare agendas in advance, allowing participants to reflect and write down their thoughts before a meeting. A crisis does not warrant an elaborate plan; ideas and agendas can show bullet points and succinctly present topics that need discussion. Asking open-ended questions can promote participation and utilize active listening skills to hear which issues and possible solutions arise and what other considerations are needed to ensure recovery from the crisis.

Finally, the most essential way to promote inclusive participation is to use forms of communication that all constituents find comfortable. This requires leaders to examine how the school community receives information. Often, communication systems are handed down from principal to principal, or districts adopt blanket communication systems, such as Robocalls (calls that are directed at everyone in the school community) or online email platforms. Given today's use of social media, online news platforms, and communication systems, however, identifying the best way to communicate provides leaders with the opportunity to reach captive audiences, even if this is not accomplished through traditional routes of school communication. Consider utilizing social media and creating a school announcements page that is linked to online content used for instructional delivery. School leaders should also consider sending text messages to all mobile phones. Throughout this process, delivering communications is but one aspect of promoting participation; another vital factor is the message and what it says.

What Do I Say, and How Do I Say It?

In July 2023, at a middle school in Qiqihar in Heilongjiang Province, China, the roof collapsed, killing a coach and at least ten members of the school's trophy-winning girls' volleyball team who were practicing at the time. The collapse resulted from a neighboring building's construction project because the project managers stored heavy materials on the school's roof. When I read about this tragedy, I thought about my life as a principal in New York City. Competing construction projects have limited room, and I thought how easily that tragedy could have occurred in my own school, which is a decrepit old building with infrastructure challenges.[10] I was struck by news reports stating that parents were furious about the school's lack of communication after the incident. The reports explained that officials were more concerned with stopping the parents from protesting than giving them reliable information. Arjen Boin et al. state that political leaders must communicate information well, framing messages that share what they currently know as well as what they currently don't yet know.[11] Moreover, officials need to communicate with empathy. Boin et al. also provide leaders with a robust crisis leadership framework that school leaders can use. Although public officials focus on broader communication priorities, school leaders must decide how and what they will communicate on their own. This can be hard for school leaders, particularly when a crisis that has outside causes affects them internally, similar to the COVID-19 pandemic or a natural disaster. Thus, what and how leaders communicate is as important as the strategic action plan for delivering the message. Across the interviews I conducted, when a crisis arose, principals expressed deep sympathy and empathy. Charles, a principal outside of Detroit, Michigan, explained that after a medical emergency occurred in his school with a student, he needed to communicate an empathetic message to his staff that highlighted how proud he was of their response.

> Friday's communication: I wanted to commend the staff members directly involved in this case. I wanted to provide positive reinforcement for how calmly and decisively they acted. I felt like we performed effectively as a team, I felt like we followed our protocol, and that the steps necessary to provide the care of the student needed. and I was proud of my team for the way that they handled that, and so not only did I communicate that with those individuals, but I also wanted to let the entire staff know how these individuals acted, and I felt that they acted in a way that would make our entire team proud.

Constructing a message during a crisis is a particular action that requires not only honesty but also vulnerability and nuance.

Crafting a Crisis Communication

School leaders must craft a persuasive message that explains what has happened and potentially why this has happened. They must also identify potential repercussions, carefully noting the populations with whom they work. Leena explained that she regretted not being more communicative with her families of children who had special education needs who needed services for their children. She stated:

> I knew some kindergartners needed hand-over-hand mouse support to navigate their laptops, but I had no paras to go into their houses and help. So, I tried to tell them how to help their children, but how can you do that and work simultaneously? I could've done a better job communicating that. . . . No one wanted to enter their homes because they feared catching COVID. We all were. It was a real fear, but it was hard to be that direct because I felt I was letting them down.

These types of anecdotes from school leaders were common in my interviews. A similar study I conducted revealed that many leaders felt guilt when handling a crisis because they had not done more to support their families and students. When crises occur, a cognitive void makes it hard for individuals to understand the origin of the crisis as well as a future beyond it. Being direct about the repercussions is powerful because it provides an opportunity for people to handle the facts and move on accordingly.

After the Newtown, Connecticut elementary school shooting, former President Barack Obama appealed to families, sharing his empathetic grief as a fellow parent: "We come to realize that we bear a responsibility for every child because we're counting on everybody else to help look after ours; that we're all parents; that they're all our children." He also expressed that Newtown was not forgotten in their suffering:

> Here in Newtown, I come to offer the love and prayers of a nation. I am very mindful that mere words cannot match the depths of your sorrow, nor can they heal your wounded hearts. I can only hope it helps for you to know that you're not alone in your grief; that our world too has been torn apart; that all across this land of ours, we have wept with you, we've pulled our children tight. And you must know that whatever measure of comfort we can provide, we will provide; whatever portion of sadness that we can share with you to ease this heavy load, we will gladly bear it. Newtown—you are not alone.[12]

Former president Obama also used the devastating tragedy as an opportunity to build a case for change:

> In the coming weeks, I will use whatever power this office holds to engage my fellow citizens—from law enforcement to mental health professionals to parents and educators—in an effort aimed at preventing more tragedies like this. Because what choice do we have? We can't accept events like this as routine.[13]

Obama was an eloquent orator during times of crisis. He spoke during these times in ways that positioned the tragedy victims as survivors, transforming and elevating these survivors into heroes. His emphasis on survivors instead of victims promoted a sense of hope and inclusion for them as well as the whole country by empowering people to move on from the tragedy. When leaders craft their messages, especially related to crises, they must consider these elements. Ask: How do I empathize with the victims of this tragedy? What can I do to change or mitigate issues presented by the crisis event? At the same time, do not overpromise your response. Obama positioned his call to action and change by saying he would do "everything in his power," which offers hope yet also limits expectations.

After the Message Has Been Delivered

The school I led was part of a network of schools, and we all had norms to follow and adhere to. One norm that we shared was "one voice." When we met as a network of schools, we discussed many issues; although we may not have agreed on the outcome, we still all had "one voice," which meant that we communicated the same views and ideas across our schools. Our disagreements were restricted to leadership meetings, so we were able to share a united front for larger audiences. Having one voice can provide stability during a crisis in which people are experiencing destabilization. When school leaders finish crafting their communications, they should share them first with their school leadership teams so that everyone can act as one voice when delivering the message. Crises spur ambiguity, confusion, conflicting beliefs, and innate survival. Thus, establishing one voice demonstrates that someone is running the show and serving as an anchor for the whole community.

CREATING YOUR INCLUSIVE COMMUNICATION PLAN

Crafting an inclusive message is the start of creating a communication plan. After doing so, leaders must evaluate how they will deliver their message. Even during a high-stakes crisis, leaders must determine where stakeholders are getting their information and align their message with those platforms.

According to a study on sensemaking and crisis communication, comprehensive crisis communication plans are needed in preK–12 public school systems in the United States.[14] The National Resource Center Communication Team has found that effective communication begins with a strong strategic plan developed for an initiative in conjunction with partners and stakeholders. Creating and relying on a well-considered plan provides a strategic road map for a leader's communication activities. It also can be a critical component of any program's implementation and sustainability efforts. Identifying key people to support the strategic action plan is also important, as is knowing your audience. Who will be receiving the messages being communicated? School leaders should identify key stakeholders, including parents, teachers, staff, and community members, and tailor their communication strategies to meet their needs. Additionally, school leaders should be prepared to try different technology platforms to ensure that they can reach all stakeholders effectively.[15] According to a study on K–12 school leadership perspectives from the COVID-19 pandemic, the challenges faced by school leaders included bridging the digital divide and communicating with parents (as well as facing staffing shortages, online instructional practices, and the need for professional development).[16]

Leaders should evaluate data trends to inform their communication plan. According to research, parents are most active on platforms like Facebook, YouTube, Instagram, and Pinterest. Facebook, in particular, appears to be a popular choice among mothers between eighteen and thirty-nine years old. Fathers tend to be more active on Twitter and Reddit. Younger parents, especially mothers, are also increasingly using TikTok. When it comes to engagement, 72 percent of millennial parents use YouTube to make better purchasing decisions for their children, whereas only a quarter of US parents report using TikTok.[17] This suggests that YouTube may be an effective platform for brands and schools looking to reach parents with educational or informational content. Additionally, more than four hundred million people use Pinterest monthly, making it a valuable channel for sharing creative ideas and inspiration with families. By analyzing communication data, leaders can gain insight that previously was inaccessible. For example, they can determine the number of times parents of at-risk students have been contacted and the nature of those communications: whether those messages were informational or personal and affirming. This type of data can help administrators refine their messaging and outreach strategies to better meet the needs of their parent community. Investigating these trends during noncrisis times allows schools and districts to develop an effective and streamlined system for communicating with families, which can be especially crucial when crisis do occur. Leaders who take the time to understand their audience and optimize their communication channels are better positioned to engage parents and support student success.

Finally, school leaders should make their communication plan public and repeat it, adjusting strategies, audiences, and tactics as needed to meet communication goals.[18] School leaders should also ensure that the plan is accessible to all stakeholders so they can be aware of the communication channels available. Repeating the plan can help ensure that all stakeholders are indeed aware of the communication strategies and can help school leaders build trust and encourage parent involvement and engagement. The following key steps are essential toward building an inclusive communication plan.

Key Steps to Crafting an Inclusive Communication Plan

- Identify data trends in parent communication.
- State the objective of the plan and its purpose.
- Identify key people to support the strategic action plan.

- Be prepared to try different technology platforms.
- Make the plan public and repeat it.

Chapter Reflection and Guiding Questions

- How can school leaders promote participation from various stakeholders within the school community, especially from marginalized populations? What are some practical approaches to ensure the shared allocation of voices?
- What are the key elements of inclusive communication, and how can school leaders incorporate them into their communication strategies during a crisis?
- How can you use mindful reflection to improve communication during a crisis? What are the benefits of mindful reflection in the context of crisis communication?
- What are specific challenges you may face when utilizing active listening skills to address issues and seek recovery from a crisis? How can you ensure that all school stakeholders in your community feel included and receive necessary information during a crisis?
- How can you identify critical stakeholders and tailor your communication strategies to meet their needs?
- How can you (or do you, currently) address the digital divide, staffing shortages, or online instructional practices in communicating with parents and the broader school community during a crisis?
- What critical steps might you take to evaluate your communication systems and structures for equity and resilience, particularly during a crisis, such as natural disasters? How might you engage your specific community to develop and share ownership of an equity-based policy framework?

Case Study

ELIZA

Principal, South United States

> My parents didn't even know that we were sending out communication because they weren't checking to see when to come to the school and pick up laptops or things of that nature, so the technology was the biggest equity gap.

Eliza is an exuberant novice principal with three years of experience. During our interview, Eliza discussed leading through the initial months of the COVID-19 pandemic. Eliza began her leadership tenure as an assistant principal at the campus she leads. Despite the fact that the town where her school is located has approximately 20 percent of families living in poverty, Eliza's school is located in a high-poverty area, with 85 percent of students qualifying for reduced lunch. Her school has a Title 1 designation and is composed of African American students (55 percent), Latino students (20 percent), and a mix of Asian Americans and Caucasians (25 percent combined). Eliza is a young, enthusiastic African American woman who described her leadership as reflective and careful in analyzing the impact of her decisions. Eliza also explained that becoming a principal on her campus, which includes a Spanish immersion program, was rife with challenges regarding why and how she became a principal. She explained, "At times, I had to work twice as hard to communicate that this was not just a job given to me, but it was earned." Eliza knew she had substantial and varying dilemmas centered around her novice leadership. Yet, she detailed how she pushed forward to identify how to make communication more inclusive, leaning on her technology strengths to accomplish this goal.

Eliza described her first year as a principal during pre-pandemic times as a stark contrast to her current leadership climate. She explained, "Pre-pandemic, it seemed like, you know, there was a focus on student achievement, there was a strong parental support and involvement level within our school, but as soon as the pandemic hit, it went into survival mode for everyone." Eliza noticed that during the COVID-19 crisis, most parents needed to be more engaged in school communications. Communication during a crisis is paramount for those experiencing a cataclysmic event, and this requires leaders to think differently. Information inequality is a real and growing problem, with systematic inequalities around age, gender, income, and education in how people engage with information about a crisis.[19] Eliza explained that after implementing her plan, she noticed that student engagement with remote learning improved.

For school leaders, in particular, communication during a crisis must also incorporate the instructional aspect of learning. During the early days of the COVID-19 pandemic, when students were engaged in remote learning, Eliza stated, "We tried to do the best that we could with academics, you know, teaching from behind a laptop and doing virtual learning, and we have about three neighborhoods that we serve here in this area. So, there was much managing the different families and their expectations." She explained that as a first-year principal, she needed more skills and experiences that would support her. Yet, she noticed particular equity issues arising during the pandemic and set out to correct them. Most important to the success of her students was engaging with virtual learning. She also realized that to accomplish this goal, she would need parents to support the students more than ever. Eliza then established a plan to tackle what she thought was the most pressing equity dilemma—that is, inclusive communication.

Equity-Crisis Dilemma

At the beginning of the crisis, as Eliza reflected on several issues that arose, she found that families were not communicating with her or paying attention to the transmitted communications. Before the pandemic, she described how she would do home visits, a tradition in her school "where our teachers will get on the school bus, and we drive through the neighborhoods so the teachers can see where the kids live." She felt this home neighborhood field trip was necessary given the school's distinct location serving a high-poverty neighborhood. During the pandemic, home visits were not an option, nor was sitting on a bus together driving through an area. Eliza began to notice that a different type of home visit was occurring instead—teachers were seeing directly into students' homes through video calls. She explained, "I mean, we saw everything!"

She realized that this view was essential to understanding how students and families navigated the pandemic, and she started to assess how families were engaging with the school. She began by noticing many students did not have the technology to access remote learning: "Technology was the biggest indicator that there is still an equity gap as relates to our students at the school. We knew that families may not have a Wi-Fi hotspot to get on their laptop for class." She also noticed that "most of our families were connected through Class Dojo [a learning management platform], Twitter, Facebook, and TikTok [social media outlets] because we could see the trends in our data reports." Eliza began to devise a plan to communicate with families using strategic actions guided by that data.

Equity-Oriented Crisis Solution

During a crisis, leaders must think differently about communication to ensure it is inclusive and equitable. As a novice principal, Eliza faced this challenge during the initial months of the COVID-19 pandemic. She devised a three-level plan to support inclusive communication strategically during the crisis. In her plan, she thought of three key elements that had to be embedded within each level: What activity would occur? Which communication modality would be most effective? What frequency or times would they activate for this type of communication activity?

Level 1

- Activity: Neighborhood Blitz
- Communication Modality: Flyers
- Frequency: One Time

Eliza began by meeting parents where they were receiving communication. First, with a team from her school, she delivered paper flyers to families. On this flyer, she publicized where and how students and families would receive regularly disseminated information. She asked her team to distribute flyers in mailboxes but to remained socially distanced. She explained:

> I am the principal, so I had to model the leadership I wanted. I would go out to neighborhoods and talk to the community managers in the apartment complexes and say "Hey, my babies live here. Can you pass out these flyers, or can you communicate this to them because I desperately need them to log on?" I would also go out with my social worker and my school counselor, and we would take trips to various parts of neighborhoods or homes. We were attempting to reach them in every way possible.

The flyer included the social media handles, a QR code, and phone numbers for the leadership team and teachers. Sometimes, leaders and teachers masked their phone numbers to provide privacy coverage.

Eliza was able to track the efficacy of this level of the plan by monitoring attendance rates for both students and teachers during the crisis, comparing them to precrisis levels. She explained:

> We had some parents of our families that made sure their child was online from eight to eleven and did their homework from eleven to three, and we had some families where their student had seventy, eighty, ninety days of absences. So we could track who was coming in or logging on and improve upon that number.

Eliza's data tracking demonstrated the effectiveness of her plan design; she explained how she used data from the blitz activity and its impact on her students: "I know my students, and I needed to see their online learning, so we saw improvements from those key areas that we delivered the flyers."

Level 2

- Activity: Regular and Varied Communication
- Communication Modality: Social Media
- Frequency: Ongoing

Social media was a crucial part of Eliza's strategic inclusive communication plan. She chose the social media outlets to align with the data and trends she observed but also based them on her knowledge of the age-group of her families. Moreover, Eliza did not select every social media platform. She stuck to Twitter because of its brevity, Facebook because most of the families she had used this platform, and YouTube to make videos for announcements. Additionally, because all these platforms "speak to each other," she could share across platforms with a quick press of a button. Also, by including videos, she could reach families in different ways. Finally, social media platforms were automatically translated for families, thus removing an language barrier if the communication was expressed only in English.

Level 3

- Activity: Remote and In-person Support—Designated hubs via hotlines or virtual meetings
- Type of Communication Modality: Virtual Meetings
- Frequency: Ongoing

Finally, Eliza established a web of hubs to assist students and families; this part of the communication plan was aimed to increase student academic engagement and keep a tab on family needs. Therefore, Eliza created multiple hubs and hotlines that directed families to specific individuals if they needed help. For example, she said, "We created a hotline during the day, so if a family said, 'Hey, I tried logging on, and we don't know how to access the Webex link,' they could get immediate help from a media coordinator." She recalled, "I didn't even hardly work in this office space because I was in the office with parents and troubleshooting technology and things like that." Eliza also allowed parents or students to come in during designated times or meet virtually to address these issues. She also created hubs and hotlines for social workers and school counselors to support families. Crisis not only can cause upheaval in a family's home but also can affect the mental health of the individuals in the home. Creating multiple pathways for families to seek help with one or two people for a particular concern or issue reduces barriers to receiving necessary resources.

Looking back at the initial days and weeks of remote learning, Eliza gave a long sigh and shook her head:

> I had to make sure that I was always poised; I could not break down or get upset or get frustrated visibly for people to see and make assumptions and judgments. I knew that people were watching me, so I had to make sure I communicated sound decisions and reasoning behind everything I did as a principal. Because I didn't want people to think, "Oh well, see, I told you she didn't need this job. It was a lot of pressure."

Despite the weight of leading through a crisis as a new principal, Eliza always tried to see the positive outcomes of her decisions as a leader:

> I was a little hesitant to make decisions, and especially because of the impact they [would] have on all the stakeholders, but since leading in the pandemic, I've become more confident. I understand that equity gaps still exist in our building, but coming up with solutions for addressing those gaps was essential during the crisis. Effective and inclusive communication is a huge gap that we are learning to solve. I also noticed that when we have principal meetings, many veteran principals opposed to my appointment became the ones

who depended on me for ideas because I'm a very tech-savvy principal. My advice for leaders is to understand and embrace that you won't know everything and that asking for help is okay. It's okay to toss an idea to a colleague and say what you think about x, y, and z because effective communication in a crisis is key, and all eyes are on you.

Research has shown that schools act as beacons of hope for families during times of crisis.[20] As a result, school leaders need to create equitable and inclusive communication plans to aid in stabilizing the chaos/unpredictability of a crisis. In summary, leaders can conduct inclusive communication during an emergency in the following ways:

- Meeting parents where they are receiving communication.
- Using social media platforms that align with the data and trends.
- Creating multiple hubs and hotlines to assist students and families.

CASE STUDY ANALYSIS

Individual and Small-Group Discussion Questions

- **Leadership in Times of Crisis:** Reflect on Eliza's challenges and successes as a novice principal during the COVID-19 pandemic. How might these experiences inform your leadership approach in times of crisis?
- **Impact of Family Support:** Reflect on the significance of family support in the educational leadership context, especially during challenging times like the COVID-19 pandemic. How can educational leaders effectively support the mental health and well-being of families within their school communities?
- **Impact of Technology:** Divide the class into groups and ask them to discuss the impact of technology on equity in education, particularly during the pandemic. How can educational leaders address technology-related equity gaps in their schools?
- **Family-Centered Support Systems:** In small groups, discuss the importance of creating multiple pathways for families to seek help with specific concerns or issues. How can educational leaders establish support systems that reduce barriers and promote the mental health and well-being of families within their school communities?

Whole-Class Activities

- **Discussion:** As a group, discuss the challenges Eliza faced as a novice principal during the pandemic. Encourage students to analyze her strategies for inclusive communication and equity-oriented solutions.
- **Interactive Scenario:** Create an interactive scenario in which students role-play as educational leaders facing communication challenges during a crisis. This activity can help them understand the complexities of inclusive communication and decision-making under pressure.

CHAPTER 6

Equitable Systems and Structures

Movements are born of critical connections rather than critical mass.
—Grace Lee Boggs[1]

Schools rely heavily on systems and structures to operate effectively. These systems and structures can include attendance and homework policies, school schedules, and other bureaucratic structures that determine the distribution of power and decision-making responsibility.[2] During times of crises, from natural disasters to pandemics, these systems and structures are put to the test. It is important for school leaders to recognize the impact of crises on these systems and structures and take steps to ensure they remain resilient and equitable. Creating equitable systems and structures that align with the school's goals and support all members of the school community is crucial. Equitable systems and structures enable effective integration and equitable outcomes for all stakeholders and create an environment that facilitates student outcomes.

One way to improve a school's systems and structures is through technology systems. Such systems help faculty and parents understand the school's educational routines by means other than flyers or automated calls and are essential to better student outcomes and family engagement after a crisis.[3] The COVID-19 pandemic exposed significant inequities in the digital divide. For example, in New York City, one of the wealthiest cities in the world, 2.2 million residents lack a home broadband internet subscription.[4] Additionally, low-income as well as racial and ethnic minority or non-English-speaking residents have significant disparities in broadband internet access. This lack of broadband access prevents students from reaching academic achievement. Therefore, based on the lessons learned from the pandemic, school leaders must adopt an equity orientation in their systems and structures to ensure access for all learners. Inclusive systems and structures should encompass policies that enable these marginalized populations to fully engage in a school community.

How can schools work toward equitable systems and structures, especially during a crisis, to ensure that all students have fair and equal opportunities for learning and support? One way is to establish restorative restart and transformation teams, as suggested by the Brookings Institution.[5] These teams systematically address educational inequities and opportunity gaps, thereby laying the groundwork for long-term and systemic transformation. Another example is the prioritization of student social and emotional wellbeing to support academic progress and the creation of teams to improve graduation rates, such as the Freshman Success Teams in districts like Fort Worth, Texas.[6] These kinds of initiatives provide personalized support to students and address the specific challenges they face, ultimately contributing to a more equitable learning environment during a crisis.

School leadership can and should help drive such equity-focused initiatives. The Building Equitable Learning Environments Network is one such example in Chicago Public Schools, where leaders like the chief equity officer Maurice Swinney and the superintendent at DeSoto Independent School District D'Andre Weaver have prioritized equity in their districts to effectively drive equity-focused initiatives. Swinney has prioritized the implementation of equity audits to identify and address systemic inequities within the district, ensuring that resources and support are allocated based on the specific needs of marginalized students. Similarly, Weaver has championed establishing restorative practices and social-emotional learning programs to create a more inclusive and supportive environment for all students. These leaders have leveraged the challenges posed by the COVID-19 pandemic as opportunities to make lasting systems-level changes, focusing on equitable access to technology and personalized support systems. Their proactive approaches highlight the importance of leadership in driving equitable practices within school systems. In fact, by leveraging a crisis as an opportunity for long-term equity and access, school leaders can create meaningful change and address the educational inequities that may have existed before and been exacerbated by the crisis.[7] This type of work ensures that all students, especially those from vulnerable communities, can receive the support and resources they need to thrive academically and emotionally. By implementing such initiatives, schools can mitigate the impact of any crisis on educational equity and fostering an environment in which every student has the opportunity to succeed.

In this chapter, I focus on systems and structures in schools and their importance in times of crisis. I briefly highlight the impact of crises on systems and structures in schools and discuss the need for an equity orientation in systems and structures. I explain how creating equitable systems and structures can enable effective integration and equitable outcomes for all stakeholders and emphasize the importance of evaluating these systems and structures for resilience and equity. In discussing the impact of the COVID-19 pandemic on systems and structures, I also highlight the drastic inequities revealed by scholarship on the digital divide. I conclude by emphasizing the need for school leaders to consider systems and structures through an equity orientation to provide access for all learners.

THE SIGNIFICANCE OF EQUITABLE SYSTEMS AND STRUCTURES IN EDUCATIONAL ENVIRONMENTS DURING TIMES OF CRISIS

In the educational context, a "system" is a collection of elements that work in harmony toward achieving a shared goal. These elements include the varied structures and interactions that form the educational environment, such as equitable discipline policies, student assignment structures, and communication systems. The significance of these elements during times of crisis cannot be overstated, as they either facilitate or impede outcomes and interactions within the educational environment. The establishment of restorative restart and transformation teams, for instance, can systematize how educational inequities are addressed, laying the groundwork for long-term and systemic transformation.[8]

Restorative Restart and Transformation Teams

In the realm of education, establishing restorative restart and transformation teams has emerged as a crucial strategy in combating educational inequities, particularly during times of crisis. These teams are specifically designed to methodically analyze and rectify the disparities within the education system, ensuring that all students have equal access to resources and support. The composition of restorative restart and transformation teams typically consist of diverse stakeholders, including educators, counselors, social workers, community representatives, parents, and students. Educators bring valuable insight into the day-to-day challenges faced by students and can shed light on systemic issues. Counselors and social workers focus on students' social and emotional well-being, addressing mental health needs alongside academic challenges. Community representatives offer perspectives on the needs of marginalized populations, and involving parents and students in the decision-making process ensures that the voices of those directly affected by policies and practices are heard.

The primary functions of restorative restart and transformation teams are varied yet complementary. These include assessing current policies, developing equitable practices, overseeing resource allocation, supporting community engagement, and monitoring and evaluating outcomes. By evaluating existing discipline policies, student assignment structures, and communication systems, these teams can identify areas that perpetuate inequities and work to rectify them. They also focus on creating and implementing policies that promote fairness and ensure the distribution of resources to address the specific needs of underrepresented or disadvantaged groups.

Moreover, the active involvement of families and community members in discussions about educational practices and policies fosters a collaborative environment, and continuous assessment of implemented strategies allows for adjustments based on feedback and outcomes. During crises such as the COVID-19 pandemic, restorative restart and transformation teams are crucial in identifying and addressing inequities, supporting mental health, and facilitating long-term systemic change. The pandemic highlighted existing disparities, such as the digital divide, in which students from low-income families lacked access to necessary technology for remote learning. These teams can develop targeted interventions to bridge these gaps and implement programs that prioritize mental health and provide necessary support systems. Furthermore, by laying the groundwork for equitable practices, these teams can transform educational environments, ensuring they are resilient and adaptable to future challenges. These types of restorative restart and transformation teams have emerged as essential catalysts in fostering equitable educational systems, particularly during crises. Their diverse composition and focused functions enable them to effectively address systemic inequities, ensuring that all students receive the support they need to succeed academically and emotionally.

Furthermore, prioritizing students' social and emotional well-being and creating equitable disciplinary policies can foster a more comprehensive and supportive learning environment, particularly in times of crisis. One example of the importance of equitable systems and structures can be seen in the case of Angela, a midcareer principal from the Southwest, who identified a systemic issue related to student lateness. By December of the academic year, 65 percent of students within her school were chronically late, arriving to school within minutes of the first bell. Angela discovered that the city bus timings were consistently causing tardiness among students. In evaluating the school's attendance and discipline policies, she found that the policies were generally sound, but they lacked discretionary notes for the teacher to follow or a buffer period for student arrival. In discussing this with her superintendent, Angela was able to shift the school's start time, ultimately improving student punctuality and addressing the systemic issue. This instance highlights the significance of examining and modifying the underlying structures within a school, leading to more equitable outcomes as well as a more supportive learning environment, particularly for marginalized communities.[9] During a crisis, such as school shootings or racial violence, equitable systems and structures in schools become even more critical to ensure that all students have an equal chance to succeed and receive the support they require.[10]

The COVID-19 pandemic, in particular, presented school leaders with a unique opportunity to address issues of equity in their schools. Research has shown that equitable systems and structures enable effective integration and equitable outcomes for all members of their school community. Principals who leveraged the crisis to ensure equity and access in the long term did so by recognizing the specific needs and demands of diverse populations that required greater resources.[11] Although the pandemic may not have caused educational inequities, it certainly exacerbated those that already existed. During the pandemic estimated 2.2 million residents of New York City did not have a home broadband internet subscription. This lack of internet access was even more pronounced in low-income and racial and ethnic minority communities, and as a result, these students faced challenges in engaging in remote learning, which directly affected their academic success.[12]

Archie, a veteran principal in Denver, observed that many families had difficulty accessing online learning platforms because they had to share devices among multiple family members. This situation highlighted the unequal access to technology, leading to some students being unable to participate in remote learning because of inadequate resources at home. Felicity, a novice principal in New York City, reported that although all teachers and students had laptops, the school's system was not equipped for regular check-ins during e-learning. This lack of preparation and understanding of students' digital interactions further exacerbated educational disparities during the pandemic as described by Archie. In response to these challenges, school leaders had to adopt equity-oriented approaches to ensure that all students had access to high-quality learning opportunities. This involved creating restorative restart and transformation teams to systematically address these educational inequities and opportunity gaps. Thus, it was crucial for school leaders to adopt an equity-oriented leadership approach as a result of what surfaced during the COVID-19 pandemic.[13] This approach involved providing each child with exactly what they needed to develop to their full potential, regardless of identity, and recognizing the value of all stakeholders in the decision-making process.[14]

This approach also requires recognizing potential future opportunities and implementing equity-oriented leadership practices.[15] Policy actors have urged school leaders to address the challenges of the extended nature of the COVID-19 crisis by strategically using resources that advance educational equity and maintain a student-centered educational experience, despite polarizing debates and discussions.[16] In so doing, school leaders who lead with an equity orientation during a crisis can ensure that all students have access to high-quality learning opportunities and decision-making is coordinated, coherent, and inclusive. I next turn to systems and structures that were tested during the COVID-19 pandemic and consider how leaders can strategically evaluate them for better equity alignment for the long term and not just during challenging times.

Importance of Evaluating Systems and Structures for Equity and Resilience

School leaders often deal with systems and structures that do not enhance school equity. The goal is to ensure a smooth-running school, but during a crisis, leaders can see more dramatically and vividly how systems actually operate and what needs to change. In determining whether systems are equitable and resilient, viability must be tested, even for external systems like transportation. Leaders must evaluate embedded systems, such as how student data are tracked or how drills are conducted. Every school requires different systems to function and must be resilient enough to withstand crises like COVID-19 without inefficiency, redundancy, and outdated processes.

Schools are unique to their specific contexts, and as a result, the systems and structures at each school have been predominantly or minimally designed to cater to the student population they serve. Schools are unique to their specific contexts, and as a result, the systems and structures at each school have been predominantly or minimally designed to cater to the student population they serve. For example, a rural school might implement a transportation system that includes school buses covering long distances to pick up students from remote areas, which urban schools may not need because of the proximity of students living within walking distance or using public transportation. Conversely, urban schools may have systems for managing high student density and diverse needs, such as specialized staff for handling a wide range of cultural backgrounds and languages, which may be less critical in a rural setting where the population is more homogenous.

These systems and structures are implemented according to the specific nature of each school or district setting, reflecting the distinct challenges and resources available in their respective environments. Almost anyone can develop a system during a crisis as a stopgap to a problem that is occurring. But a truly intentional, systematic evaluation of systems and structures provides leaders with the ability to better understand how they are functioning throughout as well as after a crisis. For example, recent mass shootings in many schools have introduced a variety of new systems and structures, such as lockdown drills, firmly closed entrance doors, new identification upon entering the building, and enhanced security. Although these measures are important, they are mainly stopgaps to the larger problem of student safety and gun control, and it remains important to examine whether these stopgaps are equitable. And beyond the time of the crisis, will these stopgaps become systems that last and *remain* equitable?

Equitable systems and structures are not merely buzzwords; they are, in fact, the bedrock of a thriving learning environment. Their importance reaches beyond mere compliance—they are the catalysts for a just and inclusive education in which every student, regardless of background or circumstance, has the opportunity to succeed. Leaders are aware that they play a role in choosing systems that ensure greater access for students and a role in working to discontinue systems that do not meet their intended purpose. In this chapter, however, I highlight leaders will also learn how to take a deeper look at their school's existing systems and structures to determine and evaluate their resilience and equity. The idea of resilience is critical for understanding how your systems and structures are working. To be effective, these systems and structures must withstand difficult times and deliver the services your faculty, staff, and students need during and after a crisis. It is not enough to assume that systems and structures will operate optimally during a crisis or postpone fixes to a later date. Crises uproot our cognitive and physical stability at the very moment when we need that stability to function and persevere. This is particularly important to address, because parents lean on school systems and structures to provide a stable framework and structure to support their children when their world turns to chaos. Moving forward, it's important to remember that equity is not a theoretical aspiration; it is a tangible, defined path toward achieving brighter futures for all students. By prioritizing equitable systems and structures, we unlock potential within every student, close achievement gaps, boost outcomes, and cultivate a just and inclusive learning environment for generations to come.

FROM SEGREGATED TO INTEGRATED: CREATING A JUST AND INCLUSIVE LEARNING ENVIRONMENT WITH EQUITABLE SYSTEMS AND STRUCTURES

School systems and structures are built to organize and operationalize school policies, norms, and procedures. Schools typically have countless systems and structures in place, such as the system to order school supplies or the structure of contact or call-out during an emergency snowstorm. During a crisis, however, these systems and structures are tested by and sometimes call into question their function and resilience. When disruptions occur, it is important for leaders to prepare, respond, adapt, and then revise the system or structure they have so that they become more resilient and minimize disruption.

Examples of Systems and Structures Tested During the COVID-19 Pandemic

As the pandemic spread around the globe, many countries locked down and schools closed, pivoting to online learning. The World Bank estimates that schools were closed for between 64 to 205 days, depending on the country.[17] The principals I interviewed in the United States said they had a hard time navigating online learning while their teachers were navigating their family lives. Additionally, the technology platforms they had invested in were tested to the limit, as was access to this technology. Archie, for example, shared issues with a family logging onto the platform because their child was using a computer that had to be shared by the family of four. After making the monumental pivot to online learning, it was easy for schools to expect that the heavy lifting was over, and students would be able to log on without problems. But COVID's wildfire-like spread across the nation deprived many schools of time, materials, and resources that would allow all students to have the same amount time using technology as students in other districts may have had. Archie remarked:

> We just thought that parents would log on and that their kids are having an environment to do their work and they didn't. It was really hard for a lot of the teachers to understand why their students were not logging on, and that it wasn't because I didn't want to be there, it was that they literally didn't have the resources to be there.

Even when other principals in this study had adequate technology in their schools and students had access to that technology during COVID-19, the skill and strategy needed to succeed in online learning was missing and unplanned. Teachers had to build their ships while reading the assembly instructions. The pandemic clearly illuminated the need for many schools, particularly in marginalized communities, to launch an e-learning system that would help their students engage with material. The systems already in place to support e-learning, however, were shaky and proved to be inequitable in many cases. Sandra, an assistant principal in New York City, explained that when her school had to go online, all teachers and students had laptops, but a system was not set up for regular check-ins of e-learning. Compounding this problem, they did not have a full understanding of how their students were working in digital spaces. The immediacy of the COVID-19 pandemic left little time for the school to prepare or rehearse an online push.

As in any crisis, it is imperative to comprehensively assess the components that have contributed to the current situation. In this case, the primary consideration revolved around a fundamental question: Do we possess adequate resources to support our students in the event of a school closure? The significance of this question had never been acknowledged, and the emergence of the COVID-19 pandemic underscored the critical need for education leaders to prioritize this issue. Likewise, a series of natural disasters in the past decade have illustrated the potential for schools to have to involuntarily cease operations for a period of time. Consequently, students must be able to maintain access to learning resources, regardless of the prevailing crisis. The fundamental inquiry for all leaders is whether they are providing their students with the necessary tools to navigate any situation, whether routine or exceptional.

EVALUATING YOUR SYSTEMS AND STRUCTURES FOR EQUITY

Moreover, the failure of leadership to monitor and support teachers in creating inclusive and engaging learning environments can perpetuate a cycle of inequity. This could result in teachers unconsciously favoring more vocal students or those who conform to traditional engagement norms, thereby disproportionately singling out students from marginalized backgrounds for disengagement, thus reinforcing existing stereotypes and biases. The equity audit unveiled that the lack of supervision and support for teachers within the systems in Cambridge Public Schools led to an environment in which disengagement was not holistically addressed. The focus shifted from identifying and rectifying the instructional practices leading to individual student disengagement, further perpetuating inequities within the educational system. The systemic issues within Cambridge Public Schools, which included ineffective supervision and a lack of accountability for fostering engagement, resulted in students being unfairly singled out for disengagement. Consequently, this example underscores the essential need for educational leaders to adopt a more equitable and comprehensive approach to monitoring and supporting instructional practices, ensuring that all students receive the attention and resources they need to thrive.[18]

During a crisis, these types of inequitable structures perpetuate more inequities, and the problem compounds when teachers have deficit mindsets. For example, Emilia, a veteran principal from Upstate New York, shared that when her students began their remote learning, she learned how teachers "really felt" about their students by expressing what she identified as deficit-oriented perspectives: "They kept saying that our student's lost learning and all I thought was, 'How could they lose something we never gave them or taught them?' It was almost as though they did not want to admit that they would have to think differently for our students, given what they had dealt with [the COVID-19 pandemic]."

The systems that leaders have in place must be regularly interrogated and tested to ensure that they are equitable. Many school policies and procedures are inherited by principals, as some of my participants suggested. Dan, a novice principal from Connecticut, shared, "I wanted to spend my first-year learning about the school community. I wanted to see what systems worked and which did not. Unfortunately, because of the COVID-19 pandemic, I was unable to do that and I had to go straight to work." Abraham, a veteran principal in California, concurred: "We had to support our students with learning, and I had just got there, but I was in the district for years, and I realized we had no data dashboard system. Teachers were handing out work or loading the online platforms, but we had no way of knowing how that work was connecting to the standards and how or if the kids were learning. So, I started there."

When crises occur, some systems may reveal their resilience whereas others do not. The reflections from these leaders revealed how they are able to examine the performance of their systems and structures during a crisis. For example, during the COVID-19 pandemic, leaders invested in their systems and structures to understand their degree of resilience. This cataclysmic event coerced all educators to assess how their school would perform in worst-case scenarios. Unfortunately, many of the leaders I interviewed found fundamental challenges in various systems and structures at their schools.

Building the Bridge: Tackling Challenges When Developing Equitable Systems and Structures

Although a defined vision of equitable systems and structures is clearly necessary, its implementation is rarely a smooth journey. During the COVID-19 pandemic, acknowledging the digital divide was just the first step to addressing the lack of equitability.

Resource Disparities

Access to technology varies widely, both within and across communities. Bridging this gap requires multifaceted solutions. Schools can spearhead device loan programs, partner with local initiatives for subsidized internet access, and leverage creative approaches like mobile hotspots or community technology centers. Investing in robust infrastructure and digital literacy programs for both students and families becomes crucial.

Mindset Shifts

Moving toward equitable structures often requires dismantling existing practices that have historically perpetuated imbalances. Stakeholders who are accustomed to set ways can pose resistance to changes. Leaders must champion clear communication and transparency, emphasizing the long-term benefits for all students. Ongoing training and professional development opportunities for educators can cultivate culturally responsive pedagogy and dismantle implicit biases.

Power Dynamics

Equitable systems demand power redistribution. This can be a daunting process, as entrenched hierarchies may feel threatened. Building trust and open communication with marginalized communities is key. Inclusive decision-making processes that empower students and address historical injustices are essential. Additionally, advocating for policy changes at district and state levels can create systemic shifts that support equitable practices.

Unseen Barriers

Beyond the readily identifiable challenges lie more subtle obstacles. Language barriers, transportation limitations, and cultural expectations can all hinder meaningful participation in equitable structures. Leaders must actively seek out and address these hidden hurdles. Multilingual resources, flexible scheduling options, and culturally sensitive outreach can help ensure that everyone feels welcome and included in the process.

Building equitable systems and structures is not a one-time fix, but rather is an ongoing journey of awareness, adaptation, and collaboration. By recognizing and tackling these challenges head-on, we can pave the way for a future in which every student has the opportunity to learn, grow, and thrive.

STRATEGIES TO ASSESS RESILIENCE AND EQUITY IN YOUR SYSTEMS AND STRUCTURES

When assessing the resilience and equity of systems and structures, utilizing data is a critical tool for leaders. Although data are often used to evaluate instructional outcomes and track student responses to policies, this information can also provide valuable insight into how different groups of students are affected by certain systems and structures during times of crisis. For instance, attendance remains a major concern in many schools, partly because of the aftermath of the pandemic, and leaders have continued to struggle to bring students back to school consistently. Instead of scrambling for new initiatives, however, leaders should examine their data and ask systemic questions such as, "How do attendance policies contribute to inequities?" It is important to recognize that attending school is not a simple task for every student, particularly for those children who experience a lack of transportation or the motivation to attend school. By analyzing their systems and structures, leaders can identify potential inequitable outcomes and start creating a more humanizing environment that empathizes with families and welcomes all students. One step toward achieving this environment is to seek feedback from families and consider which populations are most affected by the school's infrastructure. School leaders should also assess whether their systems remain effective during crises and, in response, tweak, change, or reimagine them accordingly. By using data to inform decision-making, leaders can ensure that their systems and structures are resilient and equitable.

- **Utilize data to assess resilience and equity of systems and structures:** During a crisis, it is essential to utilize data to assess the resilience and equity of existing systems and structures. This approach involves analyzing various indicators to understand the impact of the crisis on different segments of the population and to evaluate the effectiveness of current systems in ensuring equity and resilience.[19]
- **Evaluate how different student groups are affected by systems and structures:** During a crisis, it is crucial to evaluate how various student groups are affected by the systems and structures in place. This assessment involves examining data to identify disparities and inequities, particularly among marginalized student populations. By understanding these impacts, educational leaders can develop targeted strategies to address the specific needs of different student groups.[20]
- **Examine the impact of attendance policies on inequities through data analysis:** Data analysis can help examine the impact of attendance policies on inequities during crises. This involves assessing how attendance

requirements may disproportionately affect certain student populations, especially those facing educational disparities. By analyzing attendance data, educational institutions can identify and address inequities in attendance policies to ensure fairness and support for all students.[21]

- **Assess the effectiveness of systems and structures and make necessary adjustments based on data:** Continuous assessment of the effectiveness of systems and structures during crises is essential. By analyzing relevant data, educational leaders can identify areas that require adjustment or improvement to ensure that systems remain resilient and equitable. This proactive approach enables institutions to make data-informed decisions and implement necessary changes to better support all students, particularly those most vulnerable, during crises.[22]

Unpacking the Toolbox: Examples of Equitable Systems and Structures

With these broad strokes as a backdrop to this discussion of equitable systems and structures, diving into the more tangible and specific is essential. The following concrete examples illustrate equitable systems and structures and demonstrate what makes them successful.

Restorative Restarts and Transformation Teams

Restorative restart and transformation teams address behavioral issues through restorative practices rather than punitive measures.

- **How It Works:** Instead of traditional detention for minor offenses, students meet with trained facilitators in small groups to discuss the impact of their actions and collaboratively develop restorative solutions. This approach fosters conflict resolution skills, builds community accountability, and reduces reliance on punitive measures.
- **Equitable Elements:** This approach focuses on repairing harm rather than punishment, promotes student agency, and avoids having a disproportionate impact on marginalized groups.

Implementation in Practice

In practice, implementation involves the following:

- **Facilitated Discussions:** Students involved in minor infractions participate in small-group discussions led by trained facilitators. These discussions allow students to reflect on their actions, understand their impact on others, and collaboratively develop solutions to repair harm.
- **Building Community:** The teams foster community and accountability among students, encouraging them to support one another in resolving conflicts.

Requirements

To implement this plan effectively, schools need the following:

- **Training for Facilitators:** Staff must receive restorative practices training to guide discussions effectively.
- **Supportive Policies:** Schools need to revise discipline policies to incorporate restorative practices, ensuring they are prioritized over traditional punitive measures.

School leaders should regularly assess the effectiveness of their teams in reducing disciplinary incidents and improving student relationships. This approach transforms the disciplinary system from a punitive framework to one that emphasizes healing and accountability. Schools can dismantle inequitable disciplinary structures that disproportionately affect marginalized students by integrating restorative practices. School leaders can engage in feedback mechanisms by regularly gathering feedback from students, facilitators, and families about the effectiveness of restorative practices. This can be done through surveys, focus groups, or interviews. School leaders can also analyze data on disciplinary incidents before and after implementing restorative practices to measure student behavior and community dynamics changes. Finally, school leaders can continuously assess the training needs of facilitators and staff involved in restorative practices to ensure that they are equipped with the necessary skills and knowledge.

First-Year Success Teams

First-year success teams provide tailored support for first-year students.

- **How It Works:** Dedicated teams of advisers, mentors, and peer tutors provide personalized support to first-year students. This can include academic coaching, social-emotional learning resources, and connections to campus resources.
- **Equitable Elements:** Proactive intervention addresses potential pitfalls of failure early, combats first-generation student anxieties, and provides targeted support where needed.

Implementation in Practice

Implementation of first-year success teams may include the following:

- **Mentorship Programs:** Pairing incoming students with mentors who can guide them through the transition to high school.
- **Academic and Emotional Support:** Offering resources such as tutoring, counseling, and workshops on study skills and time management.

Requirements
Successful implementation requires the following:

- **Dedicated Staff:** Schools must allocate staff members specifically for these roles, ensuring they have the time and resources to support students effectively.
- **Collaboration with Community Resources:** Schools should partner with local organizations to provide additional support services, such as mental health resources.

First-year success teams address structural barriers to student success by providing proactive, personalized support. This approach helps to ensure that all students, particularly those from underserved backgrounds, have the resources they need to thrive academically. First-year success teams require tracking the academic and social-emotional progress of first-year students receiving support, including grades, attendance, and engagement levels. Data should be used to identify areas where support may need to be adjusted or enhanced, such as additional tutoring or mentoring resources. Schools should also collect feedback from former students who participated in success teams to assess long-term impacts on their academic journeys.

Culturally Responsive Teaching Practices

Culturally responsive teaching involves integrating students' cultural backgrounds into the curriculum.

- **How It Works:** Educators integrate students' cultural backgrounds, experiences, and knowledge into teaching methods and curricula. This involves diverse learning materials, incorporating historical and literary voices from various cultures, and fostering classroom discussions that respect different perspectives.
- **Equitable Elements:** This approach acknowledges and values student identities, combats implicit biases, and creates a more inclusive learning environment for all.

Implementation in Practice
Culturally responsive teaching can be implemented through the following:

- **Diverse Learning Materials:** Utilizing texts and resources that reflect students' diverse experiences.
- **Inclusive Classroom Discussions:** Encouraging dialogue that respects and values different perspectives, fostering an inclusive environment.

Requirements

To implement culturally responsive practices, schools must pursue the following:

- **Professional Development:** School should provide ongoing training for educators on cultural competency and inclusive teaching strategies.
- **Curriculum Review:** School leaders should regularly assess and update curricula to ensure that they are representative and relevant to all students.

Culturally responsive teaching practices challenge existing curricular structures that may marginalize certain voices. By embedding diverse perspectives into the curriculum, schools create a more equitable learning environment that validates all students' identities. Culturally responsive teaching practices should be evaluated through regular classroom observations to assess implementation and effectiveness in engaging students. Student surveys can gauge perceptions of inclusivity and representation in the curriculum, while a routine process for reviewing and updating curriculum materials can ensure that they remain relevant and inclusive. Ongoing training for educators on culturally responsive teaching practices is essential to inform them about new strategies and materials.

Universal Access to Technology

Universal access to technology means ensuring all students have the necessary devices and internet access to participate in learning.

- **How It Works:** Schools provide laptops, tablets, or other devices to all students, along with reliable internet access, training, and technical support. This ensures that everyone has the tools needed to participate in online learning, research, and communication.
- **Equitable Elements:** This approach eliminates the digital divide, levels the playing field for learning resources, and empowers students to take ownership of their learning.

Implementation in Practice

Ensuring universal access to technology includes the following:

- **Device Distribution:** Providing laptops or tablets to every student as well as training on how to use them effectively.
- **Reliable Internet Access:** Partnering with local internet providers to ensure that students can access high-speed internet at home.

Requirements

Successful implementation requires the following:

- **Infrastructure Investment:** Schools must invest in the necessary infrastructure to support widespread technology use.
- **Technical Support:** School should provide ongoing technical support for students and families to troubleshoot issues.

By ensuring all students have access to technology, schools can create a more equitable system that allows for equal participation in learning opportunities. Schools should monitor usage rates of provided devices and internet access among students to identify gaps in engagement. Feedback on the effectiveness of technical support services should be collected to ensure that students and families receive the assistance they need. Schools should also analyze academic performance data to assess the correlation between technology access and student achievement. Regular evaluation of technological infrastructure is necessary to ensure it meets evolving needs.

Funding Policies Based on Student Needs

Equitable funding policies ensure that resources are allocated based on the specific needs of students.

- **How It Works:** Resources are allocated to schools and programs based on factors like student poverty levels, language needs, and special education requirements. This ensures that schools with higher concentrations of underserved students receive the necessary support to close achievement gaps.
- **Equitable Elements:** This approach directs resources to areas where they are most needed, combats resource scarcity in disadvantaged communities, and promotes equal opportunities for all students.

Implementation in Practice

Equitable funding policies allocate resources as follows:

- **Needs-Based Funding Models:** This approach allocates more resources to schools with higher concentrations of low-income students or those requiring additional support.
- **Targeted Programs:** This approach develops programs that specifically address the needs of English language learners or students with disabilities.

Requirements

To implement equitable funding policies, schools need the following:

- **Data Analysis:** Schools should conduct thorough analyses of student demographics and needs to inform funding decisions.
- **Policy Advocacy:** School leaders show engage with policymakers to advocate for changes in funding structures that prioritize equity.

Equitable funding policies challenge existing financial structures that perpetuate inequities. By aligning funding with student needs, schools can ensure that resources are directed to areas where they are most needed, promoting equal opportunities for all students. Equitable funding policies require reviewing how resources are allocated based on student needs. Impact studies should assess the effect of funding policies on student outcomes, particularly for underserved populations. Stakeholder engagement in discussions about funding priorities and resource allocation promotes transparency and accountability. Collecting and analyzing student demographics and needs data informs funding decisions, while regular review processes ensure policies remain aligned with equity goals and respond to changing student needs.

CONCLUSION

This chapter highlighted the importance of equitable systems and structures in schools during crises and the need for following an equity-oriented approach to ensure access for all learners during times of crisis. As we navigate through unprecedented challenges, such as the COVID-19 pandemic, it is essential that we recognize and address the limitations of our current systems and structures in schools. All school leaders should evaluate their existing systems and structures for resilience and equity and take steps to design a more inclusive and equitable educational environment for all students, particularly those from vulnerable communities. By leveraging crisis as an opportunity for long-term equity and access, we can create meaningful change and address the educational inequities that have been exacerbated by the pandemic.

Chapter Reflection and Guiding Questions

- How do crises, such as natural disasters or pandemics, test the resilience of school systems and structures? How have crisis events tested the resilience of school systems and structures in your school?

- In what ways can inequitable systems and structures exacerbate the impact of a crisis on marginalized populations within the school community?
- Why is it crucial for school leaders to adopt an equity orientation in their systems and structures, especially during times of crisis?
- What are some examples of policies, procedures, and systems that you see implemented in your school context to ensure equitable access and participation for all members of the school community?
- How can school leaders leverage the crisis as an opportunity to drive long-term equity and access within their school systems?
- What strategies can school leaders employ to respond systematically to racial inequities in schools, moving beyond isolated reactions to racist events and addressing deeper cultural and systemic issues?
- How can school leaders proactively address and rectify inequitable systems and structures to mitigate their harmful impact on marginalized populations during times of crisis?
- What proactive measures can school leaders take to address inequities that arise as a result of a crisis event and ensure equitable access for all learners, especially those from marginalized communities?

Case Study

MONTY

Principal, Eastern United States.

> I felt like the first four months, there was a crisis every day . . . I was waiting for the next shoe to drop every day just because . . . every day, I was being called to that room.

Monty, a former history teacher and K–12 curriculum supervisor, transitioned into the role of principal at a Title I school in New Jersey with a diverse student body of approximately 330 students. The demographics include 25–30 percent of students receiving free or reduced lunch and about 20 percent of the students are classified as students with disabilities. Monty inherited a school climate affected by a previous administration's hands-off approach, leading to a lack of trust among staff and escalating behavioral issues. He explained, "I feel like what I inherited was because the previous principal [was] so hands off

I don't think [the] central office really understood or know how dire the situation was with a few of the particular students."

Equity-Crisis Dilemma

Upon taking the principal position, Monty faced immediate crises, particularly with two students exhibiting violent behaviors. He explained:

> I had several crises on my hands. But the priority was two students who were very physically violent. There were several instances where teachers and school aids were getting hit, punched, or kicked in the classroom. Even the classroom was being destroyed. I felt I had to insert myself, and then there were moments where I was getting punched in the ribs and slapped in the head. I had to change something immediately.

His initial response involved establishing rapport with students, emphasizing the importance of relationships in fostering a positive school environment. He spent significant time in the classroom, engaging with students during lunch and recess and focusing on positive reinforcement through phone calls to parents. He continued, "I went into that classroom every day. I spent time talking to the students and with them at lunch, and I went out to recess just really trying to establish rapport. I initially looked for some really positive moments." Despite these efforts, the situation escalated, resulting in frequent calls for assistance to respond to these violent incidents. Monty recognized that the previous principal's lack of discipline had contributed to this culture of chaos, necessitating a more hands-on approach to leadership. He also realized he needed to build equitable systems and structures to restabilize his building so that everyone would feel safe and the adults would know how and what to do if this situation evolved again.

Equity-Oriented Crisis Solution

Monty utilized equitable systems and structures to stabilize his school community by implementing several key strategies that focused on building relationships, fostering collaboration, and addressing the distinct needs of students, particularly those with behavioral challenges. Monty's approach included building relationships, collaborative problem-solving, and equitable crisis leadership. He prioritized establishing trust with students and their families, recognizing that parental involvement was crucial in managing behaviors. He communicated regularly with parents, especially during crises, to involve them in the solution. Monty also worked closely with parents and caseworkers to implement alternate scheduling and counseling strategies. He found that some families were more receptive to suggestions than others, which affected the effectiveness of interventions. "I really made it clear to them that there was a partnership here. And that we needed them and their influence and authority over here. You know, to assist us when we were in crisis mode." As crises arose, Monty took immediate action, including involving parents directly in managing their children's behaviors at school. He emphasized the importance of a partnership between the school and families to create a supportive student environment.

Through Monty's persistent efforts, the school climate began to improve. One particularly challenging student transitioned out of the district, while another, whose family was more engaged, showed significant improvement. Monty's leadership style, characterized by empathy and a commitment to building equitable systems, ultimately contributed to a healthier school environment. Monty's experience illustrates the complexities of leading in a challenging educational landscape. Monty prioritized students' social and emotional well-being, understanding it was crucial for academic success. His efforts to build relationships, collaborate with families, and provide personalized support created a more comprehensive and supportive learning environment. His focus on relationships, collaboration, and proactive crisis management provided a framework for creating equitable structures that supported all students, particularly those with behavioral challenges.

This case study illustrates how Monty leveraged equitable systems and structures to stabilize his school community in crisis. Monty created an environment to address inequities and to foster a more inclusive learning experience, particularly for students with behavioral challenges. Monty's leadership in establishing equitable systems and structures has yielded several long-term benefits for his school community. By prioritizing personalized support for students, particularly those with behavioral challenges, he has fostered a more inclusive learning environment that ensures all students receive the necessary resources to thrive academically and emotionally. His focus on building trust and rapport among students, families, and staff has cultivated a positive school climate, enhanced student engagement, and promoted a culture of respect and collaboration. Additionally, Monty's initiatives have laid the groundwork for systemic change, allowing the school to continuously evaluate and adjust policies and practices to meet the diverse needs of its student population. This emphasis on equity equips the school to withstand future crises better, minimizing disruptions to learning and ensuring a resilient educational environment. Ultimately, Monty's approach aligns with research indicating that equitable systems lead to improved academic outcomes, helping to close achievement gaps and promote long-term success for all learners.

CASE STUDY ANALYSIS

Individual and Small-Group Discussion Questions

- How did Monty's leadership style evolve in response to the crises he faced?
- What specific strategies did he implement to build relationships with students and staff?
- In what ways did Monty's crisis management approach reflect his understanding of the unique needs of students with behavioral disabilities?
- How did the previous principal's hands-off approach contribute to the challenges Monty faced upon his arrival?
- In what ways did Monty's actions demonstrate a commitment to creating equitable systems for all students, particularly those with behavioral challenges?
- How did Monty's experiences highlight the importance of tailored interventions for students with different levels of family support and engagement?
- What strategies did Monty implement to ensure long-term improvements in the school's approach to behavioral challenges?

Whole-Group Activities

- **Equity Audit Simulation:** Divide the class into small groups representing different stakeholder perspectives (e.g., students, parents, teachers, administrators, community members). Each group will conduct a mock equity audit of a school system, identifying potential areas of inequity and proposing solutions. Groups will present their findings and recommendations to the whole class, engaging in discussions about the challenges and strategies for implementing equitable systems and structures.

- **Crisis Management Scenario:** Present a hypothetical crisis scenario (e.g., natural disaster, pandemic, or social unrest) and discuss its impact on a school's systems and structures. Facilitate a whole-group discussion on the potential inequities that may arise and how school leaders can proactively address them. Encourage participants to brainstorm strategies for building resilience and adaptability into the school's systems and structures to mitigate the effects of future crises.

Resource Allocation, Deprivation, and Diffusion

Real leaders focus resources in areas that provide the greatest opportunity rather than making across-the-board decisions.

—Charles Sonnenberg

On May 14, 2022, a year after the Christchurch Mosque shootings in New Zealand, another mass shooting occurred in the United States, with a similar motivation: hate. At 2:28 p.m., Peyton S. Gendron entered the Tops grocery store in Buffalo, New York, killing ten and wounding three people by the end of his terrorist attack. Similar to the Christchurch Mosque shooting, Gendron sought out Black and Brown people to shoot because of his white supremacist hate. The events that unraveled that day and the memorials later set up to honor those murdered shed light on another significant and inequitable problem: food security. Tops supermarket, a Black enclave of the city, was the only supermarket available in that portion of Buffalo. During the recovery, a more extensive conversation opened about the necessity for Tops to reopen so that citizens would have access to fresh fruits and vegetables and not have to rely on powdered milk. The shooting in Buffalo exemplifies how a crisis often exacerbates inequities and brings them to light and demonstrates the key resources that are needed for recovery.

The tragic shooting at Tops supermarket underscored how crises can worsen existing inequities and resource allocation challenges. The incident shed light on the community's dependence on Tops as the sole supermarket in that area of Buffalo, highlighting the critical importance of food security and access to fresh produce in underserved neighborhoods. It laid bare the vulnerability of communities relying on limited resources and emphasized the necessity for more equitable distribution of essential services, such as grocery stores, across urban areas. This crisis, like others, highlighted the pivotal role of effective resource management and allocation in both immediate response and long-term recovery efforts. The community within Buffalo who relied on Tops were all too familiar with this food desert and understood that they needed the supermarket to return to cover their basic needs for survival and thriving health. One news report called the workers' return to Tops "resilient," but it was apparent that their return was likely fueled out of necessity.[1] As we saw after the attack at Tops, resources during a crisis are always an integral part of recovery, and new ways of thinking about how to reestablish access to those resources is imperative.

On a typical school day, children arrive in the classroom with differing needs. Some needs may be more significant than others, but even so, all children should have access to an excellent and equitable education. Leaders make decisions about the needs of their student population. When I was a school leader, I remember considering who my students were, what I wanted them to have access to, and what gaps were preventing me from reaching that desired vision. For example, I thought access to more inquiry-based experiences would provide profound understanding and improved critical-thinking skills. I thought about the curricular enhancements and extracurricular activities we could offer. During a crisis, however, the decision-making turns far more basic: How can I stabilize the environment to keep everyone safe? Allocating resources equitably requires leaders to discern how, during or after a crisis, they will diffuse, allot, and justify the decisions they make about who gets what.

When leaders decide to allocate funds in schools during or after a crisis, they must consider the potential impact on various groups and the long-term effects of their decisions. For example, if funds are directed toward improving the academic achievement of a specific group, leaders should also assess the potential consequences of reallocating resources from other areas. Research has shown that deploying funds during crises, such as the Great Recession of 2007–2009 may serve as a temporary measure, but even with additional funding, schools may still face challenges. Furthermore, leaders should consider the long-term effects of resource allocation, ensuring that the decisions they make have sustainable impact. This process involves evaluating the potential benefits and drawbacks of directing resources to specific areas and understanding the broader implications for the school or district. In summary, when distributing resources during or after a crisis, leaders should carefully consider the potential impact this allocation may have on many different groups, the long-term effects of these decisions, and the sustainability of the allocated resources.

DEFINING RESOURCE ALLOCATION

The allocation of resources is crucial in education, especially for principals and educational leaders dealing with crises. In 1985, Judith D. Hackman introduced a theory of resource allocation in higher education, which emphasized how institutions distribute resources based on the centrality of various units within the organization.[2] Hackman suggested that a unit's centrality significantly influences the internal resources allocated by the institution, which is especially important during times of crisis when effective leadership requires careful resource management.

In addition to Hackman's work, Frazerph Bower's 1970 model offers a framework for understanding resource allocation processes.[3] Bower's model outlines stages, including the definition stage, in which managers identify performance gaps or investment opportunities; and the impetus stage, in which social and political dynamics influence decision-making. Senior managers play a role in establishing a structural context that facilitates these interactions, demonstrating that resource allocation is not solely a financial decision but rather a complex interplay of cognitive, social, and political factors.

In the context of educational leadership, especially during crises, principals must navigate these stages effectively to ensure that resources are allocated appropriately. They need to assess the needs of their institutions, engage with stakeholders, and make informed decisions that address both immediate needs and long-term goals. This strategic approach to resource allocation can significantly affect the resilience and adaptability of educational institutions facing challenges, emphasizing the crucial role of principled leadership in crisis management.

Viewing resource allocation through an equity lens involves recognizing and addressing historical disparities and systemic barriers that affect marginalized communities. This approach emphasizes the fair distribution of resources based on individual and community needs rather than on a one-size-fits-all model. For instance, educational leaders can apply an equity lens by prioritizing funding and support for underserved groups, such as students of color, English language learners, and those from low-income backgrounds. By asking critical questions about who benefits from resource allocation and how decisions might exacerbate existing inequalities, leaders can make informed choices that promote inclusivity and social justice. This lens not only fosters a more equitable educational environment but also ensures that all students have access to the opportunities necessary for their success, ultimately transforming educational practices and outcomes for diverse populations.

Defining Equitable Resource Allocation

The use of resources, such as people, time, and money that support the restabilization of the students' learning environment after a crisis, empowers all children and enables them to reach rigorous learning outcomes, regardless of their race or family income.

Equitable Allocation of Additional Resources

When crises happen, governments often rally to execute additional funding so schools can continue functioning. For example, after the Great Recession, the American Recovery and Reinvestment Act (ARRA) provided opportunities for schools to recover some of the revenue they had lost at that time. Throughout this financial crisis, layoffs were expected to hit every sector, yet through ARRA funds, schools were given aid to stall potential layoffs. Similarly, during the COVID-19 pandemic, the government provided funds through the COVID-19 Elementary and Secondary Schooling Emergency Relief (ESSER) initiative. The goals of ESSER funding were to assist in mitigating learning loss so schools could hire additional support and purchase necessary materials, such as laptops, hot spots, and digital platforms, for schools to manage and support remote learning. Despite the ambitious efforts of these policy goals, Kenneth Shores and Matthew Steinberg argue that the amount of aid given to schools during two major crises—the Great Recession and the COVID-19 pandemic—was inadequate to meet policy goals.[4] For example, even with the ASSR funding relief, layoffs still swept over schools in waves, and the extra funding from the ESSER did not mitigate "learning loss," as was made clear when the National Assessment of Educational Progress shared its findings of student learning and the dramatic decrease occurring over the past few years.

These two crisis examples demonstrate that when leaders are given financial aid, they can drastically improve how schools function. Thus, leaders do have opportunities to increase the equitable outcomes of students if they determine how to allocate those resources equitably while also considering the concept of resource deprivation. The literature shows that funding across crises can be consistent and robust but also poses several limitations. Additionally, as was the case with ESSR funding, the financial resources were given based on Title 1 designation—schools with high levels of poverty—and then trickled down accordingly.

During times of crisis, additional federal aid is often given to school districts. In some cases, as with the COVID-19 pandemic, in which a significant amount of funding was spent on personal protection equipment and laptops or hot spots to engage learning, choices have to be made to determine how federal funds will be spent. With federal support, such as ESSER, funding continued to pour into schools at high levels, allowing leaders to improve specific areas of need. If the policy decision for an act such as ESSER were to mitigate issues of learning loss, the funding decisions to meet these policy decisions would vary.

The school leaders interviewed for my study explained that they used their ESSER funds in different ways. Some principals used crisis funding to add positions, retain teachers, or buy curricular enhancements. Considering how these purchases would affect their students in the long term allowed these leaders to think more strategically about the funding they received. For example, one principal discussed how she spent some of the ESSER funds received post-COVID to provide equity training for her teachers:

> During the crisis, they just kept saying "Those kids." I knew what they meant because they would follow it up with anecdotes about being poor or their parents not doing enough. I had to find a way for them to understand that they were thinking with a deficit mindset, which would be a long-term issue.

Sandra, a novice principal in New York City, explained that this mindset shared by her teachers required her to think about the impact of their words and how, in the long term, that would affect their work with the students in the urban city school. She explained that she used the funding to foster a mutual understanding of her students and their experiences through professional learning. She explained that professional learning was also tethered to culturally relevant pedagogy, which further bolstered the teachers' ability to teach academically rigorous content.

To make equitable decisions about resource allocation, the dimensions of this pillar must be teased out. With resource allocation, leaders must think strategically about the impact of the category of resources being allocated as well as the potential short- and long-term effects of each decision. For example, when funds are given to schools and districts as support during a crisis, human capital is often considered to be a great opportunity. Leaders, however, need to consider the long-term vision of the human capital and be transparent about making decisions so staff understand the intention behind this additional support. Table 7.1 provides examples of different categories of resource allocation as well as potential short-term and long-term impacts.

Human Capital

Human capital is the value that people bring to their workplace. In schools, human capital is often thought of as the adults who provide for the students: teachers and staff (e.g., janitors, secretaries). During a crisis when learning outcomes may be affected, especially among the marginalized, school

TABLE 7.1 Categories of resource allocation and examples of short-term and long-term impacts

Category of Resource Allocation	*Short-term Impact*	*Long-term Impact*
Human Capital	Hiring people who can increase the efficacy of support to return the school environment to stability	Hiring individuals who bring long-term added value
Instructional and Curricular Enhancements	Remote learning modalities and technological enhancements	Establishing curricular modules for a variety of learners through a culturally responsive pedagogical lens
Family Engagement	Immediate access to school-based resources, such as free meals, technology, and instruction	Establishing a cadre of people who develop systems and structures to embed the immediate-access items into long-term structures
Learning-Ready Facilities	In the case of structural damage, construction works to support the school's recovery; also add public health structures, such as masks or safety shields to prevent the spread of pathogens, diseases, and other threats	Assessing ways to embed some learning-ready facilities to enhance the learning environment

leaders must consider human capital as a long-term investment for the frequent emergencies that plague our schools. To protect the human capital in the building, leaders must identify the resilience of their systems and structures (see chapter 6).

Education systems play a critical role in building individual, community, and systemic resilience because they support and strengthen human capital and act as a hub to share information during crises.[5] The COVID-19 pandemic eroded human capital, particularly among young people, posing long-term risks to productivity in the form of health issues, inequality, and social unrest.[6] To address these risks, urgent policy actions were (and continue to be) recommended, including vaccinations, nutritional supplementation, increased instructional time, and support for adapted training and job intermediation for youth.

Instructional and Curricular Enhancements

When the COVID-19 pandemic hit, nearly every school in the United States moved into some degree of remote learning. In California, Abraham, a mid-career principal who worked in a high-income and high-poverty area separated by a national forest, had to think dynamically about what "remote" meant for his students. Many families in his district lived in internet-accessible areas, and these children were equipped with laptops; this principal also knew that many of his families did not have internet access in their locations. As a short-term solution, he used his ESSER funds to purchase school buses and delivered paper copies of the lessons for these students so that while they were remote, they were still learning in tandem with their peers. This solution worked for the first six months of the pandemic. As students returned and resumed working with pencil and paper, however, Abraham's initial concerns solidified. The student who received lessons on paper were not as far along as the students who had interacted digitally with teachers online.

Emilia, a veteran principal from the East Coast, designed initiatives to support the learning gaps exacerbated by this type of funding. She explained:

> I always struggle with the phrase "learning loss." Conceptually, I understand it, but what I struggled with coming off of the pandemic, or even the three months we were closed [was that] the students were online and barely online at that. They didn't lose that learning; they didn't get the content to learn in the first place because of the pandemic! But it appears that they came back to school and did everything they're supposed to and should have that learning. I took the attitude when we came back last

> year like we're still going to learn. We're going to find a new way to do it because we're educators. In 2020, we did not take state tests, so it's a disconnect because I can't say year to year. We grew because I had my district tests and maps, but I didn't have state tests to compare; at the end of last school year, in the spring of 2020, we went up 6 percent on our end-of-the-year grade, if you will. And I attribute that to my statement that we have always been and that we will keep doing what's right for kids. We might have to tweak how we do it, but we're going to keep doing it, and so I think by only focusing on what we had to teach in the standards and moving our teachers and support staff around, we were able to improve outcomes.

Emilia reflected on equitable resource allocation within the context of education. She struggled with the concept of "learning loss," emphasizing that students cannot lose what they never had. Her perspective highlighted the importance of considering the distinct circumstances of each student, particularly those who were not exposed to traditional learning because of the pandemic. Her statement also underscored the resilience and adaptability of educators to find new ways to facilitate learning. This view aligned with principles of equity, which emphasize the need to provide different levels of support to address individual needs and challenges that ultimately can lead to improved outcomes.[7]

Crises happen in many forms, so short-term solutions will always take precedence over long-term solutions because they seek to disrupt the chaos that crises cause. Leaders, however, should also consider how long-term solutions can be designed, especially when additional funds are available. In Abraham's case, he had to think about the problem he was working through and create a data management system that permitted for different forms of tracking to occur. This long-term solution allowed him to consider the curricular enhancements he would need for his students. Moreover, he codesigned this new data platform with his team to provide an overview of what students were learning, what they needed to learn, and how teachers could present that curriculum.

Family Engagement

School leaders can also use additional funds from federal aid like ESSER to improve family engagement during a crisis by implementing evidence-based strategies. Research emphasizes the crucial role of parents and families in children's learning and development, especially during recovery efforts.[8] In 2022, the Brookings Institution assessed the need for a family-centered approach to COVID-19 recovery.[9] They underscored the importance of equitable family engagement practices and the need for meaningful two-way communication and collaboration between schools and families. School leaders should use additional federal funding to implement some of the recommended strategies to increase family engagement.

Equitable Family Engagement Commitment

Committing to equitable family engagement is essential. This involves recognizing families as experts who can help build more equitable education systems and involving them in decision-making processes. This commitment is crucial to foster meaningful partnerships between schools and families. Strategies for equitable family engagement include making it "business as usual," building relationships between staff and families, meaningfully involving and engaging families and trusted community advocates, and engaging outside the school building. By embracing these strategies, school leaders can create an inclusive environment that values the input and involvement of all families, ultimately leading to improved student outcomes and a more equitable education system.[10] School leaders can enact an equitable family engagement commitment by providing additional resources to parent and family coordinator offices. By prioritizing family engagement, school leaders can ensure that resources are allocated in ways that reflect the diverse needs and perspectives of all families. Because this approach identifies specific areas where additional support is needed, it allows for a more targeted and effective allocation of resources.

Strategic Use of Resources in Family Engagement

Utilizing additional resources and funds to provide direct services to families about how to work effectively with their children's school, launching strategic surveys, and providing parents with easy-to-understand and applicable information can enhance family engagement.[11] Schools and districts can allocate resources to offer workshops, training sessions, or informational materials to help families understand how to support their children's education effectively. Strategic surveys can be conducted to gather feedback from families about their needs, preferences, and challenges, which can then inform the development of more targeted and effective family engagement initiatives. Additionally, providing parents with clear and practical information, such as guidance on navigating the education system, understanding academic expectations, and accessing support services, can empower families to be more actively engaged in their children's education. These efforts can build stronger partnerships between schools and families, leading to improved student outcomes and a more inclusive educational environment.[12]

By strategically allocating resources to support family engagement initiatives, school leaders can address disparities in access to information and support among different family groups. This targeted approach ensures that all families, particularly those from marginalized backgrounds, have the resources they need to effectively engage with the school system, thereby promoting equity in educational outcomes.

Learning-Ready Facilities for Recovery and Enhancement

A learning-ready facility signifies a school setting that is designed to augment and support the educational journey of all students in a safe, adaptable, and conducive environment. These facilities are characterized by their strong structure, proper maintenance, and integration of modern technology and resources to cater to the diverse needs of students. They also feature flexible spaces that can be easily adjusted for different learning activities, as well as robust technology infrastructure to facilitate digital learning. Additionally, learning-ready facilities prioritize the incorporation of durable, easy-to-clean materials; enhanced ventilation systems; safety measures; and outdoor learning spaces that promote a healthy and engaging environment.

Furthermore, these facilities are designed with equity in mind to ensure that all students, regardless of their backgrounds or needs, have access to high-quality equipment, technology, and spaces that support their learning and development. Leaders with an equity-focused approach consider various factors to ensure that their learning facilities are equitable, such as analyzing data on facility conditions and student outcomes across different demographics, engaging diverse stakeholders in the planning and decision-making processes, incorporating culturally responsive elements in facility design, providing ongoing training for staff, and establishing partnerships with various organizations to expand learning opportunities for all students. By creating environments that are accessible and supportive for all students, school leaders can mitigate the impact of systemic inequities and provide every student with the opportunity to succeed. This approach reinforces the idea that equitable resource allocation is not just about financial resources but also about creating physical spaces that foster inclusive learning experiences.

When a crisis occurs, leaders should view the following considerations through an equitable lens and ensure the following:

- Multipurpose areas are designed to quickly accommodate various learning needs or serve as temporary classrooms in case of building damage, utilizing movable partitions, modular furniture, and versatile storage solutions to create adaptable spaces.

- Robust internet access, power outlets, and audiovisual equipment are integrated throughout the building to support both in-person and remote learning scenarios, enabling seamless transitions between learning modes in the event of structural issues in certain areas.
- Materials for walls, floors, and surfaces are selected based on impact resistance and ease of sanitization to address structural wear and tear and public health concerns. Consideration can be given to using printed wall protection systems that are durable and can display educational content or wayfinding information.
- HVAC systems are upgraded to improve air quality and reduce the spread of pathogens, with the installation of high-efficiency filters, ultraviolet air purifiers, and increased outdoor air circulation to create healthier learning environments.
- Built-in safety measures, such as plexiglass barriers, touchless fixtures, hand sanitizer stations, and clear signage for health protocols and emergency procedures, are incorporated throughout the facility.
- Outdoor classrooms or learning areas are developed to serve as alternative spaces if indoor areas are compromised, promoting connection with nature and providing additional options for socially distanced learning.
- Smart sensors and monitoring systems are installed to detect early signs of structural issues, enabling proactive maintenance to reduce the risk of sudden building damage.

By adopting these strategies, schools can create learning environments that are resilient, adaptable, and health conscious and that are better prepared to handle structural challenges while enhancing the overall educational experience.

STRATEGICALLY PLANNING FOR LONG-TERM FACILITATION ENHANCEMENTS POSTCRISIS

In the aftermath of a crisis, educational institutions face the critical task of not just recovering but also evolving to meet future challenges. Strategic planning for long-term facilitation enhancements is essential to build resilience, improve adaptability, and ensure continued educational excellence. This process involves a comprehensive approach that goes beyond mere restoration of precrisis conditions. Instead, it focuses on leveraging lessons learned, embracing innovative technologies, and fostering a culture of continuous improvement. By strategically enhancing facilitation capabilities, schools can create more robust, flexible, and inclusive learning environments that are better equipped to navigate uncertainties and capitalize on new opportunities. The following strategies outline a road map for educational leaders to transform crisis-driven changes into sustainable, long-term improvements in facilitation and overall institutional effectiveness.

Assessing and Learning from Crisis Response

By evaluating actions and creating a database of lessons learned, principals can ensure that the voices of all stakeholders, particularly those from marginalized communities, are heard. This inclusive approach helps identify specific needs and gaps in resource allocation, allowing for targeted interventions that address inequities.

- Following each crisis event, conduct after-action reviews to evaluate the response.
- Implement a database of lessons learned that is accessible to all staff.
- Utilize data analytics to identify patterns in crisis response effectiveness.

Strategy: Develop a standardized crisis response evaluation framework that incorporates quantitative metrics and qualitative feedback from stakeholders.

Developing Adaptive Facilitation Models

Creating modular facilitation plans and hybrid meeting protocols ensures that all students, regardless of their circumstances, can engage meaningfully in their education. This adaptability is crucial for equitable resource allocation, as it allows leaders to respond to diverse student needs and ensure that resources are effectively diffused across various formats and modalities.

- Create modular facilitation plans that can be easily adapted for different formats.
- Design hybrid meeting protocols that seamlessly blend in-person and virtual participation.
- Establish a toolkit of facilitation techniques that are suitable for various scenarios.

Strategy: Implement a "facilitation playbook" outlining best practices for different meeting types and contexts to ensure consistency and adaptability.

Investing in Technology Infrastructure

Conducting a technology audit to identify gaps in access enables principals to allocate resources equitably. By investing in technology that supports all students, particularly those in underserved areas, leaders can bridge the digital divide and promote equal opportunities for learning.

- Conduct a comprehensive technology audit to identify gaps and opportunities.
- Implement cloud-based collaboration platforms for seamless information sharing.
- Invest in high-quality audiovisual equipment for enhanced virtual engagement.

Strategy: Develop a multiyear technology road map aligned with facilitation needs, including regular updates and staff training.

Enhancing Facilitator Skills

Establishing a facilitator certification program that emphasizes equity ensures that all educators are better equipped to meet the diverse needs of their students. This investment in human capital is essential for long-term success and supports the notion that equitable resource allocation includes developing the skills of staff to better serve all students.

- Establish a facilitator certification program within the organization.
- Provide regular workshops on emerging facilitation techniques and technologies.
- Encourage peer-to-peer learning through facilitator communities of practice.

Strategy: Create a Facilitator Academy that offers tiered training programs from basic skills to advanced techniques to develop a pipeline of skilled facilitators.

Integrating Resilience into Strategic Planning

By incorporating resilience metrics into key performance indicators, principals can evaluate the effectiveness of their resource allocation decisions over time. This strategic focus allows leaders to assess how well their decisions support equitable outcomes and adapt their approaches as necessary.

- Conduct regular scenario planning exercises focused on potential crises.
- Incorporate resilience metrics into organizational key performance indicators (KPIs).
- Develop and regularly update business continuity plans that include facilitation strategies.

Strategy: Implement an annual Resilience Week, including workshops, simulations, and strategic planning sessions focused on enhancing organizational adaptability.

Prioritizing Inclusive Facilitation

Implementing a suggestion system for facilitation improvements encourages feedback from all stakeholders, ensuring that resource allocation decisions are informed by diverse perspectives. This continuous feedback loop is vital for maintaining equity in resource distribution.

- Develop guidelines for inclusive language and practices in all facilitated sessions.
- Implement technology solutions that support participation from diverse groups (e.g., real-time translation, closed captioning).
- Provide training on cultural competence and unconscious bias for all facilitators.

Strategy: Establish an Inclusion Ambassador role within facilitation teams to ensure that diverse perspectives are consistently incorporated into facilitation practices.

Aligning Facilitation with Organizational Goals

Integrating facilitation objectives into performance plans ensures that equity is a priority at all levels of the organization. This alignment helps principals make informed decisions about resource allocation that support the broader goals of equity and inclusivity.

- Integrate facilitation objectives into departmental and individual performance plans.
- Regularly review and adjust facilitation strategies based on organizational strategic priorities.
- Develop KPIs that link facilitation effectiveness to organizational outcomes.

Strategy: Create a Facilitation Alignment Task Force that meets quarterly to ensure facilitation practices are supporting and driving key organizational objectives.

By implementing these considerations, approaches, and strategies, principals can begin to effectively navigate the complexities of resource allocation during and after crises. They can ensure that resources are not only distributed equitably but also aligned with the specific needs of their student populations, fostering an educational environment that promotes success for all students.

ACKNOWLEDGING THE DEPRIVATION OF RESOURCES

When leaders allocate emergency funds to address specific needs, such as declining reading scores as a result of a crisis, they must also consider the potential impact on other groups. For instance, in providing resources to improve the academic achievement of a particular group, leaders should assess how this allocation may affect other areas and the potential outcomes of their decision. This involves a careful examination of how funding and human resources could be distributed elsewhere. ESSER is one such program that provides substantial financial support to address the impact of COVID-19 on elementary and secondary schools across the United States. The American Rescue Plan also established the Higher Education Emergency Relief Fund (HEERF) to provide emergency funds to institutions and their students, which allocated $76.2 billion to emergency funds.[13] States are required to distribute at least 90 percent of ESSER funds to local education agencies based on their proportional share of Elementary and Secondary Education Act Title I-A funds.[14] Additionally, more than $6 billion of the HEERF funds must be allocated directly to students in the form of emergency financial aid grants.[15] These funds support institutions of higher education in serving students and ensuring that they have access to the necessary resources during and after the crisis. Another aspect leaders should consider when considering distributing resources is the long-term effects of this financial bolster to a particular area. In the case of the deployment of ARRA funds during the Great Recession, research found that it was a stop-gap measure for schools—that is, the funding helped solve only partial problems but did little to address systemic inequities.[16] As a result, schools still faced layoffs and revenue drops even with the extra federal funding.

The equitable allocation of resources during a crisis is a complex and critical task for leaders. When distributing funds, leaders must consider the potential impact on various groups and the long-term effects of their decisions. Research has highlighted the need for diverse representation in policy development and the importance of ensuring that policies are feasible, practical, and acceptable to all stakeholders.[17] In the context of crisis response in schools, leaders must be prepared to make difficult decisions and assess their reality to ensure that the policies are aligned to the particular characteristics of their school. During a global food crisis, for example, policymakers seek to increase food production, improve distribution, and provide social assistance to vulnerable populations. Adequate funding for specialized institutions and international organizations, as well as International Monetary Funding financing, is crucial to support countries in meeting their external financing needs associated with the food shock.[18] The allocation of resources within the context of the COVID-19 health crisis sparked debates about the consistency of preventive measures. Health economists and medical ethicists have long grappled with the challenge of fair and sensible health-care resource allocation, particularly in the face of increasing health-care costs and limited budgets. Although economic "efficiency" has become popular in informing funding decisions, health economists have shown little support for political decisions on resource allocation to COVID-19 preventive measures.[19] Similarly, in a school setting, administrators must navigate complex resource allocation decisions during crises like food shortages or health emergencies, balancing immediate needs with long-term educational goals and equity considerations.

The equitable distribution of resources does not mean equal distribution. Additional resources, including more than just funding, should be allocated to students with the greatest needs. Equitable resource allocation also involves ensuring access to highly qualified teachers and creating a culture of collaborative decision-making around resource allocation.[20] School leaders play a critical role in understanding the connections among leadership, equity, and resource allocation to create school resource equity. They need to mobilize the right combination of resources to ensure high-quality learning experiences for all students, regardless of their race or family income. The ability to do so requires paying attention to several dimensions, including providing professional development, embedding social-emotional learning, and connecting students and families with outside partners.[21]

Resource Diffusion

As suggested throughout this chapter, when a crisis occurs, resources to recover from the crisis usually follow. Federal aid can be given to school districts as well as local resources. Leaders must consider how these resources get into the hands of the students and families who need them. In this way, leaders must consider how to diffuse resources across their communities. When considering how to diffuse resources across their communities after a crisis, leaders must ask several important questions to guide their decision-making and ensure that resources are distributed effectively.[22] Some key questions to consider include the following:

- How are community members feeling about the crisis and its aftermath? It is essential to understand the emotional state of the community to provide appropriate support and resources.
- What are the most pressing needs of the community at this time? By identifying the most urgent needs, leaders can prioritize resource allocation and ensure that they meet the most critical challenges.
- Can any existing systems or processes be leveraged to distribute resources? It is essential to use any existing infrastructure to ensure that resources are distributed efficiently and equitably.
- How can resources be distributed in a way that is fair and equitable? Leaders need to avoid potential biases or disparities in resource allocation and ensure that resources are distributed fairly to all community members.
- What communication strategies can be used to ensure community members are aware of available resources and how to access them? Clear and transparent communication is essential to ensure that community members are aware of the available resources and know how to access them.

Finally, according to the School Crisis Recovery and Renewal Resources, school mental health leaders play a crucial role in containing a crisis, minimizing subsequent trauma, and restoring equity and equanimity in the school environment. The National Center for School Crisis and Bereavement provides online resources to help schools support their students through crisis and loss, including guidelines on promoting adjustment and helping children cope.[23] The Readiness and Emergency Management for Schools Technical Assistance Center supports schools, school districts, and higher education institutions in developing high-quality emergency operations plans and comprehensive emergency management planning efforts. These resources can be valuable for leaders looking to diffuse resources effectively across their communities during and after a crisis.

How to Consider Allocating Resources Equitably

School leaders are responsible for ensuring that resources are deployed efficiently and equitably, particularly in a crisis. Research has shown that resource equity can support academic excellence, but making decisions that support an equitable allocation of resources is often difficult.[24] Diffusing resources that have been allocated based on an equity-oriented stance can create a political nightmare. Allocating resources equitably in schools, especially during a crisis, presents significant challenges. The COVID-19 pandemic, for example, shed light on funding inequities, learning gaps, and a growing disparity between different communities.[25] During an economic downturn, state education leaders should advocate for federal support to prevent substantial cuts that disproportionately affect low-income students and students of color.[26] Leaders must collect and analyze school-level data beyond per-pupil funding to ensure that they distribute resources equitably.

During natural disasters, allocating resources such as food, water, and shelter is crucial for the well-being of affected populations. In addition to these necessities, research has shown that the level of resources also affects schools during crises and their explicit allocation can affect educational outcomes.[27] For example, in the aftermath of a natural disaster, schools may face challenges in allocating resources to ensure the safety and well-being of students and staff. This can include allocating funds for building repairs, providing counseling services for traumatized students, and distributing educational materials to replace those that have been lost or damaged. In some cases, schools may need to allocate resources to support the broader community, such as providing food and shelter to displaced families. The effective allocation of resources during and after a natural disaster is essential to ensure that schools can continue to provide a safe and supportive learning environment for students.[28]

The type of resources for which school leaders are responsible can range from instructional time and attention to teaching quality to tangible resources, such as laptops and hotspots. Therefore, effective leaders must use data to allocate these resources strategically. Leaders must then work collaboratively with staff and districts while monitoring data and implementing a continuous cycle of analysis to examine, assess, and refine resource use. These leaders, along with their teams, should pose the following questions to aid their decision-making:

- What are the varying needs of our students, and how do we allocate resources equitably to address priorities?
- Are we doing anything that is not aligned with our goals?
- What is the impact of the programs we are funding?
- How do we use instructional coaches, mentors, and other teacher leaders to improve instructional practice?

For leaders to decipher which resources they should allocate, to whom, and for whom, decision-making must be data-driven. According to a study by Berger et al., data-driven decision-making in resource allocation leads to more effective and efficient use of resources, ultimately improving organizational performance.[29] Diana's case study at the end of this chapter provides a practical example of this pillar in action. Furthermore, Diana's approach to tackling instructional time during and after the crisis was critical to their resource allocation strategy. Gavin Brown's research also has highlighted the significance of maintaining instructional continuity during crises, and Diana's experience serves as a valuable case study in this regard.[30]

Chapter Reflection and Guiding Questions

- Why is it essential for leaders to understand the emotional state of the community in the aftermath of a crisis? How can this understanding help in the effective distribution of resources?
- What are the potential challenges in identifying the most pressing needs of a community after a crisis? How can leaders overcome these challenges to prioritize resource allocation?
- Discuss the importance of leveraging existing systems or processes to diffuse resources efficiently and equitably. Provide examples of such systems and how they can be utilized.
- What potential biases or disparities do leaders need to be mindful of when allocating, depriving, and diffusing resources after a crisis? How can these biases be avoided?
- Why is clear and transparent communication essential in ensuring community members know how to access available resources? What are some effective communication strategies that can be employed in this context?

Case Study

DIANA

Principal, Puerto Rico

> *Soy un líder educativo quien tiene una posibilidad de utilizar todos estos recursos que tiene el distrito y la escuela, pero nunca hay responsabilidad sin saber cuáles son nuestros recursos emocionales.*
>
> I am an educational leader who has a possibility to use all these resources that the district and the school have, but there is never responsibility without knowing what our emotional resources are.

In the aftermath of Hurricane Maria, Diana was at the helm of a school community in crisis. The hurricane had devastated Puerto Rico, leaving the island waterlogged, destroying buildings, and knocking down

80 percent of the utility poles and all transmission lines. Power, cell phone service, and municipal water supplies were lost to essentially all of the island's 3.4 million residents.[31] The differential response and recovery times across US communities hit by the 2017 storms had raised concerns about disparities in response after Maria in Puerto Rico compared with the impact on the mainland states by other hurricanes.[32]

Equity-Crisis Dilemma

As a school leader, Diana was acutely aware of the need for equitable allocation of resources, considering the deprivation and diffusion in her school community. She understood the critical nature of timely aid distribution, as delayed responses could lead to serious adverse outcomes. She was aware of the critical nature of getting aid to its target promptly, given that slow responses also contribute to serious adverse outcomes.[33] She was also aware, however, that given the new policy, Ley de Reforma Educativa de Puerto Rico, funds were not readily available to public schools. She explains: "Now, there's a lot of money on the island for charter schools, but there is no money for [traditional] public schools." As a result, Diana began to look at how she could use her allocated funding to diffuse materials and resources to her population while also acknowledging that some members of her community would be deprived of resources they may want.

Research on education and disaster management has shown the importance of school leadership on student outcomes and the need for school leaders to build traits and capacities that will address challenges to learning recovery and system resilience. Diana was determined to lead her school community to recovery, leveraging the crisis to address equity issues. She knew strong leadership and school management were crucial to facilitate educational continuity and disaster recovery. Despite these challenges, she was committed to ensuring that all her students had an equal opportunity to recover and thrive in the aftermath of the disaster. She developed a dual-prong approach to facilitate resource diffusion. First, Diana looked at the funding streams that were being allocated for certain areas, such as new materials to replace those that were damaged. She found her building structure was fine, but water had seeped into all classrooms as a result of the flooding and ruined all of the technology in the building. After conferring with her team, they made the decision to invest in Chromebooks and projectors as opposed to Smartboards, which required installation. By focusing on the projectors, this made the item portable for teachers to take to different classrooms or share while they continued to rebuild.

Equity-Oriented Crisis Solution

Diana looked at the human capital to assess which faculty members attended to the needs of certain groups of students. She conferred with her team to understand how the faculty could provide more direct support to students. For example, teachers were broken up into pods and worked with their students for all content areas while providing data-driven supports. She also took stock of the teachers states of mind and needs. For example, some teachers already had generators and running water, whereas others did not. Some teachers had regular electricity, whereas others did not. Diana considered these decisions as best she could to support reductions in faculty tardiness and attendance, knowing that it was imperative to have a stable structure to support the students' return to school. She explained, "There is never accountability without knowing what the emotional resources are of the teachers in your building." Diana felt that she had to understand how the teachers were managing their emotions and lives before she could expect to hold them accountable to working under the strained conditions and to supporting students. "We want to develop talent, even after the hurricane crisis, but there's a difference now because of the hurricane and in my leadership I want to improve their quality of life, but we have to do it in a different way." By evaluating the current conditions as well as what was needed, Diana was able to release the tension created by the crisis. Faculty had expressed concerns about the lack of materials and organization around their duties.

Diana's efforts to provide emotional support to her students were informed by her understanding of the critical role that school leadership plays in disaster management. She was aware of the research highlighting the importance of strong leadership in facilitating educational continuity and disaster recovery. Diana was determined to lead her school community to recovery in the aftermath of Hurricane Maria, and she knew that addressing the emotional needs of her students was a crucial part of that process. By prioritizing emotional support, Diana demonstrated her commitment to the well-being of her students and her dedication to ensuring that all her students had an equal opportunity to recover and thrive post-disaster. Her proactive approach to providing emotional support set an example for other school leaders, highlighting the importance of addressing the emotional needs of students in the wake of a disaster.

Research and experiences from Puerto Rico after the hurricane emphasize the significance of schools in providing support for mental health and well-being. A study found that schools were the primary source of support from which families and communities sought help after the hurricane.[34] Thus, schools play a central role in addressing a disaster's emotional as well as its physical impact. To this end, Diana prioritized emotional support for students after their crisis and effectively managed resource allocation to her school community. During community meetings, Diana discussed with her faculty and staff the population that had stayed through the hurricane, those who left the island, and those who were returning. Faculty expressed concerns that students were struggling to make sense of the natural disasters. Diana recognized the importance of community outreach and collaboration in supporting those in need. This approach was exemplified by the experiences of UCA-Mayagüez graduate students and faculty members who overcame both tangible and intangible barriers to mental health by providing resources for basic needs, offering empathy and support, and making referrals for more intensive mental health treatment. Additionally, Diana's efforts aligned with best practices outlined in Save the Children's Hurricane Maria Response Strategy, which emphasized the importance of working with local volunteers, teachers, and community leaders to identify critical distribution needs and support psychosocial recovery.[35]

CASE STUDY ANALYSIS

Individual and Small-Group Activities

- **Case Analysis:** Ask each participant to read Diana's case study individually and note their observations, questions, and potential solutions.
- **Reflection:** Encourage participants to reflect on Diana's emotional and practical challenges and identify the key leadership traits and capacities she demonstrated.

- **Roundtable Discussion:** Divide participants into small groups and facilitate a roundtable discussion in which each participant shares personal observations from the case analysis. Encourage participants to discuss the case's implications for school leadership in crises.
- **Role-Playing:** Assign roles such as Diana, teachers, and community members to the participants and ask them to role-play a meeting to discuss the allocation and diffusion of resources and emotional support for the students. Also, discuss who could be deprived of these resources.

Whole-Group Activity

- **Fishbowl Discussion:** Conduct a fishbowl discussion in which a small group of participants discuss the case study in the center of a circle while the rest of the group observes. After a set time, the observers can join the discussion, and the initial group becomes the observers. This activity encourages active listening and diverse perspectives.

Advocacy for Radical Change

After all, radical simply means "grasping things at the root."
—Angela Davis[1]

The term *radical* often gets misunderstood. In reality, it signifies the intention to tackle the core of an issue at hand. School leaders can radically shift and reimagine their roles during crises to improve equity for their students and families.[2] This requires leaders to understand the root causes of inequities and commit to transformative change, even in the face of instability resulting from a crisis. In this chapter, I delve into the role of school leaders in advocating for radical change. I focus on advocacy by examining the responses to marginalized populations for long-term impact and success. Next, I discuss the bold actions leaders can take to uproot perpetuating systems of oppression. Then, I share a way to look at systemic changes on behalf of marginalized populations by providing strategies and examples of how school leaders can radically transform their schools or districts. Finally, I discuss how leaders can be advocates for radical change by sharing the case study of Alice, a school leader in Los Angeles, and summarize critical strategies and actions for long-term radical change. School leaders can make lasting changes that challenge systemic oppression and promote equity in education by grasping everything by its root.

At the time of the COVID-19 pandemic lockdown, several principals explained how they met the discrete needs of their families. Myah a principal in Minneapolis, discussed how she had to recalibrate her understanding of her families' needs. As Myah stated, "I have to learn the new needs of the students and the families and then consider the needed materials. Do we have what we need to give to students to be successful at home or in person? I tell my staff, we are here to serve our kids and our families, and, you know, if we have the means and the way, let's go." The pandemic provided an opportunity for school leaders to engage with families and advance equity in ways that were not previously considered, embodying Angela Davis's quote at the chapter's opening.[3]

Similarly, the pandemic consistently illuminated racial inequities that require a radical approach to grasp the root causes of these issues. Several leaders I interviewed described the racial inequities that permeate their schools. Racism, particularly systemic racism, can indeed be considered a crisis in the educational context. Systemic racism in education refers to the barriers within the US education system that disproportionately affect underrepresented communities.[4] This crisis of racism manifests in various ways, such as racial disparities in school discipline, academic achievement gaps, and unequal access to educational resources.[5] Racial discrimination in schools can significantly affect students' engagement and mental health, hindering their motivation to engage at school. This discrimination can take the form of hostile behaviors like bullying, hate speech, and hate crimes, which can impede access to an equitable education.[6] Moreover, racism in schools interrupts the healthy social development of young people, leading to negative consequences for their mental and physical health, standard of living, and well-being. Systemic racism in education also includes school curricula that overlook or diminish diverse perspectives and histories as well as disciplinary policies and actions that unfairly target students from underrepresented communities. These barriers make it difficult for underrepresented students to access the same quality of education as other students.[7] In response to this type of crisis, school leaders advocating for radical change can apply Davis's concept of "grasping things at the root" to address the root causes of systemic racism in education, such as racial biases, unequal funding, and unfair disciplinary actions.[8] This approach also involves acknowledging and challenging the systemic barriers that perpetuate racial inequities in schools.[9] For instance, school leaders can implement strategies for antiracist and decolonized teaching, which involves acknowledging biases and privileges and making courses and curricula actively antiracist.[10] School leaders can also advocate for radical change by working to diversify school staff, leadership, and governance and to ensure that school curricula and special education are inclusive and equitable.[11]

In the context of natural disasters, school leaders play a critical role in emergency response.[12] They need to understand the root causes of vulnerabilities leading to disaster learning loss and advocate for radical changes to mitigate them. According to the National Association of Elementary School Principals, school leaders should proactively identify potential hazards, develop emergency response plans, and ensure that staff and students are well prepared for various types of disasters.[13] By understanding the root causes of vulnerabilities, school leaders can take steps to address issues, such as building safety, communication systems, and community partnerships, to enhance disaster resilience in schools.

In the context of school shootings, school leaders advocating for radical change need to address the root causes of such incidents. This approach could involve advocating for stricter gun control laws, improving mental health support for students, and implementing comprehensive safety measures in schools. According to the American Federation of Teachers, school leaders should create a safe and supportive school environment by addressing the underlying causes of violence, including access to firearms, mental health issues, and the impact of trauma on students. By advocating for radical changes in these areas, school leaders can help reduce the possibility of school shootings and ensure the safety of their students and staff.

In all these contexts, "grasping things at the root" suggests a deep understanding of the systemic issues at play and a commitment to transformative change. It involves challenging long-held understandings, confronting oppression, and advocating for equity and justice. This is the essence of advocacy for radical change. According to the National Association of Secondary School Principals (NASSP), school leaders should be change agents who create a more just and equitable school system by addressing the root causes of inequity and advocating for policies that promote fairness and opportunity for all students.[14] School leaders can drive meaningful and lasting change in their schools and communities, again by grasping things at the root.

UNDERSTANDING THE ROLE OF SCHOOL LEADERS IN ADVOCACY FOR RADICAL CHANGE

The variety of crises and pervasive state of crisis that school leaders must face requires them to think innovatively and equitably. To advocate for radical change, leaders must address various equity issues within their schools, such as unequal resources and funding, and continuously advocate for equitable policies. Archie, a veteran principal from Denver, shared, "Running a school right now feels impossible and thankless. I have to be strong, positive, and brave for everyone. I'm exhausted."

Several principals echoed Archie's sentiments, sharing how taxed they were by responding to back-to-back crises. All the principals I interviewed, however, recognized the need for fundamental changes that targeted the root of the inequities they experienced. During the pandemic, although funding was made available for schools to purchase laptops and hotspots or wireless connection devices, many principals had to focus on short-term ways that students could gain access to remote learning while also considering long-term implications. Archie continued:

> I remember spending an entire day with a box full of hotspots in my trunk and driving around some of the most impoverished neighborhoods in Denver, knocking on doors and trying to find the people that I was looking for, which you know, sometimes did live, where the address was. One time I showed up at a student's house and it turned out to be an auto body shop and nobody was living there, but that was the address they used in order to ensure their child attended our school, or perhaps they were homeless. Whatever the case, I visited a couple of shelters and needed to get in there and provide equipment, including hotspots. This was a real opportunity to overcome some equity gaps regarding technology access.

For Archie, this experience of delivering hotspots to families who did not have internet access sparked new thinking about how he could ensure long-term access so that students could always access the internet, which, for them, would be a valuable learning tool during and after this crisis.

School leaders have firsthand insight about how their school manages a crisis and can advocate for long-term remedies for inequitable solutions. School leaders who advocate for radical change call out institutional racism or xenophobia and publicly advocate against structural oppression during a crisis. Radical change promotes inclusive learning spaces while also preserving stable and workable systems for the instruction of all students.[15]

Advocating for Radical Change Requires Transformational Leaders

Leaders enter into the task of advocacy at a variety of levels with vastly different perspectives and starting places that can look quite different, depending on the context. One common place to start is with undertaking a transformational leadership stance.[16] Rita Basu has emphasized the strength of transformational leadership in altering employees' mindsets to expedite the organizational change process.[17] It is essential, however, to be cognizant of the complex nature of any change during or after a crisis that changes a fundamental structure, which could potentially fail if leaders are not given the appropriate support they need.

Examining Responses to Marginalized Populations for Long-Term Impact and Success

As discussed in the previous chapters, leaders must identify and communicate with community members to solve long-term problems, such as underfunding and lack of personnel and resources, if they are to advocate for marginalized communities.

Advocating for radical change occurred throughout 2022 and 2023 by way of a string of teacher strikes. Unlike the strikes in 2018, in which teachers and educators demanded more funding for schools, the more recent strikes included a push to address more deeply rooted social issues, such as bringing air conditioning to schools in the wake of climate change and ensuring housing assistance for families to establish stable home environments that can improve outcomes for all children. These strikes are becoming more popular because of their efficacy.[18] For example, in 2019, Chicago Public School teachers went on strike for eleven days, demanding an increase in support staff such as nurses, librarians, and social workers. As a result, the Chicago Public School district reached an agreement with the teachers' union to provide a nurse at every public school every day of the school year.[19] School nurses provide medical care and triage for students and "play a pivotal role in the health and wellbeing of children and contribute to improved health and education outcomes."[20] In a study conducted by the National Association of School Nurses, they found that "the intensity of policies and programs in school health services [is] significantly related to graduation rate."[21] The case for school nurses has a significant impact on students' long-term academic and medical health. For children in marginalized urban or rural neighborhoods, access to health care becomes tethered to their overall trajectory.

It is clear that school leaders can play a crucial role in prioritizing long-term impact and success in their advocacy efforts. Regardless of the specific issue at hand, some of the ways leaders can and have enacted change include the following:

- **Establishing a proactive, collaborative school mindset:** School leaders can create a positive school culture by setting a proactive, collaborative school mindset. This includes supporting and enhancing staff, motivating student engagement and well-being, and committing collectively to foster improvement and promote and sustain success for schools that serve a range of advantaged and disadvantaged communities.[22]
- **Prioritizing equity and evidence:** Education leaders must prioritize equity and evidence to help students recover from the pandemic as well as

other potential crises. Short-term recovery efforts can lead to long-term transformation if states and districts invest resources in evidence-based, holistic strategies, particularly those proven to accelerate learning for historically underserved students. Education leaders should measure student progress and use data to advance learning, target interventions for students whose learning has suffered disproportionately, and continuously adjust to reflect evidence of what is working, particularly for historically underserved students.[23]

- **Providing professional development activities for district and school leaders:** School leaders can offer professional development activities for district leaders to establish and strengthen organizational leadership. This can help customize each school's level of autonomy for personnel hiring, placement and replacement, and other key decisions based on school capacity.[24]
- **Recognizing and supporting emotional health:** School leaders can acknowledge and uphold the emotional health of students and teachers. They can provide teachers and school counselors with the tools needed to become more skillful educators, such as talking about emotional health, sharing school and community resources, and modeling healthy self-care.[25]

Bold Actions to Uproot Perpetuating Systems of Oppression

The public school system across the United States needs to be more equitable. The global landscape also illustrates how some communities are given more resources, while others are not.[26] Advocating for radical change requires leaders to consider how they foster inequities by perpetuating systems of oppression. These systems are tangible, like discipline policies and school culture norms, but they are also implicitly active, as in the case of implicit bias or unconscious racial bias. In their book *Unconscious Bias in Schools: A Developmental Approach to Exploring Race and Racism*, authors Tracey Benson and Sarah Fiarman explained that implicit bias is part of all systems and structures in schools.[27] Thus, it requires an awareness and alertness to racial equity within the work teachers and leaders engage in every day. Benson and Fiarman further note that uprooting inequities and uncovering implicit biases involve a complex process requiring that requires solutions that may not be readily available. The steps in this process include:

- **Establishing a clear vision:** School leaders can define a clear vision for their schools or districts that all stakeholders will share. This vision should be based on the values and beliefs of the school community and should be communicated effectively to all stakeholders.[28]

- **Fostering a positive school climate:** School leaders can support a positive climate by modeling the values, beliefs, and behaviors they wish to see in their school community. Transformational leaders can accomplish this by creating a culture of collaboration, empowering teachers, and inspiring and motivating staff and students to achieve a shared vision of excellence.[29] School leaders can also foster a positive climate during a crisis by acknowledging how the event has caused instability and unpredictability. They can also elicit an empathetic approach that allows their staff and faculty to maneuver the crisis. For example, I interviewed Tom, a veteran principal in New York City, who explained that during Hurricane Maria in Puerto Rico, some of his staff had lost family members in the devastation: "I gave them days off because I knew they needed to ensure their families were okay. I did not put in the paperwork. I just couldn't. I wanted to give them the time and not worry about paperwork, days off, et cetera." Leaders whose staff experience crises that occur in other parts of the world can use empathy to foster a positive school culture that is also inclusive.
- **Empowering teachers:** School leaders can empower their teaching staff by supporting their professional growth and development in equity-oriented practices, such as culturally relevant teaching and restorative circles. Transformational leaders understand that teachers are the primary drivers of student success and actively seek to support their professional growth.[30] During the COVID-19 crisis, Darla, a novice principal in New York City, shared that her teachers were operating from a deficit mindset: "They [teachers] would say 'these kids' and I would say, 'No, they are our kids.' " Radical change occurs when teachers are empowered to think reflectively during both typical and turbulent times. In this way, leaders can foster empowerment by providing professional learning and examining equity-oriented practices.
- **Aligning staffing and resources with instructional priorities:** School leaders can help staffing and resources to ensure that their curriculum, instruction, and assessments align with state standards. They can also strengthen the capacity of leaders and school staff to analyze and use data for decision-making.[31]
- **Monitoring progress and acting on it:** School leaders can closely watch, discuss, report, and act on the progress of schools that are undertaking rapid improvement. They can provide tailored support to each school by conducting a cause analysis of deeply rooted issues and a comprehensive needs assessment to inform its priorities for improvement.

In the wake of a crisis, school leaders can create real change for their communities. By taking bold steps like the ones noted here, they might transform their schools and districts in meaningful ways, for example by ensuring that students without access to technology are not left behind, or ensuring that all teachers have high expectations for their students without falling into the trap of a savior complex (more to come on this issue).

Examining Systemic Changes for Equity and Liberation

School leaders have an opportunity to drive systemic changes toward equity and liberation. They can do this by advocating for more resources and questioning systemic processes, such as discipline policies and metrics used in their school. For example, the COVID-19 pandemic significantly affected school attendance in the United States. Before the pandemic, about 15 percent of students nationwide were chronically absent—that is, they missed 10 percent or more of the school year. By the end of the 2021–2022 school year, that percentage grew to 28.5 percent, an increase of 6.5 million students. In California specifically, nearly two million students were chronically absent by the end of the 2021–2022 school year, an increase of 13 percentage points prepandemic.[32] In the Los Angeles Unified School District, one of the country's largest school districts, the chronic absentee rate was 46 percent during the following 2022–2023 school year, compared to an average of 19 percent in the three years prepandemic.[33]

Students reported anxiety about getting sick and the impact of prolonged isolation contributing to chronic absenteeism.[34] Vulnerable student groups are most likely to experience these challenges, which can lead to chronic absenteeism that significantly affects student performance. Students who are chronically absent are at higher risk of falling behind, scoring lower on standardized tests, and even dropping out.[35] The pandemic made it harder to address chronic absenteeism; some students have elected to stay home because of finances, housing instability, illness, transportation issues, anxiety, depression, bullying, and feeling unwelcome at school.[36] Increased mental health concerns and heightened caution around sending potentially sick children to school have also challenged attendance.[37]

School leaders can begin to tackle this sort of complex, systemic inequity by advocating for radical change and gradually working toward creating a more equitable and inclusive environment for all students, families, and staff.[38] Based on scholarly literature and expert insight, researchers have identified several strategies to guide school leaders in this transformative work. Nelda Cambron-McCabe and Martha McCarthy emphasized the importance of educating school leaders for social justice, highlighting the need for authentic educational justice leaders whose views aligned with social justice for equity and inclusion.[39] Furthermore, Paul Miller discussed the evidence of school leaders leading antiracism and inclusion efforts, emphasizing the importance of addressing systemic racism and building more inclusive environments.[40] Moreover, the National Education Association provided insight into the sources of systemic education inequities and the role of families, communities, and partners in advocating for equity as well as tools and strategies to help participants organize and advocate for change at the institutional level.[41] Additionally, New Leaders for Just Schools stressed the need for equity-focused leaders to contribute passionately to systemic change and advocates for the removal of barriers to student success.[42]

This scholarly insight underscores the significance of school leaders' role in addressing systemic inequities and provides a foundation for guiding their transformative work with the identified strategies. By integrating these scholarly perspectives, school leaders can advocate for and implement change to create more equitable and inclusive educational environments. School leaders can deploy several strategies to transform systemic inequities while advocating for radical change:[43]

- **Engage in reflection around positionality:** School leaders should engage in reflective practices to understand how their positionality influences their leadership style within the context of a crisis. This involves critically examining their experiences and biases to recognize how specific factors may affect decision-making and interactions with marginalized groups, especially during challenging times.
- **Develop racial literacy:** In a crisis, school leaders should prioritize the development of racial literacy for themselves as well as their school community to address any crisis-related disparities. This includes fostering a school culture that values diversity and inclusivity, providing professional development opportunities for staff and students, and creating crisis-specific policies and practices that promote equity and social justice.
- **Facilitate shared visions and collective responsibility:** Creating a shared vision to address a crisis and build collective responsibility among stakeholders is essential. School leaders can achieve this by engaging in dialogue with students, families, and community members to understand their needs and perspectives in the context of the crisis.

- **Build the capacity of stakeholders:** Efforts should be made to build the capacity of stakeholders to address a crisis and the impacts it has on social justice and equity. School leaders should build the capacity of stakeholders to engage in transformative work. This involves providing crisis-specific training and support for staff, students, and families to develop the skills and knowledge needed to promote equity and social justice during challenging times.
- **Develop critical alliances through community involvement:** School leaders should develop critical alliances with community members and organizations to promote equity and social justice. This can involve partnering with local organizations to provide crisis-specific resources and support for marginalized groups, as well as engaging in advocacy efforts to address crisis-related disparities and promote policy changes.
- **Shift to an aggressive advocacy mode:** During a crisis, school leaders should shift to an advocacy and activist role for their most marginalized student and family populations. This can involve demanding that their school communities receive more resources to address crisis-related challenges and altering staff beliefs about families from vulnerable populations in the context of the crisis.[44]
- **Address deficit mindsets:** Efforts should be made to address deficit mindsets within their teaching staff regarding students and families from vulnerable populations in a crisis. This can involve challenging and altering staff beliefs to create a more inclusive and supportive environment for all students, especially during challenging times.[45]
- **Advocate for mental health programmatic improvements:** School leaders are crucial in advocating for mental health programmatic improvements during a crisis. Additionally, they should lobby for more funds to improve mental health services in schools, as highlighted by the NASSP campaign.[46] Furthermore, school leaders must engage parents in mental health conversations and ensure that students become aware of the mental health supports available on campus. Several leaders I interviewed expressed being stressed themselves and suggested the importance of treating those who provide mental health support at the administrative level, thus signaling the significance of mental health support in the school environment. Advocating for mental health services as state policy and promoting social and emotional competency are also crucial aspects of the role of school leaders in advocating for mental health improvements during a crisis.[47] By advocating for mental health improvements, school leaders can create positive, safe, and

affirming school environments and ensure that students have the necessary support and resources to address their mental health needs.[48]

School leaders face concrete challenges. The COVID-19 pandemic, for example, had a significant impact on the mental health of P-21 students and led to a range of challenges and concerns. Research by the Kaiser Family Foundation found that adolescents, young children, LGBTQ young people, and children of color may be especially vulnerable to pandemic-related mental health consequences, such as anxiety and depression.[49] Additionally, data from the Centers for Disease Control and Prevention revealed that in 2021, more than one-third (37 percent) of high school students reported experiencing poor mental health during the COVID-19 pandemic, with 44 percent reporting persistent feelings of sadness or hopelessness. College students have also faced mental health challenges, including stress, relationship difficulties, low self-confidence, and issues around sex and sexuality, as highlighted in a scoping review of the mental health consequences of the pandemic among college students.[50] Pandemic-related stresses, such as job insecurity and loss, have contributed to poor mental health among children and adolescents.[51] The closure of universities and social isolation have further affected the mental health of both students and academic staff.[52] The pandemic's adverse effects on Black and Latino adults, including higher rates of illness and death from COVID-19, negative financial impact, and poor mental health outcomes, have also had an adverse impact on the mental health of children from these communities.[53] These challenges underscore the urgent need for comprehensive support and interventions to address the mental well-being of students across all educational levels. In light of these specific inequities (and with the considerations and mindsets listed previously in mind), school leaders can pursue the following efforts:

- **Raise awareness and lobby for funding:** Principals can raise awareness about mental health challenges and lobby for more funds to improve mental health services in schools. This can involve engaging parents in mental health conversations, ensuring students are aware of the mental health supports available on campus, and offering mental health support at the administrative level, which can send an important signal that mental health is a priority.[54]
- **Advocate for mental health services within state policy:** School leaders can advocate for mental health services as part of state policy. This may involve contacting local elected officials to identify strategies that bolster support for mental health policies, advocating for mental health

literacy in classrooms, and identifying solutions to hire more school-employed mental health professionals.[55]

- **Promote social and emotional competency:** School leaders can promote social and emotional competency and build student resilience. This can help create a positive, safe school environment and reinforce positive behaviors and decision-making, which are essential for supporting mental health during a crisis.[56]
- **Advocate for youth mental health:** School leaders can advocate for more education, services, and support to address the youth mental health crisis. This may involve promoting youth leadership at the local, state, and national levels to improve youth mental health in schools and advocating for effective school-based mental health services and supports.[57]
- **Enhance school-based mental health personnel:** School administrators should consider how their mental health personnel are engaged and advocate for more staff members, if necessary. This includes school psychologists, counselors, and social workers who can offer assessment and counseling to students and consult with families and teachers to provide effective interventions and support.[58]
- **Create inclusive, positive, safe, and affirming school environments:** School leaders can introduce positive, safe, and affirming school environments. This involves ensuring that schools are places where students can learn new knowledge and skills, develop close relationships with peers and supportive adults, and access help to manage mental health challenges.[59]

By implementing these strategies, school leaders can effectively advocate for mental health improvements during a crisis, ensuring that students have the necessary support and resources to address their mental health needs.

CHALLENGES AND OPPORTUNITIES IN IMPLEMENTING SYSTEMIC CHANGES

Former New York City Public Schools Chancellor Richard Carranza once said, "Never waste a good crisis to transform a system. We see this as an opportunity to finally push and move and be very strategic in a very aggressive way what we know is the equity agenda for our kids."[60] Carranza made this statement during a virtual panel of the National Association of Latino Supervisors and Superintendents held in mid-April 2020. He encouraged other educational leaders to capitalize on the deadly upheaval caused by the COVID-19 pandemic to change how students learn, teachers teach, and administrators lead. Carranza saw the pandemic as an opportunity to overhaul the education system and push for an equity agenda for students. He believed that the pandemic forced them to change how they accomplish their goals and that they should use this opportunity to transform the system, particularly by disrupting inequities.[61] But it can be difficult to do such work. Here, I'll explore some potential challenges (and related opportunities) when implementing radical systemic change.

The Courage to Be an Advocate for Radical Change

Leading for radical change requires courage, self-awareness, and effective communication. Courage is essential to pause empathetically and identify areas that require change.[62] Courage is needed to be a change agent and disrupt the status quo, particularly when discussing equity issues. For example, in the book *Ruthless Equity: Disrupt the Status Quo and Ensure Learning for ALL Students*, author Ken Williams explained that disrupting the status quo can be essential to achieve educational equity.[63] Furthermore, he argued that disrupting the status quo is necessary to provide equitable opportunities for every student. But that does not mean it is easy.

Leaders must have the courage to combat fear-based organizational barriers that inhibit engagement.[64] Educational leadership scholar Kenneth Leithwood reviewed sixty-three empirical studies and reviews of research to identify school leadership practices that improve equity in schools. He found that leaders with high expectations for students, staff, and parents were essential for improving school equity. The study also found that leadership practices such as building relationships, creating a shared vision, and promoting collaboration are essential for achieving equity in education.[65] Leaders must have the courage to address deficit mindsets among their teaching staff about students and families, shift to aggressive advocacy mode, and demand that their school communities receive more resources.[66] Leaders must also have self-awareness and effective communication skills to lead for radical change. Self-awareness is imperative for leadership, and school leaders must understand the importance of communication.[67] They must also have the humility to listen to feedback from the community to determine what works and what does not work in response to a crisis or challenge.[68] Leaders must have the courage to find a voice rooted in confidence so that they do not lower their standards.[69] Finally, leaders must be courageous enough to pause and identify areas that require transformation, combat fear-based organizational barriers, and be agents of change.

Enacting Advocacy for Radical Change

Enacting advocacy for radical change in a crisis requires taking a focused approach to prioritizing equity. Advocacy efforts should be grounded in theories of change that help to identify causal connections supported by research.[70] Advocates should also be aware of the broader political environment and understand the context around opportunities for change before undertaking advocacy. Effective advocacy requires a combination of short-term and long-term thinking, an understanding of the points of resistance and the means to gain traction, the readiness to form alliances, and the flexibility to seize windows of opportunity.[71] Advocates should focus on building relationships with key stakeholders, developing a unified solution, and galvanizing support through public meetings.

Advocacy also occurs on a continuum. Leaders often believe that enacting radical change requires them to risk it all, but they do not have to take an all-or-nothing approach. Leaders should begin by reviewing the strategies they feel most comfortable pursuing and evaluating what makes them uncomfortable. This strategy then becomes their continuum to lean into change. Change is a process that requires taking small steps, monitoring progress, engaging stakeholders, and celebrating success.[72] The following strategies can be implemented to support change:

- **Identify clear objectives:** Determine the specific goals of the advocacy campaign and develop a strategic plan that establishes where you are, where you want to go, and how you will get there.
- **Eliminate deficit thinking:** School leaders should work to end deficit thinking among staff and students by providing professional development opportunities that promote equity and social justice.
- **Implement structural strategies:** School leaders should implement structural strategies that improve the school's professional culture and promote inclusive practices.
- **Understand marginalized identities:** School leaders should understand the identities of marginalized students and implement teaching strategies that support them in the classroom.
- **Identify and address barriers:** School leaders should identify and address the barriers facing marginalized students, including those related to socioeconomic status, cultural and linguistic backgrounds, and other factors.
- **Utilize a systemic approach:** School leaders should develop and use a systemic approach to social and emotional learning that acknowledges the connections between students' immediate context and proximal setting.

Advocacy efforts should focus on questioning policies at fundamental levels instead of making administrative or rule changes to existing policies.

Advocates need to understand the context surrounding opportunities for change before undertaking advocacy, as the broader political environment should inform an advocate's selection of influencing strategies.

The Savior Complex: A Pitfall to Avoid

The savior complex is a psychological construct that describes a person's need or compulsion to save others, often neglecting their own needs in the process.[73] The savior complex can originate from various sources and often is deeply ingrained in a person's past experiences. For some, it may be rooted in childhood experiences in which a person had to assume responsibility for the well-being of family members. For others, it may stem from low self-esteem and the desire for validation, which a person seeks by being indispensable to others. The savior complex can manifest in many ways but is most evident in relationships. Individuals with a savior complex may gravitate toward people they perceive need help or rescue. They often find themselves in relationships with other individuals who have addictions, emotional issues, or serious problems. In these relationships, they believe they can or must "save" those with whom they are involved. In some instances, the savior complex can lead to codependent relationships, in which the person with the savior complex becomes emotionally dependent on the person they are trying to "save," and their self-esteem becomes tied to their perceived success or failure in this role. Although often rooted in empathy and a genuine desire to help, the savior complex can lead to unhealthy dynamics in relationships and personal distress.

In the context of a school setting, the savior complex has expanded to describe the belief that individuals in a place of power, often white individuals, can "save" marginalized communities.[74] Schools with marginalized communities see a manifestation of this complex in situations in which white teachers express the belief that they are the only ones who can help their students succeed because their students are inherently flawed and need to be "fixed."[75] Unfortunately, this approach is counterproductive because it reinforces the notion that the teacher is the hero without recognizing the strengths and brilliance of the students.[76] This approach can also contribute to a lack of understanding about the distinct needs and experiences of the students; thus, meaningful discussions about culture, race, and white supremacy fail to occur.[77]

To combat the savior complex in schools with marginalized communities, school leaders and teachers must approach their work with humility and a willingness to learn from their students.[78] Teachers should recognize that their students have multiple strengths; teachers are not there to "save" them but rather to collaborate with them. This requires a critical understanding of the hierarchical relationships present in the classroom and a focus on working in solidarity with students to struggle collaboratively against the institutions that sustain oppression.[79] Teachers should also be willing to examine their privileges and biases and create a more just and equitable educational system for all students.[80]

During or after a crisis, the savior complex may cause adults in the school to gravitate toward helping marginalized children, perceiving them as needing rescue. This approach, however, can create a problematic dynamic whereby the person with the savior complex assumes a position of power and control over the children being helped. As a result, colonial relationships are reinforced, and the idea that marginalized communities need outsiders is perpetuated.[81] In *Other People's Children*, Lisa Delpit insists that teachers and other school staff need to care for and work genuinely with the children they serve.[82] Individuals with a savior complex must recognize these patterns and work on building self-esteem and a sense of self-worth. It is also important to challenge societal messages and cultural norms that reinforce the belief that saving anyone is necessary. Instead, leaders should create healthier, more equitable relationships by recognizing the importance of individual agency and autonomy in the classroom.[83] In so doing, it can be possible to avoid perpetuating harmful dynamics and fostering mutual growth and development.[84]

Especially during a crisis, school leaders can avoid the savior complex by recognizing the importance of individual agency and autonomy. They should build relationships with the community they serve rather than the one they save; they should not assume a position of power and control over their community. Instead, they should challenge the societal messages and cultural norms that reinforce the savior complex.[85] School leaders should communicate constantly with their community and work together toward mutual growth and development. They should also seek guidance and support from experts in the field and be open to feedback and suggestions.[86] Additionally, school leaders should prioritize self-care and recognize their limitations.[87] After a crisis, leaders can partner with community members, securing additional funds and resources to support their students. By trusting the community with which they are working, leaders can avoid assuming positions of power and control. Finally, leaders can challenge societal messages and cultural norms that reinforce the belief that any one person needs to save another. Instead, leaders should consider how each individual can *help* another.

CONCLUSION

School leaders can advocate for radical change during crises to improve student and family equity. Advocacy for radical change requires transformational leaders who can call out institutional racism or xenophobia and publicly advocate against structural oppression during a crisis. School leaders can act boldly in their schools or districts by implementing strategies such as developing racial literacy, facilitating shared visions and collective responsibility, building the capacity of stakeholders, and developing critical alliances through community involvement. Leaders must have the courage to be change agents and disrupt the status quo, combat fear-based organizational barriers, and address deficit mindsets held by their teaching staff about their students and families. School leaders must have self-awareness and effective communication skills to lead for radical change. They must have the humility to listen to feedback from the community to determine what did and did not work in response to a crisis or challenge.

In this chapter, I emphasized the importance of school leaders advocating for radical change to address systemic issues of inequity in education. I provided strategies and examples of how school leaders can take bold actions to transform their schools or districts radically and promote equity and social justice. I also highlighted the challenges and opportunities inherent in implementing systemic changes and the characteristics of transformational leaders who can lead to radical change.

Chapter Discussion Questions

- What barriers do marginalized students face in your school or district, and how can school leaders address them?
- How can school leaders utilize a systemic social and emotional learning approach to support marginalized students?
- What strategies can school leaders use to advocate for radical change during crises, and how can they build alliances to support their efforts?
- How can school leaders develop their racial literacy and cultural competence to support marginalized students and families better?
- What are some examples of successful advocacy for radical change in schools or districts, and what can we learn from these examples?
- How can school leaders balance short-term and long-term thinking when advocating for radical change, and what challenges may they face in doing so?
- What role do community members and stakeholders play in advocating for radical change in schools, and how can school leaders engage them in the process?

Case Study

ALICE

Principal, Western United States

> I got sick and tired of the central office leaders saying they were social justice and equity-oriented and then kept inequitable policies in place, so I decided to change the system.

Alice is a veteran principal leading a Title I school in Los Angeles. She began her leadership at the school as a dean of culture, with her role primarily centered around school culture issues. Alice discussed leading through an influx of students from Puerto Rico after Hurricane Maria. Alice's school has a total enrollment of approximately one thousand students and a student-teacher ratio of 11:1. The school serves primarily BIPOC students, with 63.9 percent Hispanic, 33 percent Black, and the remaining percentage composed of other races. Additionally, 97 percent of the students are economically disadvantaged. The school is located between an up-and-coming gentrified area and a high-poverty area. As with many metropolises, demographics are shifting around the school. Alice, a daughter of Mexican immigrants, described her beliefs about social justice and equity: "I used to be some of my students, so I lead with the belief that I have to provide an environment for them to thrive."

Hurricane Maria devastated the island of Puerto Rico in September 2017 and caused widespread destruction, including prolonged power outages and damage to hundreds of schools. By November, Hurricane Maria had driven many students from Puerto Rico to cities across the United States. In total, nearly 2,300 students displaced from Puerto Rico entered New York schools.[88] The cumulative stresses of Hurricane Maria also contributed to thousands of schoolchildren developing symptoms of post-traumatic stress disorder (PTSD), further highlighting the impact of the hurricane on the education and well-being of students in Puerto Rico.[89] During this time, US schools were preparing for an influx of students, because they had McKenny-Vento funding. Alice found, however, that the policies in place at the school were inequitable, causing migrating students to fall further behind in their education and not feeling a sense of belonging in their school. Alice decided to challenge the district to make substantiative changes.

Equity-Crisis Dilemma

Alice was confronted with a challenging dilemma. The district's policies on grading and accountability, compounded by the social problems of the students, families, and community, were detrimental to those who had recently migrated to the city after the natural disaster. One student, Carlos, struggled to adapt to the new school environment and fell behind in his classes. The district's rigid grading policies, however, left Alice with little room to maneuver and with little support to help Carlos and other students who also were struggling. Determined to advocate for her students and address the systemic issues, Alice challenged the district's grading and accountability policies. In a meeting with her superintendent, Alice exclaimed, "You guys all say you are socially just leaders and you care about equity, but these policies are not equitable." Alice felt that her comments fell on deaf ears, reflecting the challenges many urban school leaders face when addressing systemic issues, such as grading and accountability. Research has shown that high-stakes accountability policies, which often rely on standardized tests and narrow performance measures, can have detrimental effects on urban schools, particularly those serving disadvantaged communities. These policies may neglect capacity building, poverty, and institutional racism in favor of standardized tests and evaluations, ultimately harming student and teacher outcomes. In urban areas, scholars have suggested that policymakers' preoccupation with external measures has ultimately harmed student and teacher outcomes, highlighting the need for more expansive and equitable forms of accountability.[90] Despite these challenges, school leaders like Alice must continue advocating for their students and seeking alternative forms of accountability that promote more equitable outcomes. Another study found that school responses to high-stakes accountability policies depend on school context, and in low-performing schools, responses often focus narrowly on complying with policy demands, which may not address the underlying needs of students from disadvantaged backgrounds.[91] This issue underscores the importance of considering the specific needs of urban schools and implementing accountability measures that consider the distinct challenges they face. By challenging the district's policies on grading and accountability, Alice was taking a crucial step to promote a more equitable and supportive environment for her students, particularly those who recently migrated to the city after a devastating hurricane.

Equity-Oriented Crisis Solution

Alice was well aware of the additional demands and challenges of working in an urban school district, including lack of resources and socioeconomic factors that affect students and their families. She knew that challenging the district's policies would be difficult, but she also understood the importance of standing up for what suited her students. Alice began by gathering data on the impact of the district's policies on students who had migrated to the city after the natural disaster. She found that many of these students faced challenges much as Carlos did, and the district's policies only exacerbated their difficulties. With these data, Alice approached the district superintendent to discuss the issue. She proposed a pilot program allowing schools in the area to use alternative grading methods for students who had migrated after the hurricane. After much deliberation, the superintendent agreed to the pilot program. Ultimately, it led to a districtwide policy change that provided more flexibility and support for students in situations that were similar to Carlos's situation.

Thanks to Alice's leadership and advocacy, students like Carlos received the support they needed to succeed in school, despite the challenges they faced from both the hurricane and the district policies. This experience also highlighted the importance of addressing systemic issues that affect urban school districts and the need for greater flexibility and support to ensure that all students are given equal opportunities to succeed. Alice's determination and commitment to her students eventually led to positive changes that benefited the entire school community.

CASE STUDY ANALYSIS

Individual and Small-Group Discussion Questions

- What were the specific challenges that Alice faced as a principal of a Title I school in a large urban city?
- What key lessons can other school leaders learn from Alice's experience in advocating for radical change in the district's policies?

- What were the district's policies on grading and accountability, and how did they affect students who had recently migrated to the city after a natural disaster?
- What are some of the challenges that urban school leaders face when trying to address systemic issues, such as grading and accountability policies?
- What are examples of high-stakes accountability policies in your school or district, and how do they affect your school during a crisis?
- What unique challenges do urban schools face during a crisis, and how can school leaders address them?

Whole-Group Activities

- **Role-Playing:** Divide the participants into groups and ask them to role-play a meeting between Alice and the district superintendent, in which they discuss the district's policies on grading and accountability.
- **Panel Discussion:** Invite a panel of urban school leaders to discuss their challenges and strategies to address systemic issues and support their students, particularly during a crisis.

Reflection

When people now think of crises, they often signal COVID-19 as a significant disruptor of education for children, particularly in the United States. Since I began writing this book, however, there were fifty-one school shootings in 2022, thirty-eight school shootings in 2023, and twenty school shootings as of July 2024.[1] That is more than one hundred school shootings resulting in fatalities or injuries (both mental and physical) in three academic school years. Similarly, over the past five years, the United States has experienced an average of $18 billion in climate disasters annually. In 2023, climate disasters caused $175.2 billion in damage and resulted in 474 fatalities.[2] In 2024, the Armed Location and Event Data organization declared that ten global armed conflicts are currently threatening the stability and safety of humans.[3] Although these cataclysmic events rage on, school leaders are tasked with maintaining the efficacy of their school and meeting academic improvements.

As I collected stories from interviews with leaders across the country and in Puerto Rico, I found narratives that were not aligned with what I was hearing in the news. Were principals burnt out? Yes! They also felt immense hope, however, and were eager to move toward recovery. Collins, a first year principal, articulated this feeling of hope:

> Many people feel hopeless right now, and I keep hearing things like "teacher shortage." They're looking at this crisis and saying, "You know we're on a downward trend . . . " and I'm excited! I think it's a very exciting time in education. Equity and inclusion are the things that I've been waiting to see. So I'm hopeful that we don't forget the feelings of waiting for the other shoe to drop and the constant anxiety and fear that nobody can sustain. I hope that all of that goes away. I really do hope and pray. But the feelings of caring deeply for each other, that we united under this crisis, I hope that those are made and propelled into something better because we all deserve it. I'm not even just going to say our students deserve it, because we all deserve it.

The leaders who shared their stories and explained how they navigated crises all used equity as a starting or ending point in their leadership. Their reflections show the complexity of equity and its manifestations in crisis leadership. The stories shared in this text provide insight into how leaders can pause, be proactive, and engage in long-term beneficial equity work for all students. Research has shown that equity benefits all students. Thus, it is imperative to walk away from reading this book with a deep understanding that equity is for everyone, because we are all not the same and we need different things during a crisis. Although it may be perceived as a hardship for leaders to consider all these issues during or after a crisis, assessing equity allows leaders to think more strategically and make better plans for school communities during recovery. Because leadership is iterative, leaders must understand the changing landscapes, demographics, and needs of families. The leaders featured in this book show how they concretely do this work.

KEY THEMES

As we come to a close, I want to explore several key themes that emerged throughout this book that underscore the complexities of crisis management in educational settings.

Understanding Polycrisis

The concept of polycrisis is central to the discussion, illustrating how multiple crises can intertwine and create compounded effects on educational systems. The COVID-19 pandemic, alongside other global challenges, such as political strife and climate change, has highlighted the interconnectedness of these crises. This multifaceted nature of crises necessitates a comprehensive approach to crisis management, as the impacts are not isolated but often affect various aspects of life, including education, health, and social equity.

The Role of School Leaders

School leaders are positioned at the forefront of crisis management, tasked with navigating the complexities that arise during emergencies. Their experiences, as shared through interviews, reveal that crises can take many forms, and effective leadership requires a nuanced understanding of each situation's distinct challenges. Leaders must possess strong communication skills, emotional intelligence, and the ability to make swift decisions under pressure while addressing the inequities that crises often exacerbate.

Equity in Crisis Response

A recurring theme is the necessity of equity in crisis response. In this book, I emphasize that crises disproportionately affect marginalized groups. As a result, school leaders need to prioritize equity in their decision-making processes. This involves recognizing the diverse needs of students and communities, particularly those vulnerable or disadvantaged. By adopting an equity-focused approach, leaders can ensure that all students receive the support they need to navigate crises effectively.

Impacts on Education

I also discussed the significant educational disruptions caused by crises, notably the COVID-19 pandemic. Data indicate a decline in student performance and widening educational inequalities, particularly among marginalized populations. The narrative stresses the importance of maintaining educational continuity and access to quality resources during crises, as these factors are crucial for fostering resilience and recovery in affected communities.

Innovative Communication Strategies

Effective communication emerges as a vital component of crisis management. I have highlighted the need for school leaders to adapt their communication strategies to meet the diverse needs of their communities, especially in times of crisis. This includes utilizing various platforms and methods to ensure that all families receive timely and relevant information regardless of their background.

Ultimately, the themes explored in this book underscore the intricate challenges of crisis management in educational settings. Understanding the concept of polycrisis, the pivotal role of school leaders, the importance of equity, the impacts on education, and the necessity for innovative communication strategies are essential for navigating the complexities of crises and fostering resilient school communities.

THE IMPORTANCE OF EQUITY

Equity is not merely a desirable goal during crises; it is a fundamental principle that must guide all actions and decisions made by educational leaders. Crises stemming from natural disasters, pandemics, or social unrest often exacerbate existing inequalities within educational systems. This reality underscores leaders' need to address disparities that disproportionately affect marginalized groups proactively.

In crisis leadership, equity involves recognizing and responding to the unique needs of diverse student populations. Unlike equality, which offers everyone the same resources or opportunities, equity focuses on providing tailored support that considers individual circumstances. For example, during the COVID-19 pandemic, students from low-income households faced significant barriers to online learning because of a lack of technology and internet connectivity. School leaders must ensure that these students receive the necessary resources, such as devices and internet access, to continue their education effectively.

DISPROPORTIONATE IMPACT ON MARGINALIZED GROUPS

Crises tend to disproportionately affect marginalized groups, including low-income families, students with disabilities, and those from racially minoritized backgrounds. Historical data shows that during events like Hurricane Katrina, these communities suffered the most significant losses, not only in terms of physical resources but also in educational opportunities. Leaders I spoke with explained how they actively work to support marginalized groups during a crisis to benefit everyone. The COVID-19 pandemic further highlighted these disparities, as research has indicated that marginalized students experienced greater declines in academic performance than their peers. The Malala Fund reports that girls, particularly in low-income regions, are at greater risk of dropping out of school during crises. Similarly, the National Assessment of Educational Progress (NAEP) has documented a stark decline in performance among students from disadvantaged backgrounds since the onset of the pandemic. Such evidence illustrates the urgent need for leaders to prioritize equity in their crisis response strategies.

ADDRESSING DISPARITIES

The imperative for educational leaders is clear: They must actively work to identify and address the inequities that crises reveal and exacerbate. This requires a multifaceted approach that includes all the elements of crisis leadership explored throughout the chapters of this book, but especially the following:

- **Resource Allocation:** Leaders must ensure that emergency funding is distributed equitably, targeting those who most need it. For instance, schools with a high percentage of low-income students may require additional resources to provide support services such as tutoring and counseling.

- **Culturally Responsive Communication:** Effective communication strategies must be inclusive and sensitive to students' and families' diverse backgrounds. This includes providing information in multiple languages and utilizing platforms that reach families where they are most comfortable.
- **Targeted Interventions:** It is crucial to implement specific programs and supports tailored to the needs of marginalized students. This might involve mental health resources, academic support, or community engagement initiatives designed to foster a sense of belonging and connection.

Equity is a critical component of effective crisis management in education. By understanding and addressing the unique challenges marginalized groups face, school leaders can create a more inclusive and supportive environment that helps students navigate crises and promotes long-term resilience and success.

FUTURE IMPLICATIONS FOR EDUCATION

The landscape of education is on the brink of substantial change amid ongoing and emerging crises, especially as we continue to grapple with the repercussions of the COVID-19 pandemic. The COVID-19 pandemic has accelerated the pace of change, revealing and amplifying existing inequalities in educational systems. Remote learning transitions have disproportionately affected students from marginalized backgrounds, resulting in limited access to technology, inadequate support structures, and heightened mental health struggles. The long-term consequences of these disparities could lead to a generation of students who find it challenging to catch up academically and socially. Furthermore, the pandemic has underscored the fragility of educational infrastructures, prompting a reconsideration of educational delivery methods. Although online learning and hybrid models may continue, without deliberate efforts to ensure equitable access, these innovations could deepen existing inequalities. Future educational policies must prioritize inclusivity, guaranteeing that all students have access to quality education and resources regardless of socioeconomic status. Apart from the pandemic, other global challenges, such as climate change, political unrest, and economic instability will continue to mold the educational landscape. These crises can disrupt schooling, leading to increased dropout rates and further marginalization of vulnerable populations. Schools must be ready to face these challenges with resilience and adaptability, fostering environments that support all students.

Although educational systems adapt to these challenges, it is crucial to consider the potential long-term impacts on educational equity and access. Even as the world and the education sector move past the global pandemic, its effects linger. For instance, absenteeism has remained high since the pandemic's onset and has not returned to prepandemic levels. Additionally, leaders contend with severe teacher shortages, compounded by longstanding educational inequities and challenges. Research on educational leaders also indicates disruptions in sleep patterns and burnout. Leaders have gleaned valuable lessons during this period, but they still have many more to uncover. At the core of this approach to educational equity, we all must adopt an equity-focused mindset to support the future of education in a world grappling with multiple crises.

In light of these challenges, it is crucial for educators, policymakers, and community leaders to prioritize crisis preparedness and equitable practices. To bolster preparedness for crises, educational institutions need to create thorough crisis management plans that encompass staff training, effective communication strategies, and the prioritization of resources for marginalized students. Additionally, leaders must advocate for policies that rectify systemic inequities by ensuring that funding and resources are distributed based on specific needs rather than employing a uniform approach. Furthermore, it is essential to continue conducting research and engaging in open dialogue about crisis leadership in education. This will facilitate the ability to share best practices and learning from one another, ultimately working toward a more resilient educational system capable of withstanding future crises.

CLOSING THOUGHTS

Crises, despite their difficulties, offer the chance for educational systems to grow and evolve. They encourage us to reconsider our leadership methods and skills, give priority to equity, and cultivate inclusive settings that cater to all students. Reflecting on the process of writing this book, I have gained deep insight into the resilience and adaptability of educational leaders when faced with crises. Every interview and case study showcased the strength of community and an unwavering commitment to student success, even in the most challenging situations. The leaders in this book demonstrated a wide range of expertise and talent, a strong emphasis on empathy, and the desire to improve outcomes for all students. They have remained focused on enhancing their equity literacy by confronting their implicit biases, challenging deficit mindsets, and addressing inequitable policies. In times of crisis, they relied on a foundation of hope to guide them, enabling them to be strategic and leverage their strengths to bring about change. The book has taught me that school leaders often confront crises head on, seeking the best solutions and support for all community members while never shying away from danger. For some, this experience has taken a significant emotional toll; for everyone, however, it has provided the strength to persevere. I found the work of these leaders to be truly humbling. I have shared these stories to offer practical insight on leading during and after a crisis, with a proactive approach to being better prepared for the future. These leaders may not be flawless, but their perseverance is genuinely admirable. Above all, I hope these stories give you the same strength, humility, and courage to continue striving for a more equitable future.

Methods

For this study, I employed qualitative methods, which are instrumental for two significant reasons. First, following William G. Tierney's essential components for a meaningful scholarship, qualitative methodology enables profound exploration, leading to a newer understanding of reality, ourselves, and truth.[1] Second, the distinct experiences of the principals provide a crucial opportunity to gain deep insight into their orientation and the implementation of equity or equality-oriented leadership activities, underscoring the importance of this research in the field of educational leadership and crisis management.

DATA COLLECTION

For this study, I undertook a rigorous data collection process, focusing on interviews with fifty public school principals. These interviews were audiotaped and transcribed, ensuring the preservation of every detail. Study participants were identified using purposeful sampling, which emphasizes the selection of "information-rich cases."[2] My selection of principals who experienced a crisis during their tenure as a principal was meticulous, covering a wide range of crises from natural disasters, medical trauma, criminal violence, racial harm, and the COVID-19 pandemic, among others.

Each interview ranged from thirty-five to sixty minutes and was conducted between 2019 and 2022. The semistructured interviews consisted of twelve questions intended to address how interviewees experienced a crisis,[3] navigated a crisis, and considered equity-oriented responses.[4] The interview protocol included questions about how they responded to a crisis, how their identities intersected with their crisis leadership response, how they made sense of the crisis through the equity lens, and the equity factors that influenced how they responded. The interview protocol included specific questions, such as: "How did you consider equity during the crisis?" Other questions were broad to allow interviewees the opportunity to describe in depth their multiple trains of thoughts throughout the crisis, such as: "What lessons did you learn as a result of experiencing this crisis?" Table A.1 lists the demographics of all participants.

TABLE A.1 Study participant demographics

Pseudonyms	*Race or Ethnicity*	*Gender*	*Age*	*Years as a Principal*	*School Location*	*Grade Band Level*
Abraham	White	F	41	3	West	Elementary
Alice	White	F	42	6	West	Elementary
Angela	White	F	39	4	Southwest	K–8
Annalise	White	F	42	3	Southwest	K–8
Archie	White	M	47	8	West	K–8
Barbara	White	F	45	5	East	Elementary
Betsy	Black	F	47	14	East	Middle School
Brenda	White	F	47	11	East	Elementary
Cassandra	White/Latinx	F	47	9	East	Elementary
Celine	White	F	38	6	East	Elementary
Charles	White	M	44	6	Midwest	Elementary
Collins	White	F	41	1	East	Middle School
Curtis	White	M	47	11	Midwest	Elementary
Dante	White	M	44	3	East	Elementary
Darla	Black	F	33	1	East	Elementary
Darryl	White	M	55	8	East	Elementary
Deborah	Black	F	42	5	East	Middle School
Dexter	Black	M	36	1	East	Elementary
Diana	White	F	43	8	Puerto Rico	Elementary
Dominik	White	M	34	1	East	K–8
Elizai	Black	F	44	7	South	Elementary
Emilia	White	F	55	19	East	Elementary

Fannie	Latinx	F	56	3	East	Middle School
Felicity	Latinx	F	32	3	East	Elementary
Flora	White	F	44	4	East	Elementary
Franklin	Latinx	M	38	4	East	Elementary
Frazer	Latinx	M	45	16	East	Elementary
Grace	White	F	56	10	East	Elementary
Guy	White	M	43	7	Midwest	K–8
Harley	White	F	43	7	West	Elementary
Iris	White	F	39	7	Midwest	Elementary
Isabel	White	F	40	2	East	Middle School
Ismail	White	M	51	11	Midwest	Elementary
Kiara	LatinX	F	49	8	East	Elementary
Larry	White	M	32	1	East	Elementary
Leena	White	F	37	1	East	K–21
Lily-Rise	White	F	46	1	Midwest	Middle School
Marlon	Black	M	63	22	East	High School
Marshall	White	M	38	8	West	Middle School
Maxine	Black	F	56	27	East	Elementary
Millie	Latinx	F	51	20+	East	Elementary
Monty	White	M	42	4	East	Elementary
Myah	Black	F	44	6	Midwest	Elementary
Nicolas	White	M	49	7	Midwest	Middle School
Patrice	White	F	43	4	Midwest	Elementary
Samuel	White	M	38	12	Northeast	Middle School
Sandra	Black	F	34	1	East	Elementary
Shreya	Black	F	34	5	Northeast	Elementary
Tom	White	M	52	10	East	Elementary
Victoria	White	F	41	9	East	Elementary
Yusuf	Black	M	36	2	East	Middle School

DATA ANALYSIS

To gain theoretical insight into the problem, qualitative methods based on grounded theory enable working with emerging phenomena, concepts, and theories.[5] I adopted these methods to analyze and compare two overarching leadership frameworks and reflect on the intersection of these two areas. In the educational leadership field, the goal is often to engender change by developing practical frameworks for leaders to use to support the ever-changing landscape of the public education system. To this end, I applied a conceptual framework analysis method. I used different sources of information and compared and interpreted them in several steps to gradually develop a new perspective on the problem.[6] Analysis was conducted with support from Atlas.ti qualitative analysis software while employing an iterative process of open and axial coding to identify themes and patterns across interviews.[7]

An initial understanding of the role of school leaders in responding to a crisis was developed in previous research by Larry Smith and Dan Riley, who applied a crisis leadership framework for a comprehensive analysis of the K–12 setting.[8] Crisis leadership is significant for school leaders, especially when incorporating equity issues. In this research, I examined how the Smith and Riley role of leaders, as highlighted by the crisis leadership framework, has been further explored in more recent literature.[9] Given that attention has been paid to the concept of equity-oriented crisis leadership, I developed an analytical tool to reflect the presence of this element in different contexts. The tool was drafted as a simple generalization of the Smith and Riley framework to allow for the categorization of equity-oriented elements.

I used a theoretical open-coding method to verify the draft tool's validity and applicability and its appropriateness for analysis.[10] The Smith and Riley crisis leadership framework provided theoretically grounded categories. I used codes outlined from the Smith and Riley framework to identify relevant domains and designed categories to uncover leaders' equity-oriented actions when responding to a crisis. I discussed the results of this step, along with other concepts and frameworks.

Tools and Protocols

EQUITY-ORIENTED MINDSET WORKSHEET

Identifying Disparities

- How have recent crises highlighted disparities in access to resources and support within our organization?
- What specific groups have been disproportionately affected, and how can we gather data to better understand their experiences?

Understanding Challenges

- What challenges are our marginalized populations facing in fully engaging with our services or educational offerings?
- How do these challenges affect their overall well-being and outcomes?

Assessing Staff Well-Being

- How has the crisis affected the emotional and mental well-being of our staff?
- In what ways does this affect our ability to support students or community members effectively?

Recognizing the Need for Equity

- What observations have led me to recognize the urgent need for equity-focused actions within our organization?
- How can I ensure that these observations translate into meaningful change?

Key Components of an Equity-Oriented Mindset

- What are the key components of an equity-oriented mindset that I need to embody as a leader?
- How can I apply these components to address the challenges posed by the current crisis?

CRITICAL REFLECTION PROTOCOL

School leaders can benefit from incorporating mindfulness practices into their leadership, especially during a crisis. Mindful breathing is a simple yet effective technique that can help school leaders manage stress and make sound decisions. The following critical reflection protocol is useful for school leaders leading through a crisis that begins with mindful breathing:

- **Mindful Breathing:** Start the reflection protocol with a few minutes of mindful breathing. This can be done by finding a comfortable and quiet space, sitting or standing in a relaxed position, and focusing on the natural breath for a few minutes. Mindful breathing can help in reducing stress and promoting a sense of calm and clarity.[1]
- **Reflection Questions:** After the mindful breathing exercise, school leaders can reflect on the following questions:
  - What are the current challenges and stressors we are facing as a school community?
  - How am I personally responding to these challenges, and what emotions are arising within me?
  - In what ways can I support the well-being of the staff, students, and parents during this crisis?
  - What decisions or actions require careful consideration, and how can a mindful approach help in addressing them?
- **Mindfulness Strategies:** Next, explore other mindfulness strategies beyond mindful breathing, such as guided meditation and movement, to support well-being and decision-making during the crisis.[2]
- **Well-being and Impact:** Gradually expand your frame of mind, reflecting on the well-being of the school community, including administrators, teachers, students, and parents.

By integrating mindful breathing and other mindfulness practices into their leadership approach, school leaders can cultivate a greater sense of presence, resilience, and emotional regulation, which are essential for effectively navigating through a crisis.[3]

INCLUSIVE DECISION-MAKING WORKSHEET

Self-Reflection

Identify Your Values

- What values guide your leadership, especially in crisis situations? How do these values influence your approach to inclusive decision-making?

Assess Your Leadership Style

- Describe your leadership style (e.g., collaborative, directive). How does your style affect inclusivity during crises?

Understanding Team Dynamics

Identify Team Strengths

- What unique contributions do team members bring, particularly in times of crisis? How can these strengths be leveraged to support equitable decision-making?

Recognize Power Dynamics

- Are there existing power dynamics that may hinder open communication during a crisis? How can you create a safe environment that encourages all voices to be heard?

Decision-Making Frameworks

Choose a Decision-Making Framework

- Which framework will you use to ensure inclusivity (e.g., consensus-building, participatory decision-making)? How does this framework promote equity and inclusivity?

Establish Decision Rules

- What explicit rules will guide how decisions are made during a crisis? Who will be involved in the decision-making process, and how will you ensure diverse representation?

Engaging Diverse Perspectives

Identify Stakeholders

- Who are the key stakeholders affected by the decisions made during a crisis? How will you ensure that marginalized voices are included in the decision-making process?

Active Listening Techniques

- What methods will you use to encourage input from all team members (e.g., focus groups, anonymous surveys)? How will you ensure that feedback is genuinely considered and valued?

Addressing Challenges

Recognize Barriers to Inclusivity

- What barriers (e.g., biases, communication issues) could impede inclusive decision-making during a crisis? How will you address these barriers proactively?

Training and Development

- What training will you provide to your team on equity and inclusive practices? How will you foster ongoing learning and development in this area?

Implementation and Follow-Through

Action Plan

- What specific actions will you take to implement inclusive decision-making during the crisis? How will you monitor progress and outcomes to ensure equity?

Feedback Mechanisms

- How will you solicit feedback from stakeholders on the decision-making process? What metrics will you use to assess the inclusivity and equity of your decisions?

Reflection and Continuous Improvement

Evaluate Outcomes

- After implementing decisions, how will you evaluate their effectiveness in promoting equity? What lessons learned can be applied to future crisis decision-making processes?

INCLUSIVE COMMUNICATION WORKSHEET

Assess your level of preparedness worksheet	
Identify data trends of parent communication.	
State the objective of your plan: Why do you want or need to communicate with parents? What is the purpose?	
Identify key people to support the strategic action plan toward building a more inclusive communication plan.	
Be prepared to do something different (e.g., there are several technology platforms). Which will you try to be more inclusive?	
How will you or your team make your plan consistently public?	

EQUITABLE SYSTEMS AND STRUCTURES PROTOCOL

Assessing Current Systems and Structures

Identify Existing Systems

- List the current systems (e.g., attendance policies, communication methods, technology access).
- Evaluate how these systems support or hinder equity.

Evaluate the Impact of Crises

- Reflect on how recent crises (e.g., COVID-19) have exposed inequities in your systems.
- Document specific examples where inequities were evident.

Stakeholder Feedback

- Gather input from diverse stakeholders (teachers, students, parents, community members).
- Use surveys or focus groups to understand their experiences with current systems.

Establishing Restorative Restart and Transformation Teams

Team Composition

- Form teams that include educators, counselors, social workers, community representatives, parents, and students.
- Ensure diversity in perspectives to address systemic issues effectively.
  - Team Functions: Define the primary functions of the team; assess current policies.
  - Develop equitable practices.
  - Allocate resources equitably.
  - Engage with the community.
  - Monitor and evaluate implemented strategies.

Meeting Schedule

- Establish a regular meeting schedule to discuss progress and challenges.
- Create an agenda focused on equity and systemic change.

Developing Equitable Practices

Policy Review

- Review existing policies (e.g., discipline, student assignments) for equity.
- Identify areas that perpetuate inequities and propose modifications.

Resource Allocation

- Analyze how resources are currently distributed.
- Ensure that marginalized populations receive the necessary support.

Community Engagement

- Develop strategies for engaging families and community members in decision-making processes.
- Create platforms for ongoing dialogue and feedback.

Monitoring and Evaluation
Set Equity Goals

- Define clear, measurable equity goals for your school.
- Align these goals with the school's overall mission and vision.

Data Collection

- Establish a system for collecting data on student outcomes and experiences.
- Use this data to assess the effectiveness of implemented changes.

Continuous Improvement

- Regularly review and adjust strategies based on feedback and data.
- Foster a culture of continuous improvement focused on equity.

EQUITABLE RESOURCE ALLOCATION, DEPRIVATION RATIONALE WORKSHEET

1. Identify the crisis or situation and describe the current crisis or situation affecting your school/district.
2. List the primary challenges posed by this crisis.
3. Complete a basic resource inventory.

Available financial resources	
Available human resources	
Available material resources	
Available technological resources	

4. Complete a needs assessment:
   a. List the most pressing needs of your students.
   b. List the most pressing needs of your staff.
   c. List the most pressing needs of your community.
5. Prioritize:
   a. Rank the identified needs in order of urgency and impact.
   b. Explain the rationale for your prioritization.

6. Complete a resource allocation plan.

Need	Resource to be allocated	Rationale for allocation	Potential short-term impact	Potential long-term impact

7. Think through resource deprivation considerations:
   a. Identify areas or groups that may receive fewer resources.
   b. Explain the rationale for these decisions.
   c. Describe potential mitigation strategies for negative impacts.
8. Think through equity considerations:
   a. How does this allocation plan address equity issues?
   b. Are there any potential biases in the allocation decisions?
   c. How will you ensure fair distribution across different student groups?
9. Monitor and evaluate:
   a. Describe how you will track the impact of resource allocation.
   b. Outline a timeline for reviewing and adjusting the allocation plan.

ACTION PLANNING TEMPLATE FOR ADVOCACY FOR RADICAL CHANGE

Understand the Root Causes of Inequities

Activities

- Conduct a thorough analysis of the systemic issues and barriers that perpetuate inequities in your school or district.
- Identify the specific challenges faced by marginalized populations.
- Examine how crises exacerbate existing inequities, and also create new ones.

Develop a Vision for Transformative Change

Activities

- Based on your reflections, articulate a clear and compelling vision for a more equitable and inclusive school system.
- Identify the key stakeholders and allies who can support your efforts for radical change.
- Establish measurable goals and objectives to track progress toward achieving your vision.

Implement Antiracist and Decolonized Practices
Activities

- Implement strategies for antiracist and decolonized teaching, such as ways to acknowledge biases/privileges and actively working to infuse antiracism into courses and curricula.
- Diversify school staff, leadership, and governance to better reflect the student population.
- Ensure that school curricula and special education programs are inclusive and equitable.

Advocate for Equitable Policies and Funding
Activities

- Advocate for policies that promote fairness and opportunity for all students at the school, district, and state levels.
- Secure equitable funding for schools serving marginalized communities to address resource gaps.
- Partner with community organizations and advocacy groups to amplify your voice and influence.

Engage and Empower the School Community
Activities

- Aim to foster a culture of inclusivity, belonging, and support for all students and families.
- Provide professional development for staff on topics such as cultural responsiveness, implicit bias, and trauma-informed practices.
- Engage students, families, and community members as partners in the change process.

Monitor Progress and Adapt Strategies
Activities

- Regularly assess the impact of your efforts on student outcomes and experiences.
- Gather feedback from stakeholders and adjust strategies as needed to ensure continuous improvement.
- Share successes and lessons learned with other school leaders to inspire and support their advocacy efforts.

EQUITABLE RESOURCE DIFFUSION WORKSHEET

1. Resource identification:
   a. List the resources to be diffused.
   b. Describe the intended beneficiaries for each resource.
2. Community assessment:
   a. Describe the current emotional state of the community.
   b. Identify any potential barriers to resource access.
3. Distribution methods:
   a. Identify existing systems that can be leveraged for resource distribution.
   b. Describe new methods or processes needed for effective distribution.
4. Equity considerations:
   a. How will you ensure equitable access to resources across different groups?
   b. Describe any special accommodations needed for vulnerable populations.
5. Partnerships and collaboration:
   a. List potential community partners for resource diffusion.
   b. Describe how you will collaborate with these partners.
6. Timeline and milestones:
   a. Create a timeline for resource diffusion.
   b. Identify key milestones and checkpoints.
7. Feedback and adjustment:
   a. Describe how you will gather feedback on the diffusion process.
   b. Outline a plan for making adjustments based on feedback.
8. Long-term sustainability:
   a. Describe how this diffusion plan supports long-term educational goals.
   b. Identify potential challenges to sustaining resource access over time.

Notes

Introduction

1. John F. Kennedy, "Remarks of Senator John F. Kennedy, Convocation of the United Negro College Fund, Indianapolis, Indiana, April 12, 1959," John F. Kennedy Presidential Museum and Library, https://www.jfklibrary.org/archives/other-resources/john-f-kennedy-speeches/indianapolis-in-19590412.
2. "One Hundred Years of Price Change: The Consumer Price Index and the American Inflation Experience," Bureau of Labor Statistics Monthly Labor Review, April 2014, https://www.bls.gov/opub/mlr/2014/article/one-hundred-years-of-price-change-the-consumer-price-index-and-the-american-inflation-experience.htm.
3. "A Partial List of U.S. Mass Shootings in 2023," *New York Times*, July 3, 2023, https://www.nytimes.com/article/mass-shootings-2023.html; Paul LeBlanc, "America's Mass Shootings in 2023: A Continuing Crisis," *CNN*, March 6, 2023, https://cnn.com/2023/03/06/politics/america-mass-shootings-2023-gun-violence/index.html; Bill Hutchinson, "U.S. Surpasses 400 Mass Shootings in 2023," *ABC News*, July 23, 2023, https://abcnews.go.com/US/us-surpasses-400-mass-shootings-2023-national-gun/story?id=101588652; James N. Meindl and Jonathan W. Ivy, "Mass Shootings: The Role of the Media in Promoting Generalized Imitation," *American Journal of Public Health* 107, no. 3 (2017): 368–370.
4. "Disaster Risk Reduction, Climate Risk Management, and Sustainable Development," WMO Bulletin, World Meteorological Organization, 2023; "Climate Change 2022: Impacts, Adaptation, and Vulnerability," Intergovernmental Panel on Climate Change Sixth Assessment Report, February 28, 2022, https://www.ipcc.ch/2022/02/28/pr-wgii-ar6/.
5. Jeremy Allouche, Steve Metcalfe, Megan Schmidt-Sane, and Shilpi Srivastava, "Are We in the Age of the Polycrisis?," Institute of Development Studies, 2023, https://www.ids.ac.uk/opinions/are-we-in-the-age-of-the-polycrisis/; Melissa Leach, Hayley MacGregor, Ian Scoones, and Annie Wilkinson, "Post-Pandemic Transformations: How and Why COVID-19 Requires Us to Rethink Development," *World Development* 138 (2021); "G7 Hiroshima Leaders' Communiqué," The White House, May 20, 2023, https://www.whitehouse.gov/briefing-room/statements-releases/2023/05/20/g7-hiroshima-leaders-communique/.
6. *Global Annual Results Report 2022: Humanitarian Action* (New York: UNICEF, 2022), https://www.unicef.org/media/142731/file/Humanitarian%20action%20global%20annual%20results%20report%202022%20.pdf.
7. *World Public Sector Report 2023* (New York: United Nations, Department of Economic and Social Affairs, 2023), https://desapublications.un.org/publications/world-public-sector-report-2023#:~:text=The%20World%20Public%20Sector%20Report,2030%20Agenda%20for%20Sustainable%20Development; UNICEF, *Global Annual Results Report 2022*.
8. Leach et al., "Post-Pandemic Transformations."

9. *The Global Risks Report 2022*, 17th ed. (Cologny, Switzerland: World Economic Forum, 2022), https://www3.weforum.org/docs/WEF_The_Global_Risks_Report_2022.pdf.
10. *Global Humanitarian Overview 2022* (New York: United Nations Office for the Coordination of Humanitarian Affairs, 2022), https://cerf.un.org/sites/default/files/resources/Global%20Humanitarian%20Overview%202022.pdf.
11. Gema Zamarro, Andrew Camp, Dillon Fuchsman, and Josh B. McGee, "How the Pandemic Has Changed Teachers' Commitment to Remaining in the Classroom," Brookings Institution, September 8, 2021, https://www.brookings.edu/articles/how-the-pandemic-has-changed-teachers-commitment-to-remaining-in-the-classroom/.
12. Jennifer Lee and Tiffany Huang, "Why the Trope of Black-Asian Conflict in the Face of Anti-Asian Violence Dismisses Solidarity," Brookings Institution, March 11, 2021, https://www.brookings.edu/articles/why-the-trope-of-black-asian-conflict-in-the-face-of-anti-asian-violence-dismisses-solidarity/; "Hearing on Discrimination and the Civil Rights of Muslim, Arab and South Asian American Communities," 117th Congress, House Subcommittee on the Constitution, Civil Rights, and Civil Liberties, 2021, https://www.govinfo.gov/content/pkg/CHRG-117hhrg48303/html/CHRG-117hhrg48303.htm.
13. *Hate Speech and Hate Crime in the EU and the evaluation of online content regulation approaches* (Brussels, Belgium: European Parliament, 2020), https://www.europarl.europa.eu/RegData/etudes/STUD/2020/655135/IPOL_STU(2020)655135_EN.pdf.
14. *Hate Speech and Hate Crime in the EU.*
15. Matt Barnum, "NAEP Test Scores: Pandemic School Reopening," *Chalkbeat*, October 24, 2022, https://www.chalkbeat.org/2022/10/24/23417139/naep-test-scores-pandemic-school-reopening/.
16. "Malala Fund Publishes Report on Climate Change and Girls' Education," Malala Fund, 2023, https://malala.org/newsroom/malala-fund-publishes-report-on-climate-change-and-girls-education.
17. Zamarro et al., "How the Pandemic Has Changed Teachers' Commitment."
18. Kate Whiting, "This Is Why 'Polycrisis' Is a Useful Way of Looking at the World Right Now," World Economic Forum, March 2023, https://www.weforum.org/agenda/2023/03/polycrisis-adam-tooze-historian-explains/.
19. "Improving School Leadership," Organization for Economic Co-operation and Development (OECD), 2023, https://www.oecd.org/education/school/Improving-school-leadership.pdf.
20. *Improving Cultural Competence*, Treatment Improvement Protocol (TIP) Series No. 59, HHS Publication No. (SMA) 14-4849 (Rockville, MD: Substance Abuse and Mental Health Services Administration, 2014), https://store.samhsa.gov/sites/default/files/d7/priv/sma14-4849.pdf.
21. *Improving Cultural Competence.*
22. OECD, "Improving School Leadership."
23. *Deep Water: The Gulf Oil Disaster and the Future of Offshore Drilling*, Report to the President (Washington, DC: US Congress National Commission on the BP Deepwater Horizon Oil Spill and Offshore Drilling, 2023), https://www.govinfo.gov/content/pkg/GPO-OILCOMMISSION/pdf/GPO-OILCOMMISSION.pdf.
24. Jeanne Batalova, "Frequently Requested Statistics on Immigrants and Immigration in the United States," Migration Policy Institute, 2024, https://www.migrationpolicy.org/article/frequently-requested-statistics-immigrants-and-immigration-united-states; Anusha Natarajan, Mohamad Moslimani, and Mark Hugo Lopez, "Key Facts About Recent Trends in Global Migration," Pew Research Center, December 16, 2022, https://www.pewresearch.

org/short-reads/2022/12/16/key-facts-about-recent-trends-in-global-migration/; Mohamad Moslimani and Jeffrey S. Passel, "What the Data Says About Immigrants in the U.S.," Pew Research Center, July 2024, https://www.pewresearch.org/short-reads/2020/08/20/key-findings-about-u-s-immigrants/; *Changing Patterns in U.S. Immigration and Population* (Washington, DC: Pew Research Center, 2014), https://www.pewtrusts.org/en/research-and-analysis/issue-briefs/2014/12/changing-patterns-in-us-immigration-and-population; Natarajan et al., "Key Facts About Recent Trends in Global Migration."

25. Natarajan et al., "Key Facts About Recent Trends in Global Migration."
26. *Changing Patterns in U.S. Immigration and Population.*
27. Antonio Flores and Mark Hugo Lopez, "Among U.S. Latinos, the Internet Now Rivals Television as a Source for News," Pew Research Center, January 11, 2018, https://www.pewresearch.org/fact-tank/2018/01/11/among-u-s-latinos-the-internet-now-rivals-television-as-a-source-for-news/.
28. Lucila C. Vargas and Bruce J. De Pyssler, "U.S. Latino Newspapers as Health Communication Resources: A Content Analysis," *Howard Journal of Communications* 10, no. 3 (1999): 189–205.
29. https://convention2.allacademic.com/one/aera/aera23/index.php?cmd=Online+Program+View+Paper&selected_paper_id=2007348&PHPSESSID=akfp6ggv252cgqlts5q5n3hs33.
30. Jason A. Grissom, Anna J. Egalite, and Constance A. Lindsay, *How Principals Affect Students and Schools: A Systematic Synthesis of Two Decades of Research* (New York: Wallace Foundation, 2021), 30–41.
31. Margaret Grogan, Michelle D. Young, and Mónica Byrne-Jiménez, "Editorial: Education Leadership and the COVID-19 Crisis," *Frontiers in Education* 7 (2022), https://doi.org/10.3389/feduc.2022.838313.
32. Anthony S. Bryk, Louis M. Gomez, Alicia Grunow, and Paul LeMahieu, *Learning to Improve: How America's Schools Can Get Better at Getting Better* (Cambridge, MA: Harvard Education Press, 2015).
33. Viviane M. Robinson, Claire A. Lloyd, and Kenneth J. Rowe, "The Impact of Leadership on Student Outcomes: An Analysis of the Differential Effects of Leadership Types," *Educational Administration Quarterly* 44, no. 5 (2008): 635–674, https://doi.org/10.1177/0013161X08321509.
34. Patricia M. Virella, "Cultivating Critical Hope While Leading During Crisis: A Qualitative Cross-Comparative Analysis," *American Journal of Education* 130, no. 2 (2024): 275–300.
35. Jeffrey Duncan-Andrade, "Note to Educators: Hope Required When Growing Roses in Concrete," *Harvard Educational Review* 79, no. 2 (2009): 181–194.
36. Larry Smith and Dan Riley, "School Leadership in Times of Crisis," *School Leadership and Management* 32, no. 1 (2012): 57–71.
37. Smith and Riley, "School Leadership in Times of Crisis."
38. Chukwuma N. Eruchalu, Margaret S. Pichardo, Maheetha Bharadwaj, Carmen B. Rodriguez, Jorge A. Rodriguez, Regan W. Bergmark, David W. Bates, and Gezzer Ortega, "The Expanding Digital Divide: Digital Health Access Inequities During the COVID-19 Pandemic in New York City," *Journal of Urban Health* 98 (2021): 183–186.
39. Monica Anderson and Andrew Perrin, "Nearly One-in-Five Teens Can't Always Finish Their Homework Because of the Digital Divide," Pew Research Center, October 26, 2018, https://www.pewresearch.org/short-reads/2018/10/26/nearly-one-in-five-teens-cant-always-finish-their-homework-because-of-the-digital-divide/.

40. Ochega A. Ataguba and John E. Ataguba, "Social Determinants of Health: The Role of Effective Communication in the COVID-19 Pandemic in Developing Countries," *Global Health Action* 13, no. 1 (2020): 1788263.
41. Patricia M. Virella and Sarah Woulfin, "Leading After the Storm: New York City Principal's Deployment of Equity-Oriented Leadership Post-Hurricane Maria," *Educational Management Administration and Leadership* 51, no. 5 (2023): 1031–1048.
42. Smith and Riley, "School Leadership in Times of Crisis," 57.
43. Susan Sonnenschein, Elyse R. Grossman, and Julie A. Grossman, "US Parents' Reports of Assisting Their Children with Distance Learning During COVID-19," *Education Sciences* 11, no. 9 (2021): 501.
44. Chang Su-Russell, Csilla Greiner, Ashley Ermer, and Luke T. Russell, "Parents' Discussions of the COVID-19 Pandemic and Death with Young Children," *Journal of Family Nursing* 29, no. 2 (2023): 122–135.
45. Henry A. Giroux, "Chartering Disaster: Why Duncan's Corporate-Based Schools Can't Deliver an Education That Matters," *Counterpoints* 400 (2012): 49–72.
46. Virella and Woulfin, "Leading After the Storm."
47. Ann M. Ishimaru and Mollie K. Galloway, "Beyond Individual Effectiveness: Conceptualizing Organizational Leadership for Equity," *Leadership and Policy in Schools* 13, no. 1 (2014): 93–146; Rosa L. Rivera-McCutchen, "'We Don't Got Time for Grumbling': Toward an Ethic of Radical Care in Urban School Leadership," *Educational Administration Quarterly* 57, no. 2 (2021): 257–289.
48. Angela Davis, "Angela Davis Lecture, Moe Lectureship in Women's Studies," Gustavus Adolphus College, April 12, 2006.
49. Lillian Paine et al., "Declaring Racism a Public Health Crisis in the United States: Cure, Poison, or Both?," *Frontiers in Public Health* 9 (2021): 676784.
50. Sharon D. Kruse, "Schools as Soft Systems: Addressing the Complexity of Ill-Defined Problems," in *Leading Holistically*, ed. Haim Shaked, Chen Schechter, and Alan James Daly (New York: Routledge, 2018), 39–53.
51. Maija Lanas and Michalinos Zembylas, "Towards a Transformational Political Concept of Love in Critical Education," *Studies in Philosophy and Education* 34 (2015): 31–44.
52. Susan R. Madsen, "The Key to Leadership Development is Critical Reflection," *Forbes,* May 26, 2020.
53. Laura Hallberg and Louise J. Santiago, "Using Narrative Inquiry to Explore Critical Reflection and Self-Awareness in Equity Leadership Development," *Educational Leadership and Administration: Teaching and Program Development* 33 (2021): 18–39.
54. "Characteristics of Public and Private School Principals," in *The Condition of Education 2023* (Washington, DC: US Department of Education, National Center for Education Statistics, 2023), https://nces.ed.gov/programs/coe/pdf/2023/cls_508.pdf.
55. Janet Patti, Peter Senge, Claudia Madrazo, and Robin S. Stern, "Developing Socially, Emotionally, and Cognitively Competent School Leaders and Learning Communities," in *Handbook of Social and Emotional Learning: Research and Practice*, ed. Joseph A. Durlak, Celene E. Domitrovich, Roger P. Weissberg, and Thomas P. Gullotta (New York: Guilford, 2015), 442.
56. Hallberg and Santiago, "Using Narrative Inquiry to Explore Critical Reflection."
57. "Family Engagement in Schools: Common Barriers to Identify and 6 Effective Strategies for Success," *ParentSquare* (blog), 2023, https://www.parentsquare.com/blog/family-engagement-in-schools-common-barriers-to-identify-and-6-effective-strategies-for-success/.

58. Karen L. Mapp and Eyal Bergman, *Embracing a New Normal: Toward a More Liberatory Approach to Family Engagement* (New York: Carnegie Corporation of New York, 2021), https://media.carnegie.org/filer_public/f6/04/f604e672-1d4b-4dc3-903d-3b619a00cd01/fe_report_fin.pdf.
59. Ari Gerzon-Kessler, "Giving Marginalized Families a Voice," *ASCD*, August 29, 2022, https://www.ascd.org/el/articles/giving-marginalized-families-a-voice.
60. Kathy B. Grant and Julie A. Ray, *Home, School, and Community Collaboration: Culturally Responsive Family Involvement* (New York: Sage, 2010).
61. Jamel Adkins-Sharif, *The Racial Challenges Facing Black Male School Leaders Enacting Social Justice Agendas in Environments of Privilege* (EdD diss., University of Massachusetts Boston, 2020).
62. Karen L. Mapp et al., *Everyone Wins! The Evidence for Family-School Partnerships & Implications for Practice* (New York: Scholastic Professional, 2022).
63. MSUNER (June 27, 2023), MSUNER Mindfulness Institute, https://msuner.org/profiles/blogs/msuner-mindfulness-institute-june-27th-2023.
64. John B. Diamond, "Race and White Supremacy in the Sociology of Education: Shifting the Intellectual Gaze," in *Education in a New Society: Renewing the Sociology of Education*, ed. Jal Mehta and Scott Davies (Chicago: University of Chicago Press, 2018), 345–362.
65. Chen Schechter, Rima'a. Da'as, and Mowafaq Qadach, "Crisis Leadership: Leading Schools in a Global Pandemic," *Management in Education* 38, no. 4 (2022).
66. Ian E. Sutherland, "Learning and Growing: Trust, Leadership, and Response to Crisis," *Journal of Educational Administration* 55, no. 1 (2017): 2–17.
67. Christopher Day, Pam Sammons, and Kristine Gorgen, *Successful School Leadership* (Reading, England: Education Development Trust, 2020).
68. "A School Leader's Guide to Crisis Communication," *Teaching Channel* (blog), January 9, 2020, https://www.teachingchannel.com/k12-hub/blog/crisis-communication/.
69. Casey Thompson, "K–12 Crisis Communication: What Does It Look Like Now?," *Skyward* (blog), March 2022, https://www.skyward.com/blogs/ak12/2022/march/k-12-crisis-communication-what-does-it-look-like-now.
70. Thompson, "K–12 Crisis Communication."
71. Mario Jackson, "Backtalk: What Principals Need to Know to Respond to a Crisis," *Phi Delta Kappan* 104, no. 5 (2023): 66–67.

Chapter 1

1. Harvey Milk, as quoted by Shan Bitney Crone, "Hope Will Never Be Silent," *HuffPost* (blog), June 26, 2013, https://www.huffpost.com/entry/hope-will-never-be-silent_b_3500479.
2. Gillian B. White, "The Recession's Racial Slant," *The Atlantic*, June 24, 2015, https://www.theatlantic.com/business/archive/2015/06/black-recession-housing-race/396725/.
3. Diane Herbst, "Captain 'Sully' Chesley Sullenberger Reunites with Passengers from 'Miracle on the Hudson' Flight 10 Years Later," *People*, January 13, 2023, https://people.com/human-interest/captain-sully-chesley-sullenberger-passengers-reunion-miracle-hudson-anniversary-flight/.
4. "Human Nature and Survival," City Tech OpenLab, July 20, 2023, https://openlab.citytech.cuny.edu/belli-f2016-eng2420/human-nature-survival/.
5. Mireia Tintoré et al., "Management Model, Leadership and Autonomy in Portuguese and Spanish Public Schools: A Comparative Analysis," *Cogent Education* 9, no. 1 (2022): 2105553.

6. Noam Chomsky, "'Exterminate All the Brutes': Gaza 2009," in *Gaza in Crisis: Reflections on Israel's War Against the Palestinians* by Noam Chomsky and Ilan Pappe (Chicago: Haymarket, 2019), 79–124.
7. Jochen Kleres and Åsa Wettergren, "Fear, Hope, Anger, and Guilt in Climate Activism," *Social Movement Studies* 16, no. 5 (2017): 507–519.
8. Andrew J. W. Civettini, "Barack Obama and the Political Science of Hope," in *Politics and Emotions: The Obama Phenomenon*, ed. Marcos Engelken-Jorge, Pedro Ibarra Güell, and Carmelo Moreno del Río (New York: Springer, 2011), 95–106.
9. Hugo D. Critchley and Sarah N. Garfinkel, "Interoception and Emotion," *Current Opinion in Psychology* 17 (2017): 7–14; Antonio R. Damasio, "The Somatic Marker Hypothesis and the Possible Functions of the Prefrontal Cortex," *Philosophical Transactions of the Royal Society of London, Series B: Biological Sciences* 351, no. 1346 (1996): 1413–1420; India Morrison, Line S. Löken, and Håkan Olausson, "The Skin as a Social Organ," *Experimental Brain Research* 204, no. 3 (2010): 305–314.
10. Jill Anderson, "School Leadership During a Crisis," Harvard Graduate School of Education EdCast, April 16, 2020, https://www.gse.harvard.edu/ideas/edcast/20/04/school-leadership-during-crisis.
11. C. R. Snyder, *The Psychology of Hope: You Can Get There from Here* (New York: Free Press, 1994).
12. R. L. Chang, *Hope and Hopelessness: Critical Clinical Constructs* (Thousand Oaks, CA: Sage, 1998); S. J. Lopez et al., *The Oxford Handbook of Positive Psychology* (Oxford: Oxford University Press, 2009).
13. Bart De Smet, "Why All Leaders Must Centre 'Hope' in Their Messaging," World Economic Forum, May 2022, https://www.weforum.org/agenda/2022/05/why-all-leaders-must-centre-hope-in-their-messaging/.
14. Mark Comanducci, "School Leadership in Times of Crisis," *SmartBrief*, April 7, 2020, https://www.smartbrief.com/original/school-leadership-times-crisis.

Chapter 2

1. Kofi Annan, Commencement Address to the Massachusetts Institute of Technology, June 6, 1997, https://www.kofiannanfoundation.org/kofi-annan/quotes/?search=&theme=.
2. Alex Katsomitros, "Against the Odds: Ursula Burns' Extraordinary Rise to the Top," World Finance, July 19, 2024, https://www.worldfinance.com/markets/against-the-odds-ursula-burns-extraordinary-rise-to-the-top; Adam Bryant, "Xerox's New Chief: A Woman's Rise to the Top," *New York Times*, February 20, 2010, https://www.nytimes.com/2010/02/21/business/21xerox.html.
3. Elizabeth Holcombe et al., *Leading for Equity from Where You Are: How Leaders in Different Roles Engage in Shared Equity Leadership* (Washington, DC: American Council on Education and USC Rossier, 2022), https://www.acenet.edu/Documents/Shared-Equity-Leadership-Roles.pdf; Patricia M. Virella, "Introducing the Pillars of Equity-Oriented Crisis Leadership: A Conceptual Framework," *School Leadership and Management* 43, no. 4 (2023): 390–410, doi:10.1080/13632434.2023.2186848.
4. Patricia M. Virella and Casey Cobb, "Leveraging the Crisis for Equity and Access in the Long Term: A Brief Research Report," *Frontiers in Education* 6 (2021); Holcombe et al., *Leading from Equity from Where You Are.*
5. Virella and Cobb, "Leveraging the Crisis for Equity and Access"; Holcombe et al., *Leading from Equity from Where You Are.*
6. Virella, "Introducing the Pillars of Equity-Oriented Crisis Leadership."

7. Randall S. Peterson, "How to Be an Equity-Focused Leader," London Business School Think, March 23, 2023, https://www.london.edu/think/how-to-be-an-equity-focused-leader.
8. Virella and Cobb, "Leveraging the Crisis for Equity and Access."
9. Estela Mara Bensimon, "Reclaiming Racial Justice in Equity," *Change: The Magazine of Higher Learning* 50, no. 3–4 (2018): 95–98.
10. Román Liera and Steve Desir, "Taking Equity-Mindedness to the Next Level: The Equity-Minded Organization," *Frontiers in Education* 8 (2023): 1–12, https://doi.org/10.3389/feduc.2023.1199174.
11. "Overview of Equity-Focused Teaching at Michigan," Center for Research on Learning and Teaching, University of Michigan, https://crlt.umich.edu/overview-equity-focused-teaching-michigan; Sharon I. Radd et al., *Five Practices for Equity-Focused School Leadership* (Alexandria, VA: ASCD, 2021).
12. Valerie Ehrlich, "Leading with an Equity-Based Mindset," Center for Creative Leadership, March 2023, https://cclinnovation.org/news-posts/leading-with-an-equity-based-mindset/.
13. Jennifer Kuhr Butterfoss, "Equity-Focused Leadership: What Does It Look Like in Action?," *New Leaders* (blog), July 2021, https://www.newleaders.org/blog/equity-focused-leadership-what-does-it-look-like-in-action.
14. Patricia M. Virella, "Leading Through the 'Influx': Leadership Responses and the Influence of a Political Spectacle," *Journal of School Leadership* 32, no. 1 (2022): 27–50.
15. Virella, "Leading Through the 'Influx.' "
16. Ehrlich, "Leading with an Equity-Based Mindset."
17. Chris Nichols, Shoma Chatterjee Hayden, and Chris Trendler, "4 Behaviors That Help Leaders Manage a Crisis," *Harvard Business Review*, April 2020, https://hbr.org/2020/04/4-behaviors-that-help-leaders-manage-a-crisis.
18. Virella and Cobb, "Leveraging the Crisis for Equity and Access"; *Embedding Equity in Crisis Preparedness and Response in Health Systems* (Chicago: American Marketing Association, 2023), https://www.ama-assn.org/system/files/eecpr-guide.pdf; Peterson, "How to Be an Equity-Focused Leader."
19. Virella, "Introducing the Pillars of Equity-Oriented Crisis Leadership."
20. Ehrlich, "Leading with an Equity-Based Mindset."
21. Virella, "Introducing the Pillars of Equity-Oriented Crisis Leadership."
22. Gene Klann, "How to Lead Through a Crisis," Center for Creative Leadership, December 15, 2020, https://www.ccl.org/articles/leading-effectively-articles/how-to-lead-through-a-crisis/.
23. Klann, "How to Lead Through a Crisis."
24. Peterson, "How to Be an Equity-Focused Leader."
25. Virella, "Introducing the Pillars of Equity-Oriented Crisis Leadership."
26. Adrianna Kezar et al., *Shared Equity Leadership: Making Equity Everyone's Work* (Washington, DC: American Council on Education and USC Rossier Pullias Center for Higher Education, 2021), https://www.acenet.edu/Documents/Shared-Equity-Leadership-Work.pdf.

Chapter 3

1. Paulo Freire, *Pedagogy of the Oppressed* (New York: Seabury, 1970), chap. 3.
2. Max van Manen, "Linking Ways of Knowing with Ways of Being Practical," *Curriculum Inquiry* 6, no. 3 (1977): 205–228; Kenneth Zeichner and Daniel Liston, "Teaching Student Teachers to Reflect," *Harvard Educational Review* 57 (1987): 23–49; Todd Dinkelman,

"Critical Reflection in a Social Studies Semester," *Theory and Research in Social Education* 27, no. 3 (1999): 329–357.

3. John Dewey, "Natural Resources in the Training of Thought," in *How We Think* (Lexington, MA: D.C. Heath, 1910), 29.
4. Eric Kail, "Leadership Character: The Role of Reflection," *Washington Post,* April 4, 2011, https://www.washingtonpost.com/blogs/guest-insights/post/leadership-character-the-role-of-reflection/2011/04/04/gIQAdJOr1R_blog.html.
5. Kail, "Leadership Character."
6. Colleen DeGuzman, "A Third of Schools Don't Have a Nurse. Here's Why That's a Problem," *KFF Health News*, September 8, 2022, https://kffhealthnews.org/news/article/school-nurses-shortage-mental-health/.
7. Susan R. Madsen, "The Key to Leadership Development is Critical Reflection," *Forbes*, May 26, 2020; Christa Boske, "Critical Reflective Practices: Connecting to Social Justice," in *International Handbook of Educational Leadership and Social (In)justice*, ed. Ira Bogotch and Carolyn M. Shields (Dordrecht: Springer Netherlands, 2013), 289–308.
8. Laura Hallberg and Louise J. Santiago, "Using Narrative Inquiry to Explore Critical Reflection and Self-Awareness in Equity Leadership Development," *Educational Leadership and Administration: Teaching and Program Development* 33 (2021): 18–39, https://files.eric.ed.gov/fulltext/EJ1318526.pdf.
9. *The Condition of Education 2020* (Washington, DC: US Department of Education, National Center for Education Statistics, 2020), https://nces.ed.gov/programs/coe/pdf/coe_cls.pdf.
10. Janet Patti et al., "Developing Socially, Emotionally, and Cognitively Competent School Leaders and Learning Communities," in *Handbook of Social and Emotional Learning: Research and Practice*, ed. Joseph A. Durlak, Celene E. Domitrovich, Roger P. Weissberg, and Thomas P. Gullotta (New York: Guilford, 2015), 438–452.
11. Hallberg and Santiago, "Using Narrative Inquiry to Explore Critical Reflection and Self-Awareness."
12. Esther Han, "The Importance of Reflective Leadership in Business," *Harvard Business School Online*, September 5, 2023, https://online.hbs.edu/blog/post/the-importance-of-reflective-leadership-in-business.
13. Devita Bishundat, Daviree Velazquez Phillip, and Willie Gore, "Cultivating Critical Hope: The Too Often Forgotten Dimension of Critical Leadership Development," in *New Directions for Student Leadership: Leadership Development Through Campus Employment*, ed. Adam Peck and Kathleen Callahan (New York: Wiley, 2019).
14. Hari Bapuji et al., "Corona Crisis and Inequality: Why Management Research Needs a Societal Turn," *Journal of Management* 46, no. 7 (2020): 1205–1222; Sabine O'Hara and Etienne Toussaint, "Food Access in Crisis: Food Security and COVID-19," *Ecological Economics* 180 (2021).
15. Hallberg and Santiago, "Using Narrative Inquiry to Explore Critical Reflection and Self-Awareness."
16. Dawn Louise Kramer, *Culturally Responsive School Leaders: Actions, Barriers and the Impact of Critical Self-Reflection* (PhD diss., Old Dominion University, 2021), https://digitalcommons.odu.edu/cgi/viewcontent.cgi?article=1277.&context=efl_etds.
17. Barbara Jacoby, "What Is Critical Reflection?," University of Florida Division of Student Affairs, December 2010, https://www.dso.ufl.edu/documents/nsfp/What_is_Critical_Reflection.pdf.

18. Hallberg and Santiago, "Using Narrative Inquiry to Explore Critical Reflection and Self-Awareness."
19. "What Is Critical Reflection?," Western Carolina University, https://www.wcu.edu/_files/academic-enrichment/CCESL_Critical_Reflection_Models.pdf; Hallberg and Santiago, "Using Narrative Inquiry to Explore Critical Reflection and Self-Awareness."
20. Ronald A. Beghetto, "How Times of Crisis Serve as a Catalyst for Creative Action: An Agentic Perspective," *Frontiers in Psychology* 11 (2021), https://doi.org/10.3389/fpsyg.2020.600685.
21. *The Psychology of a Crisis* (Washington, DC: Centers for Disease Control and Prevention, 2019), https://emergency.cdc.gov/cerc/ppt/CERC_Psychology_of_a_Crisis.pdf.
22. Beghetto, "How Times of Crisis Serve as a Catalyst for Creative Action."
23. "The Critical Theory of Jurgen Habermas," Buffalo State University, http://physicsed.buffalostate.edu/danowner/habcritthy.html.
24. Gerry Ewert, "Habermas and Education: A Comprehensive Overview of the Influence of Habermas in Educational Literature," *Review of Educational Research* 61, no. 3 (1991), https://doi.org/10.3102/00346543061003345.
25. Paraskevi Chatzipanagiotou and Eirene Katsarou, "Crisis Management, School Leadership in Disruptive Times and the Recovery of Schools in the Post COVID-19 Era: A Systematic Literature Review," *Education Sciences* 13, no. 2 (2023): 118, https://www.mdpi.com/2227-7102/13/2/118.
26. Sameer Sampat et al., "Will Crisis Force Us to Rethink School Leadership? Insights from the South-South Exchange," World Bank, April 13, 2022, https://blogs.worldbank.org/education/will-crisis-force-us-rethink-school-leadership-insights-south-south-exchange.
27. Hairon Salleh and Charlene Tan, "Habermas and Teacher Leadership Through Reflection," *New Educational Review* 15, no. 2 (2008), https://hub.hku.hk/handle/10722/307488.
28. "Mindful Leadership in Times of Crisis," *Saint George's Magazine*, Summer 2022, https://sgs.org/wp-content/uploads/2022/06/SGMagSummer22-P10-11-Mindful-Leadership.pdf; Sharon Kruse, *Mindful Educational Leadership: Contemplative, Cognitive, and Organizational Systems and Practices* (New York: Routledge, 2023).
29. Rob Russell and Dustin Miller, "Being a More Mindful Principal," *ASCD*, October 1, 2023, https://www.ascd.org/el/articles/being-a-more-mindful-principal.
30. Kathleen King, Danny Yahya, and Julia Mahfouz, "Six Self-Care Practices for School Leaders," *Greater Good Magazine*, May 10, 2022, https://greatergood.berkeley.edu/article/item/six_self_care_practices_for_school_leaders.
31. Nick Davis, "Mindfulness Practices for School Administrators," *Edutopia,* January 10, 2023, https://www.edutopia.org/article/mindfulness-practices-school-administrators/.
32. Leora Wolf-Prusan and David Schonfeld, *School Mental Health Crisis Leadership Lessons: Voices of Experience from Leaders in the Pacific Southwest Region* (Santa Rosa, CA: MHTTC, 2020), https://cars-rp.org/_MHTTC/docs/SMH-Crisis-Leadership-Lessons-Guide.pdf.
33. Mark Cappone, "How Self-Reflection Can Help You Lead Through a Crisis," *Lead Read Today,* Ohio State University Fisher College of Business, May 19, 2020, https://fisher.osu.edu/blogs/leadreadtoday/blog/how-self-reflection-can-help-you-lead-through-a-crisis.
34. Saqib Mansoor Ahmed, "Reflection & Reaction: What to Select," LinkedIn, October 2, 2023, https://www.linkedin.com/pulse/reflection-reaction-what-select-saqib-mansoor-ahmed-%D8%AB%D8%A7%D9%82%D8%A8-%D9%85%D9%86%D8%B5%D9%88%D8%B1-%D8%A7%D8%AD%D9%85%D8%AF/.

35. Peter G. Northouse, *Leadership: Theory and Practice*, 8th ed. (Thousand Oaks, CA: SAGE, 2019).
36. "Rubrics for the Framework for Teaching, 2013 Edition (Observable Components)," Center for Teaching Excellence, University of Illinois Urbana-Champaign, https://cte-s.education.illinois.edu/documents/danielson%20-%20domain%204%20rubric.pdf.
37. "Leadership During Crises," Kellogg Insight, Northwestern University, October 15, 2021, https://insight.kellogg.northwestern.edu/article/leadership-during-crises.
38. Kara Lasater et al., "The Data Culture Continuum: An Examination of School Data Cultures," *Educational Administration Quarterly* 56, no. 4 (2020): 533–569.
39. Elena A. Makarova, "Culturally-Based and Culturally-Biased Aspects of Knowing the Other," *Universal Journal of Educational Research* 2, no. 2 (2014): 181–187.

Chapter 4

1. Terry McDaniel and Steve Gruenert, "The Making of a WEAK Principal," *School Administrator*, June 2018, https://www.aasa.org/resources/resource/2018-jun18-mcdaniel-gruenert.
2. Mollie K. Galloway and Ann M. Ishimaru, "Equitable Leadership on the Ground: Converging on High-Leverage Practices," *Education Policy Analysis Archives* 25, no. 2 (2017), https://doi.org/10.14507/epaa.25.2205.
3. Mollie K. Galloway and Ann M. Ishimaru, "Radical Recentering: Equity in Educational Leadership Standards," *Educational Administration Quarterly* 51, no. 3 (2015): 372–408; Arjen Boin, Sanneke Kuipers, and Werner Overdijk, "Leadership in Times of Crisis: A Framework for Assessment," *International Review of Administrative Sciences* 18, no. 1 (2013): 79–91; Aida Alvinius, "A Gender Perspective on Teachers as Crisis Managers," *Nordic Journal of Feminist and Gender Research* 27, no. 2 (2019): 125–138, doi:10.1080/08038740.2019.1588373; Julia B. Bear and Anita Williams Woolley, "The Role of Gender in Team Collaboration and Performance," *Interdisciplinary Science Reviews* 36, no. 2 (2011): 146–153; Jasmine Tilghman, "Examining the Role of Hardiness, Race-Related Stress, and Racial Identity on Psychological Health Outcomes of Black College Students" (PhD diss., University of Missouri-Columbia, 2015); Rosabeth Moss Kanter, *Think Outside the Building: How Advanced Leaders Can Change the World One Smart Innovation at a Time* (New York: PublicAffairs, 2020); Edgar H. Schein, *Organizational Culture and Leadership*, 5th ed. (Hoboken, NJ: Wiley, 2017); Peter G. Northouse, *Leadership: Theory and Practice*, 8th ed. (Thousand Oaks, CA: SAGE, 2019).
4. Galloway and Ishimaru, "Radical Recentering."
5. Karen Bell and Mark Reed, "The Tree of Participation: A New Model for Inclusive Decision-Making," *Community Development Journal* 57, no. 4 (2022): 595–614, https://doi.org/10.1093/cdj/bsab018.
6. Alvinius, "A Gender Perspective on Teachers as Crisis Managers."
7. Supriya Garikipata et al., "Leading the Fight Against the Pandemic: Does Gender Really Matter?," *Feminist Economics* 27 (2021).
8. Isabel Hong, "Does Unequal Access to Leadership Cause Gender Differences in Risk Aversion?" (NHSJS Report, 2024), https://nhsjs.com/2024/does-unequal-access-to-leadership-cause-gender-differences-in-risk-aversion/; Nancy Ammon Jianakoplos and Alexandra Bernasek, "Are Women More Risk Averse?," *Economic Inquiry* 36 (1998): 620–630, https://doi.org/10.1111/j.1465-7295.1998.tb01740.x; Natassia Walley and Sarah Kaplan, "The Risky Rhetoric of Female Risk Aversion," *Stanford Social Innovation Review* (2016), https://ssir.org/articles/entry/the_risky_rhetoric_of_female_risk_aversion; Nursel Durmaz Bodur et al., "Gender Differences in Risk Aversion: Evidence from Private

Pension System in Türkiye," *Women's Studies International Forum* 101 (2023), https://doi.org/10.1016/j.wsif.2023.102843.

9. Joseph Scanlon, Ira Helsloot, and Jelle Groenendaal, "Putting It All Together: Integrating Ordinary People Into Emergency Response," *International Journal of Mass Emergencies and Disasters* 32, no. 1 (2014): 43–63.
10. Scanlon et al., "Putting It All Together"; *Hacking Diversity with Inclusive Decision Making* (Cloverpop, 2017), https://www.cloverpop.com/hubfs/Whitepapers/Cloverpop_Hacking_Diversity_Inclusive_Decision_Making_White_Paper.pdf; Jonathan Westover, "Embracing Diversity: Navigating Challenges in Implementing Inclusive Decision-Making Processes," Innovative Human Capital, August 27, 2023, https://www.innovativehumancapital.com/post/embracing-diversity-navigating-challenges-in-implementing-inclusive-decision-making-processes; Erik Larson, "When It Comes to Business Decisions, Diversity Is Not Propaganda," *Forbes,* October 24, 2018, https://www.forbes.com/sites/eriklarson/2018/10/24/when-it-comes-to-decisions-diversity-is-not-propaganda/.
11. Michael W. Apple, *Ideology and Curriculum*, 3rd ed. (New York: Routledge, 2004); Richard Delgado and Jean Stefancic, *Critical Race Theory: An Introduction*, 3rd ed. (New York: New York University Press, 2017).
12. H. Richard Milner IV, *Rac(e)ing to Class: Confronting Poverty and Race in Schools and Classrooms* (Cambridge, MA: Harvard Education Press, 2010); Sonia Nieto, *Affirming Diversity: The Sociopolitical Context of Multicultural Education*, 6th ed. (Boston: Pearson, 2018); Beverly Daniel Tatum, *Why Are All the Black Kids Sitting Together in the Cafeteria? And Other Conversations About Race* (New York: Basic Books, 2017).
13. Gloria Ladson-Billings, "From the Achievement Gap to the Education Debt: Understanding Achievement in U.S. Schools," *Educational Researcher* 35, no. 7 (2006): 3–12, https://doi.org/10.3102/0013189X035007003.
14. Delgado and Stefancic, *Critical Race Theory*; Ladson-Billings, "From the Achievement Gap to the Education Debt."
15. Mohammad Selim, "Inclusiveness in Decision Making and Avoiding Unnecessary Costs for Successful Decision Making," International Conference on Decision Aid Sciences and Application (DASA, 2021), 809–812; Larson, "When It Comes to Business Decisions, Diversity Is Not Propaganda"; *Hacking Diversity with Inclusive Decision Making*; Westover, "Embracing Diversity."
16. Susan E. Jackson, Karen E. May, and Kristina Whitney, "Understanding the Dynamics of Diversity in Decision-Making Teams," in *Team Effectiveness and Decision Making in Organizations,* ed. Richard A. Guzzo and Eduardo Salas (New York: Wiley, 1995), 261.
17. David P. Baker and Gerald K. LeTendre, *National Differences, Global Connections: Conceptual Frameworks for Comparative Education* (Stanford, CA: Stanford University Press, 2005); Anthony S. Bryk and Barbara Schneider, *Trust in Schools: A Core Resource for Improvement* (New York: Russell Sage, 2003); Michael Fullan, *Leading in a Culture of Change* (San Francisco: Jossey-Bass, 2001); Adam Kahane, *Collaborating with the Enemy: How to Work with People You Don't Agree with or Like or Trust* (Oakland: Berrett-Koehler, 2017); Peter M. Senge, *The Fifth Discipline: The Art and Practice of the Learning Organization* (New York: Doubleday, 1990).
18. Mackenzie Cramblit et al., "How Nonprofits Can Structure Inclusion Practices for Greater Impact," McKinsey and Company, August 7, 2023, https://www.mckinsey.com/capabilities/people-and-organizational-performance/our-insights/the-organization-blog/how-nonprofits-can-structure-inclusion-practices-for-greater-impact.

19. Karyn Twaronite, "How to Strengthen Inclusive Leadership in Times of Crisis," EY, April 17, 2020, https://www.ey.com/en_us/diversity-inclusiveness/inclusive-leadership-in-times-of-crisis.

Chapter 5

1. Gerald R. Ford, quoted in M. S. Rao, "Grace the Stage in Public Speaking," *Training Magazine*, September 25, 2020, https://trainingmag.com/grace-the-stage-in-public-speaking/.
2. Tracey Salamondra, "Effective Communication in Schools," *BU Journal of Graduate Studies in Education* 13, no. 1 (2021): 22–26, https://files.eric.ed.gov/fulltext/EJ1303981.pdf.
3. Liz Hollingworth et al., "Initiating Conversations and Opening Doors: How Principals Establish a Positive Building Culture to Sustain School Improvement Efforts," *Educational Management Administration and Leadership* 46, no. 6 (2017).
4. Salamondra, "Effective Communication in Schools."
5. Yvonne Bender, *The Tactful Teacher: Effective Communication with Parents, Colleagues, and Administrators* (Norwich, VT: Nomad, 2005).
6. Paulo Freire, *Pedagogy of the Oppressed: 30th Anniversary Edition* (New York: Bloomsbury, 2014) 63.
7. "Implicit Bias," American Psychological Association, https://www.apa.org/topics/implicit-bias.
8. Siddika S. Mulchan, Emily O. Wakefield, and Melissa Santos, "What COVID-19 Teaches Us About Implicit Bias in Pediatric Health Care," *Journal of Pediatric Psychology* 46, no. 2 (2021): 138–143.
9. Rhonda Magee, "How Mindfulness Can Defeat Racial Bias," *Greater Good Magazine*, Greater Good Science Center, University of California, Berkeley, May 2015, https://greatergood.berkeley.edu/article/item/how_mindfulness_can_defeat_racial_bias.
10. Adam Forman, "NYC's Silent Infrastructure Challenge: Aging Public Buildings," *City Limits*, Center for an Urban Future, March 2014, https://nycfuture.org/research/city-limits-nycs-silent-infrastructure-challenge-aging-public-buildings#:~:text=The%20average%20public%20school%20building,(OMB)%20asset%20management%20report.
11. Arjen Boin et al., "The Crisis Approach," in *Handbook of Disaster Research*, ed. Havidán Rodríguez, Enrico L. Quarantelli, and Russell R. Dynes (New York: Springer, 2007), 42–54.
12. Barak Obama, "President Obama at Sandy Hook Prayer Vigil," transcript, NPR, December 16, 2012, https://www.npr.org/2012/12/16/167412995/transcript-president-obama-at-sandy-hook-prayer-vigil#:~:text=As%20a%20community%2C%20you've,how%20Newtown%20will%20be%20remembered.
13. Obama, "President Obama at Sandy Hook Prayer Vigil."
14. Kara Grasser, "Sensemaking and Crisis Communication: How School Leaders Communicate in Times of Crisis" (EdD diss., George Washington University, 2022).
15. "Strategic Communication Planning for Success and Sustainability," National Resource Center for Mental Health Promotion and Youth Violence Prevention, https://healthysafechildren.org/sites/default/files/NRC-Communication-Workbook-Final.pdf.
16. Aura Wharton-Beck et al., "K–12 School Leadership Perspectives from the COVID-19 Pandemic," *Policy Futures in Education* 22, no. 1 (2024): 21–42.
17. Molly E. Waring et al., "Social Media Use Among Parents and Women of Childbearing Age in the US," *CDC Preventing Chronic Disease* 20 (2023).

18. *Creating a Communications Plan: Workbook A* (New York: Wallace Foundation, 2023), https://wallacefoundation.org/sites/default/files/2023-09/Workbook-A-Communication.pdf.
19. Kleis Nielsen et al., "Communications in the Coronavirus Crisis: Lessons for the Second Wave," *Reuters Institute*, October 27, 2020, https://reutersinstitute.politics.ox.ac.uk/communications-coronavirus-crisis-lessons-second-wave.
20. "Schools Are a Beacon of Hope in a Society," UNESCO International Institute for Educational Planning (IIEP), September 9, 2022, https://www.iiep.unesco.org/en/schools-are-beacon-hope-society-14282.

Chapter 6

1. Grace Lee Boggs, Scott Kurashige, and Danny Glover, *The Next American Revolution: Sustainable Activism for the Twenty-First Century* (Berkeley: University of California Press, 2012).
2. Larry Smith and Dan Riley, "School Leadership in Times of Crisis," *School Leadership and Management* 32, no. 1 (2012): 57–71.
3. Hans d'Orville, "COVID-19 Causes Unprecedented Educational Disruption: Is There a Road Towards a New Normal?," *Prospects* 49, no. 1 (2020): 11–15.
4. Samantha Handler, "As Census Moves Online, City Comptroller Warns of Digital Divide and Recommends Steps to Bridge It," *Gotham Gazette*, July 24, 2019, https://www.gothamgazette.com/city/8692-as-census-moves-online-city-comptroller-stringer-warns-of-digital-divide.
5. Heather J. Hough, "COVID-19: The Educational Equity Crisis and the Opportunity Ahead," Brookings Institution, April 29, 2021, https://www.brookings.edu/articles/covid-19-the-educational-equity-crisis-and-the-opportunity-ahead/.
6. Heather Schwartz and Matthew M. Chingos, "COVID-19, the Educational Equity Crisis, and the Opportunity Ahead," Brookings Institution, April 29, 2021, https://www.brookings.edu/articles/covid-19-the-educational-equity-crisis-and-the-opportunity-ahead/.
7. Patricia Virella and Casey D. Cobb, "Leveraging the Crisis for Equity and Access in the Long Term: A Brief Research Report," *Frontiers in Education* 6 (2021), https://doi.org/10.3389/feduc.2021.618051.
8. Hough, "COVID-19: The Educational Equity Crisis and the Opportunity Ahead."
9. Josh Parrish, "Creating More Equitable Schools Amid a Pandemic: Yes, It Can Be Done!," *The Education Trust*, May 4, 2022, https://edtrust.org/the-equity-line/creating-more-equitable-schools-amid-a-pandemic-yes-it-can-be-done/.
10. Hough, "COVID-19: The Educational Equity Crisis and the Opportunity Ahead."
11. Alec I. Kennedy, Ana María Mejía-Rodríguez, and Andrés Strello, "Inequality in Remote Learning Quality During COVID-19: Student Perspectives and Mitigating Factors," *Large-Scale Assessments in Education* 10 (2022): 29.
12. Hough, "COVID-19: The Educational Equity Crisis and the Opportunity Ahead"; Chukwuma Eruchalu et al., "The Expanding Digital Divide: Digital Health Access Inequities During the COVID-19 Pandemic in New York City," *Urban Health* 98, no. 2 (2021): 183–186; "Broadband and Equal Access to the Internet in New York City," New York City Council, https://council.nyc.gov/data/internet-access/#:~:text=About%20a%20quarter%20of%20New,have%20high%2Dspeed%20broadband%20service.
13. Mario Jackson, "What Principals Need to Know to Respond to a Crisis," *Phi Delta Kappan* 104, no. 5 (2023): 66–67, https://kappanonline.org/principals-crisis-response-jackson/.

14. Salimah Jasani-Nelson, "Advancing Educational Equity in Times of Political Crisis," *Education Elements* (blog), September 26, 2023, https://www.edelements.com/blog/advancing-educational-equity-in-times-of-political-crisis.
15. Scott McLeod and Shelley Dulsky, "Resilience, Reorientation, and Reinvention: School Leadership During the Early Months of the COVID-19 Pandemic," *Frontiers in Education* 11 (2021), https://doi.org/10.3389/feduc.2021.637075.
16. Jasani-Nelson, "Advancing Educational Equity in Times of Political Crisis"; Jennifer O'Day and Dale Marsden, *Educational Leadership in Crisis: Reflections from a Pandemic* (California Collaborative on District Reform, 2022), https://files.eric.ed.gov/fulltext/ED622164.pdf.
17. Jamele Rigolini, Rafael de Hoyos, and Ha Thi Hong Nguyen, *Protecting Human Capital Through Shocks and Crises: How Lessons Learned from the COVID-19 Response Across Eastern Europe and the South Caucasus Can Be Used to Build Better and More Resilient Human Development Systems* (Washington, DC: World Bank, 2023).
18. "Cambridge Public Schools - Massachusetts," Niche, 2023, https://www.niche.com/k12/d/cambridge-public-schools-ma/; "Inequitable School and Classroom Experiences," Cambridge Public Schools, https://www.cpsd.us/building_equity_bridges/barriers_to_equity/inequitable_school_and_classroom_experiences.
19. Carine Rongier et al., "Towards a Crisis Performance Measurement System," *International Journal of Computer Integrated Manufacturing* 26, no. 11 (2013): 1087–1102; D. Hanfling, J. L. Hick, and C. Stroud, eds., *Committee on Crisis Standards of Care: A Toolkit for Indicators and Triggers* (Washington, DC: Board on Health Sciences Policy, Institute of Medicine, 2013).
20. Rongier et al., "Towards a Crisis Performance Measurement System."
21. "Evaluation During a Crisis or Disaster: Evaluation Toolkit," National Sexual Violence Resource Center, https://www.nsvrc.org/prevention/evaluation-toolkit/evaluation-during-crisis-or-disaster.
22. Nagl, "How Educational Leaders Impact Diversity, Equity, and Inclusion in Schools"; Jaime Saavedra, "A Silent and Unequal Education Crisis: And the Seeds for Its Solution," *World Bank Education* (blog), January 5, 2021, https://blogs.worldbank.org/education/silent-and-unequal-education-crisis-and-seeds-its-solution.

Chapter 7

1. Deena Zaru and Briana Stewart, "Buffalo Supermarket Reopens, While Community 'Food Desert' Concerns Remain," *ABC News*, July 15, 2022, https://abcnews.go.com/US/buffalo-supermarket-reopens-community-food-desert-concerns-remain/story?id=86696929.
2. Judith D. Hackman, "Organization and Environment: A Theory of Resource Allocations for Higher Education," ASHE Annual Meeting Paper (1984).
3. Joseph L. Bower, *Managing the Resource Allocation Process: A Study of Corporate Planning and Investment* (Boston: Harvard Business School Press, 1970).
4. Kenneth Shores and Matthew P. Steinberg, "Fiscal Federalism and K–12 Education Funding: Policy Lessons from Two Educational Crises," *Educational Researcher* 51, no. 8 (2022), https://doi.org/10.3102/0013189X221125764.
5. "Collapse and Recovery: How COVID-19 Eroded Human Capital and What to Do About It," World Bank, February 16, 2023, https://www.worldbank.org/en/publication/human-capital/publication/collapse-recovery-how-covid-19-eroded-human-capital-and-what-to-do-about-it.

6. Carol Mutch, "How Schools Build Community Resilience Capacity and Social Capital in Disaster Preparedness, Response and Recovery," *International Journal of Disaster Risk Reduction* 92 (2023), https://www.sciencedirect.com/science/article/pii/S2212420923002157.
7. Devin Vodicka, "4 Ways to Increase Inclusion and Engagement When Allocating Resources," *Learner-Centered Collaborative*, https://learnercentered.org/blog/4-ways-to-increase-inclusion-and-engagement-when-allocating-resources/.
8. Megan Kuhfeld et al., "The COVID-19 School Year: Learning and Recovery Across 2020–2021," *AERA Open* 8, no. 1 (2022), https://journals.sagepub.com/doi/full/10.1177/23328584221099306.
9. Rachel M. Perera, Ayesha K. Hashim, and Hayley R. Weddle, "Family Engagement Is Critical for Schools' COVID-19 Recovery Efforts," Brookings Institution, December 6, 2022, https://www.brookings.edu/articles/family-engagement-is-critical-for-schools-covid-19-recovery-efforts/.
10. "Strategies for Equitable Family Engagement," US Department of Education, accessed July 18, 2024, https://oese.ed.gov/resources/oese-technical-assistance-centers/state-support-network/resources/strategies-equitable-family-engagement/.
11. "Biden-Harris Administration Announces More Than $11 Million to Expand and Support Parent Education and Family Engagement Efforts," US Department of Education, October 11, 2023, https://www.ed.gov/news/press-releases/biden-harris-administration-announces-more-11-million-expand-and-support-parent-education-and-family-engagement-efforts.
12. Catherine Jacques and Alma Villegas, *Strategies for Equitable Family Engagement* (Washington, DC: US Department of Education, 2018), https://oese.ed.gov/files/2020/10/equitable_family_engag_508.pdf.
13. "American Rescue Plan (ARP) Act of 2021," US Department of Education, https://www2.ed.gov/about/offices/list/ope/arp.html.
14. "Elementary and Secondary School Emergency Relief Fund Tracker," National Conference of State Legislatures, January 25, 2022, https://www.ncsl.org/in-dc/standing-committees/education/elementary-and-secondary-school-emergency-relief-fund-tracker.
15. "NASFAA Higher Education Emergency Relief Fund (HEERF I) Reference Page," National Association of Student Financial Aid Administrators, March 7, 2022, https://www.nasfaa.org/covid19_heerf.
16. Michael D. Meyer, *Impact of Program Implementation on the Effectiveness of the American Recovery and Reinvestment Act: The Case of Transportation*, Special Report 312 (Washington, DC: National Academies Press, 2013), https://nap.nationalacademies.org/resource/18628/sr312Meyer.pdf.
17. Hayley B. Gershengorn, "Inequitable Resource Allocation Amidst a Pandemic—A Crisis Within a Crisis," *Journal of the American Medical Association* 5, no. 9 (2022), https://jamanetwork.com/journals/jamanetworkopen/fullarticle/2790110.
18. Kristalina Georgieva, Sebastián Sosa, and Björn Rother, "Global Food Crisis Demands Support for People, Open Trade, Bigger Local Harvests," *International Monetary Fund* (blog), September 30, 2022, https://www.imf.org/en/Blogs/Articles/2022/09/30/global-food-crisis-demands-support-for-people-open-trade-bigger-local-harvests.
19. Julian W. März, Søren Holm, and Michael Schlander, "Resource Allocation in the Covid-19 Health Crisis: Are Covid-19 Preventive Measures Consistent with the Rule of Rescue?," *Medicine, Health Care and Philosophy* 24, no. 4 (2021), https://www.ncbi.nlm.nih.gov/pmc/articles/PMC8364940/.

20. Jason Willis et al., *Resource Allocation Strategies to Support the Four Domains for Rapid School Improvement* (San Francisco: WestEd, The Center on School Turnaround, 2019), https://files.eric.ed.gov/fulltext/ED602981.pdf.
21. "School Leaders as Equity Leaders," Education Strategies, https://www.erstrategies.org/toolkits/school_leaders_as_equity_leaders.
22. Erika James and Lynn Perry Wooten, "In a Crisis, Great Leaders Prioritize Listening," *Harvard Business Review*, September 2022, https://hbr.org/2022/09/in-a-crisis-great-leaders-prioritize-listening.
23. "School Crisis Recovery and Renewal Resources," School Crisis Healing, https://schoolcrisishealing.org/school-crisis-recovery-renewal-resources/.
24. Jonathan Travers, "What Is Resource Equity?," ERS Working Paper, October 2018, https://files.eric.ed.gov/fulltext/ED593369.pdf.
25. "The Problems of Equity in Resource Allocation," Ohio Leadership Advisory Council, https://ohioleadership.org/problem-of-equity-in-resource-allocation.
26. David S. Knight et al., "Prioritizing School Finance Equity During an Economic Crisis," *Educational Finance and Policy* 17, no. 1 (2022): 188, https://direct.mit.edu/edfp/article/17/1/188/106761/Prioritizing-School-Finance-Equity-during-an.
27. Diane Pan et al., *Examination of Resource Allocation in Education: Connecting Spending to Student Performance* (Austin, TX: Southwest Educational Development Laboratory, 2003), https://sedl.org/pubs/policyresearch/policydocs/Examination.pdf.
28. Kimberly Ann Harris, "Effects of Resource Allocation on Student Academic Achievement and Self-Perceptions of Success in an Urban Setting" (Bachelor's thesis, Dominican University, September 2014), https://scholar.dominican.edu/senior-theses/4; Michael Hansen, Jon Valant, and Nicolas Zerbino, "Do School Districts Allocate More Resources to Economically Disadvantaged Students?," Brookings Institution, December 16, 2022, https://www.brookings.edu/articles/do-school-districts-alloca; Brian J. Caldwell, *Principles and Practices in Resource Allocation to Schools Under Conditions of Radical Decentralization* (Washington, DC: National Center for Education Statistics, 1997), https://nces.ed.gov/pubs97/97535h.pdf.
29. L. Berger et al. "Uncertainty and Decision-Making During a Crisis: How to Make Policy Decisions in the COVID-19 Context?," University of Chicago, Becker Friedman Institute for Economics working paper (2020-95).
30. Gavin T. L. Brown, "Schooling Beyond COVID-19: An Unevenly Distributed Future," *Frontiers in Education* 5 (2020): 82.
31. Peter Anagnostakos et al., "Banks Versus Hurricanes: A Case Study of Puerto Rico After Hurricanes Irma and Maria," Federal Reserve Bank of New York Staff Reports, No. 1078, 2023, https://www.newyorkfed.org/medialibrary/media/research/staff_reports/sr1078.pdf?sc_lang=en.
32. "Earth 107: Introduction to Earth Science," Penn State E-Education, https://www.e-education.psu.edu/earth107/node/1664.
33. Sameer Sampat et al., "Will the Crisis Force Us to Rethink School Leadership? Insights from the South-South Exchange," *World Bank* (blog), April 13, 2022, https://blogs.worldbank.org/education/will-crisis-force-us-rethink-school-leadership-insights-south-south-exchange.
34. J. Goswick et al., "Lessons Identified by the Joplin School Leadership After Responding to a Catastrophic Tornado," *Journal of Contingencies and Crisis Management* 26, no. 4 (2018): 544–553.
35. https://preprod.savethechildren.org/content/dam/usa/reports/emergency-response/hurricane-maria-1-yr-report-sept-2018.pdf.

Chapter 8

1. Angela Y. Davis, *Women, Race and Class* (New York: First Vintage, 1983).
2. Leticia Alvarez Gutiérrez et al., "Community-Centered School Leadership: Radical Care and Apertures During COVID-19," *AERA Open* 8, no. 1 (2022): 1–14.
3. Chauncey K. Robinson, "Angela Davis: 'Education Must Not Be Sacrificed at the Altar of Profit.'" *People's World*, June 19, 2018, https://www.peoplesworld.org/article/angela-davis-education-must-not-be-sacrificed-at-the-altar-of-profit/.
4. Robert F. Smith, "Understanding Systemic Racism in Education," *Robert F. Smith* (blog), August 22, 2023, https://robertsmith.com/systemic-racism-in-education/.
5. Jessika Bottiani et al., "Buffering Effects of Racial Discrimination on School Engagement: The Role of Culturally Responsive Teachers and Caring School Police," *Journal of School Health* 90, no. 12 (2020): 1019–1029; Kirsten Weir, "Inequality in School: How Racial Bias Affects Student Achievement," *Monitor on Psychology* 47, no. 10 (2016), https://www.apa.org/monitor/2016/11/cover-inequality-school.
6. Bottiani et al., "Buffering Effects of Racial Discrimination on School Engagement"; *K–12 Education: Students' Experiences with Bullying, Hate Speech, Hate Crimes, and Victimization in Schools* (Washinton, DC: US Government Accountability Office, GAO-22-104341, 2021), https://www.gao.gov/products/gao-22-104341.
7. Smith, "Understanding Systemic Racism in Education."
8. Weir, "Inequality in School."
9. "Racism as a Public Health Crisis in Schools," American Public Health Association, Center for School, Health and Education, January 2022, http://schoolbasedhealthcare.org/cshe-bulletin/january-2022.
10. "Racism as a Public Health Crisis in Schools"; Anamika Twyman-Ghoshal and Danielle Carkin Lacorazza, "Strategies for Antiracist and Decolonized Teaching," *Faculty Focus*, March 2021, https://www.facultyfocus.com/articles/equality-inclusion-and-diversity/strategies-for-antiracist-and-decolonized-teaching/.
11. Jamilah Pitts, "What Anti-Racism Really Means for Educators," *SPLC Learning for Justice*, September 11, 2020, https://www.learningforjustice.org/magazine/what-antiracism-really-means-for-educators.
12. Kaleen Daneil Weiland, "Don't Let Their Future Blow Away: An Integrated Methodology to Inform School Leaders of the Dimensions and Determinants of School Vulnerability Leading to Disaster Learning Loss" (PhD diss., Morgridge College of Education, 2019).
13. K. C. Cowan et al., *A Framework for Safe and Successful Schools* [Brief] (Bethesda, MD: National Association of School Psychologists, 2013), https://www.naesp.org/sites/default/files/Framework%20for%20Safe%20and%20Successful%20School%20Environments_FINAL_0.pdf.
14. Cowan et al., *A Framework for Safe and Successful Schools.*
15. Bill Mulford, "School Leaders: Challenging Roles and Impact on Teacher and School Effectiveness," Commissioned Paper, Organization for Economic Co-operation and Development, April 2003.
16. Eleanor Drago-Severson, Jessica Blum-DeStefano, and Deborah Brooks Lawrence, *Growing for Justice: A Guide for Educators* (Thousand Oaks, CA: Corwin, 2023).
17. Rita Basu, "Emotional Intelligence and Transformational Leadership Skills of Correctional Officers of West Bengal," *Management Today* 5, no. 2 (2015): 67–74.

18. Madeline Will, "Teacher Strikes Explained: Recent Strikes, Where They're Illegal, and More," *Education Week*, October 2023, https://www.edweek.org/teaching-learning/teacher-strikes-explained-recent-strikes-where-theyre-illegal-and-more/2023/10.
19. "Chicago Teachers Strike: What You Need to Know," American Bar Association, *Health Law Section News*, November 2019, https://www.americanbar.org/groups/health_law/section-news/2019/11/chi-tea/.
20. "The Case for School Nursing," National Association of School Nurses, 2012, https://higherlogicdownload.s3.amazonaws.com/NASN/3870c72d-fff9-4ed7-833f-215de278d256/UploadedImages/PDFs/Advocacy/advocacy_The_Case_for_School_Nursing.pdf.
21. "The Case for School Nursing."
22. Christopher Day, Pam Sammons, and Kristine Gorgen, *Successful School Leadership* (Reading, UK: Education Development Trust, 2016), https://files.eric.ed.gov/fulltext/ED614324.pdf.
23. Lindsay Dworkin and Karyn Lewis, "To Help Students Recover from the Pandemic, Education Leaders Must Prioritize Equity and Evidence," Brookings Institution, October 13, 2021, https://www.brookings.edu/articles/to-help-students-recover-from-the-pandemic-education-leaders-must-prioritize-equity-and-evidence/.
24. "Domain 1: Instructional Leadership," Colorado Department of Education, https://www.cde.state.co.us/fourdomains/domainone.
25. "7 Ways Teachers & School Leaders Can Support Students in a Post-Pandemic Year," *PBS Education*, September 16, 2021, https://www.pbs.org/education/blog/7-ways-teachers-school-leaders-can-support-students-in-a-post-pandemic-year.
26. "Thriving Communities, Healthy Landscapes," Rainforest Alliance, November 29, 2022, https://www.rainforest-alliance.org/in-the-field/thriving-communities-healthy-landscapes/.
27. Tracey Benson and Sarah Fiarman, *Unconscious Bias in Schools: A Developmental Approach to Exploring Race and Racism* (Cambridge, MA: Harvard Education Press, 2020).
28. Benson and Fiarman, *Unconscious Bias in Schools.*
29. Jacqueline Kareem et al., "Transformational Educational Leaders Inspire School Educators' Commitment," *Frontiers in Education* 8 (2023), https://doi.org/10.3389/feduc.2023.1171513; Sonja Bloetner, "Transformational Leadership: The Most Impactful Actions for School Improvement," LinkedIn, May 7, 2023, https://www.linkedin.com/pulse/transformational-leadership-most-impactful-actions-school-bloetner/.
30. Bloetner, "Transformational Leadership."
31. Sylvia Segura Pirtle and Don Doggett, "Leadership Actions for Transforming Schools," *SEDL Insights* 1, no. 1 (2013), https://sedl.org/insights/1-1/leadership_actions.pdf.
32. Carolyn Stein, "In the Wake of COVID-19, One Million California Students Were Chronically Absent. Why Are Kids Missing So Much School?," *Mercury News*, August 12, 2023, https://www.mercurynews.com/2023/08/10/in-the-wake-of-covid-19-one-million-california-students-were-chronically-absent-why-are-kids-missing-so-much-school/.
33. Paloma Esquivel, "Nearly Half of LAUSD Students Have Been Chronically Absent This Year, Data Show," *Los Angeles Times,* March 31, 2022, https://www.latimes.com/california/story/2022-03-31/lausd-students-chronic-absent-amid-covid-pandemic.
34. Stein, "In the Wake of COVID-19, One Million California Students Were Chronically Absent."
35. Emma García and Elaine Weiss, "Student Absenteeism: Who Misses School and How Missing School Matters for Performance," Economic Policy Institute, September 25, 2018, https://www.epi.org/publication/student-absenteeism-who-misses-school-and-how-missing-school-matters-for-performance/.

36. Bianca Vasquez Toness, "The Pandemic's Missing Students," Associated Press, August 11, 2023, https://apnews.com/article/back-to-school-attendance-pandemic-chronic-absenteeism-90c05e3013b72802439565250d1adc33.
37. Jonaki Mehta, "3 Years Since the Pandemic Wrecked Attendance, Kids Still Aren't Showing Up to School," *NPR*, March 2, 2023, https://www.npr.org/2023/03/02/1160358099/school-attendance-chronic-absenteeism-covid.
38. Chuck Flores and Jack Bagwell, "Social Justice Leadership as Inclusion: Promoting Inclusive Practices to Ensure Equity for All," *Educational Leadership and Administration: Teaching and Program Development* 1 (2021): 31–43, https://files.eric.ed.gov/fulltext/EJ1318516.pdf.
39. Nelda Cambron-McCabe and Martha M. McCarthy, "Educating School Leaders for Social Justice," *Educational Policy* 19, no. 1 (2005): 201–222.
40. Paul Miller, "School Leaders Leading Anti-Racism and Inclusion: Evidence from Schools in England," *Equity in Education and Society* 3, no. 1 (2024): 46–60.
41. *Understanding and Advocating for Equity in Education: Program Report 2021* (Washington, DC: National Education Association, 2021), https://www.nea.org/sites/default/files/2021-10/LJS%20Program%20Report%202021%20FINAL.pdf.
42. "Shining a Light on Inequity in Education: Actions You Can Take," *New Leaders* (blog), March 22, 2022, https://www.newleaders.org/blog/shining-a-light-on-inequity-in-education-actions-you-can-take.
43. Deirdra Preis, "Transformational School Leadership to Dismantle Inequitable Systems," https://oxfordre.com/education/display/10.1093/acrefore/9780190264093.001.0001/acrefore-9780190264093-e-1815, *Oxford Research Encyclopedia of Education* (Oxford: Oxford University Press, 2023).
44. Patricia Virella and Casey Cobb, "Leveraging the Crisis for Equity and Access in the Long Term: A Brief Research Report," *Frontiers in Education* 6 (2021), https://doi.org/10.3389/feduc.2021.618051.
45. Virella and Cobb, "Leveraging the Crisis for Equity and Access in the Long Term."
46. Denisa R. Superville, "How Principals Can Help Support Students Through a Mental Health Crisis," *Education Week*, May 29, 2023, https://www.edweek.org/leadership/how-principals-can-help-support-students-through-a-mental-health-crisis/2023/05.
47. Eva Alisic, "Teachers' Perspectives on Providing Support to Children After Trauma: A Qualitative Study," *School Psychology Quarterly* 27, no. 1 (2012): 51.
48. *Protecting Youth Mental Health: The U.S. Surgeon General's Advisory* (Washington, DC: US Department of Health and Human Services, 2021), https://www.ncbi.nlm.nih.gov/books/NBK575986/; Katie Eklund, "Advocating for School Mental Health Services Within State Policy," *NASP Research and Policy Matters* (blog), https://www.nasponline.org/research-and-policy/policy-matters-blog/advocating-for-school-mental-health-services-within-state-policy.
49. Rebecca T. Leeb et al., "Mental Health–Related Emergency Department Visits Among Children Aged <18 Years During the COVID-19 Pandemic—United States, January 1–October 17, 2020," *CDC Morbidity and Mortality Weekly Report* 69, no. 45 (2020): 1675–1680.
50. "New CDC Data Illuminate Youth Mental Health Threats During the COVID-19 Pandemic," *CDC Newsroom*, March 31, 2022, https://www.cdc.gov/media/releases/2022/p0331-youth-mental-health-covid-19.html.
51. Jasmine A. L. Raw et al., "Examining Changes in Parent-Reported Child and Adolescent Mental Health Throughout the UK's First COVID-19 National Lockdown," *Journal of*

Child Psychology and Psychiatry 62, no. 12 (2021): 1391–1401, https://doi.org/10.1111/jcpp.13490.

52. Anna Ordóñez et al., eds., *Child and Adolescent Mental Health During the Covid-19 Pandemic* (Child and Adolescent Psychiatry and Mental Health, BMC Psychiatry, 2024), https://www.biomedcentral.com/collections/camh-covid19.
53. Leeb et al., "Mental Health–Related Emergency Department Visits Among Children."
54. Superville, "How Principals Can Help Support Students Through a Mental Health Crisis."
55. Eklund, "Advocating for School Mental Health Services Within State Policy."
56. "For Educators: How to Talk About Mental Health," Substance Abuse and Mental Health Services Administration, https://www.samhsa.gov/mental-health/how-to-talk/educators.
57. Sydney Daniello et al., *Addressing the Youth Mental Health Crisis: The Urgent Need for More Education, Services, And Supports* (Alexandria, VA: Mental Health America, 2020), https://mhanational.org/addressing-youth-mental-health-crisis-urgent-need-more-education-services-and-supports.
58. "School Violence Prevention: Guidelines for Administrators and Crisis Teams," National Association of School Psychologists, https://www.nasponline.org/resources-and-publications/resources-and-podcasts/school-safety-and-crisis/school-violence-resources/school-violence-prevention/school-violence-prevention-guidelines-for-administrators-and-crisis-teams.
59. *Protecting Youth Mental Health: The U.S. Surgeon General's Advisory* (Washington, DC: US Department of Health and Human Services, 2021), https://www.ncbi.nlm.nih.gov/books/NBK575986/.
60. Selim Algar, "De Blasio Schools Boss Carranza Lauds 'Opportunity' of Deadly Coronavirus: 'Never Waste a Good Crisis,'" *New York Post,* May 5, 2020, https://nypost.com/2020/05/05/richard-carranza-calls-for-nyc-doe-overhaul-amid-coronavirus-crisis/.
61. Virella and Cobb, "Leveraging the Crisis for Equity and Access in the Long Term."
62. Maribel E. Paulino, "Lead Self to Lead Others: Intersection of Courage, Self-Awareness, and Leadership Communication for Self-Leadership and Development" (Master's thesis, Baruch College, City University of New York, August 21, 2023), https://academicworks.cuny.edu/cgi/viewcontent.cgi?article=1176&context=bb_etds.
63. Ken Williams, *Ruthless Equity: How to Disrupt Learning for Students of Color* (Unfold the Soul, 2022).
64. Paulino, "Lead Self to Lead Others."
65. Rene O. Guillaume, Noelle Witherspoon Arnold, and Azadeh F. Osanloo, eds., *Handbook of Urban Educational Leadership*, 2nd ed. (Lanham, MD: Rowman and Littlefield, 2021).
66. Frances Hesselbein, "Leadership Tip of the Week: Being the Change Means Radical Courage," *Fisher Leadership Initiative*, August 2, 2022, https://fisher.osu.edu/blogs/leadreadtoday/blog/leadership-tip-of-the-week-being-the-change-means-radical-courage.
67. Paulino, "Lead Self to Lead Others."
68. Cory Colton, "Busting Systemic Exclusion Takes Humility, Curiosity, and Courage," LinkedIn, July 19, 2020, https://www.linkedin.com/pulse/busting-systemic-exclusion-takes-humility-curiosity-courage-colton/.
69. Paulino, "Lead Self to Lead Others."
70. Sarah Stachowiak, *Pathways for Change: 10 Theories to Inform Advocacy and Policy* (Seattle, WA: Organizational Research Services Impact, Center for Evaluation Innovation, 2013).
71. Steve Buckley, "Advocacy Strategies and Approaches: Overview," Association for Progressive Communications, https://www.apc.org/en/advocacy-strategies-and-approaches-overview.

72. Wayne Visser and Polly Courtice, "Sustainability Leadership: Linking Theory and Practice," *SSRN* (October 21, 2011), https://ssrn.com/abstract=1947221.
73. Crystal Raypole, "A Savior No One Needs: Unpacking and Overcoming the White Savior Complex," *Healthline*, July 14, 2021, https://www.healthline.com/health/white-saviorism; Colleen Murphy, "What Is White Savior Complex and Why Is It Harmful?," *Health*, August 17, 2023, https://www.health.com/mind-body/health-diversity-inclusion/white-savior-complex.
74. Murphy, "What Is White Savior Complex and Why Is It Harmful?"
75. Maya Elie, "Authors' Advice for White Teachers in Urban Schools: Drop the Savior Complex and Learn from Students," *NEA Today*, July 2016, https://www.nea.org/nea-today/all-news-articles/authors-advice-white-teachers-urban-schools-drop-savior-complex-and-learn-students.
76. *Understanding and Advocating for Equity in Education.*
77. Raypole, "A Savior No One Needs."
78. Christopher Emdin, *For White Folks Who Teach in the Hood . . . and the Rest of Y'all Too: Reality Pedagogy and Urban Education* (Boston: Beacon, 2017).
79. Eva Harrell, "Combating White Saviorism in Community-Engaged Learning," (MEd thesis, Merrimack College, 2022), https://scholarworks.merrimack.edu/cgi/viewcontent.cgi?article=1073&context=soe_student_ce.
80. Teju Cole, "The White Savior Industrial Complex," *The Atlantic*, March 21, 2012, https://www.theatlantic.com/international/archive/2012/03/the-white-savior-industrial-complex/254843/.
81. Eric Rosen and Katherine Cowan, "The Role of Schools in Supporting Traumatized Students," *Principal's Research Review* 8, no. 6 (2013): 1–8.
82. Lisa Delpit, *Other People's Children: Cultural Conflict in the Classroom* (New York: New Press, 1995).
83. Sarah A. Benton, "The Savior Complex," *Psychology Today*, February 2017, https://www.psychologytoday.com/us/blog/the-high-functioning-alcoholic/201702/the-savior-complex.
84. Larry Ferlazzo, "Education Funders Need to Ditch the Savior Complex," *Education Week*, July 21, 2023, https://www.edweek.org/policy-politics/opinion-education-funders-need-to-ditch-the-savior-complex/2023/07.
85. Rosen and Cowan, "The Role of Schools in Supporting Traumatized Students."
86. Sindhu Kutty, "How to Mitigate the Destructive Force of Insecure Leaders," *Forbes*, September 23, 2020, https://www.forbes.com/sites/forbesbusinesscouncil/2020/09/23/how-to-mitigate-the-destructive-force-of-insecure-leaders/?sh=38a29348288a.
87. Alisic, "Teachers' Perspectives on Providing Support to Children After Trauma."
88. Elizabeth A. Harris, "Displaced by Storm, Puerto Rican Students Land in New York," *New York Times*, January 28, 2018, https://www.nytimes.com/2018/01/28/nyregion/hurricane-maria-puerto-rican-college-nyc.html; Josh Einiger, "New York City Schools Brace for Influx of Students from Puerto Rico," *ABC7 New York*, October 12, 2017, https://abc7ny.com/hurricane-maria-new-york-city-puerto-rico-education/2525779/; Joseph Spector, "After Hurricane Maria: Rochester Absorbs More Displaced Students Than Other NY Districts," *Democrat and Chronicle*, March 23, 2018, https://www.democratandchronicle.com/story/news/politics/albany/2018/03/23/hurricane-maria-rochester-ny-puerto-rican-students/395305002/.
89. Carmen Heredia Rodriguez, "Hurricane Maria's Legacy: Thousands of Puerto Rican Students Show PTSD Symptoms," *PBS*, April 27, 2019, https://www.pbs.org/newshour/nation/hurricane-marias-legacy-thousands-of-puerto-rican-students-show-ptsd-symptoms.

90. Chantal Francois and Jennie Weiner, "Internal, Moral, and Market Accountability: Leading Urban Schools During the Covid-19 Pandemic," *Urban Education* (2022), https://www.ncbi.nlm.nih.gov/pmc/articles/PMC9047607/.
91. John B. Diamond and James P. Spillane, "High Stakes Accountability in Urban Elementary Schools: Challenging or Reproducing Inequality?," *Teachers College Record* 106, no. 6 (2004): 1145–1176.

Chapter 9

1. "Billion-Dollar Weather and Climate Disasters," US NOAA National Centers for Environmental Information, 2024, https://www.ncei.noaa.gov/access/billions/.
2. Penny Gusner and Les Masterson, "Natural Disaster Facts and Statistics 2024," *Forbes*, modified June 7, 2023, https://www.forbes.com/advisor/homeowners-insurance/natural-disaster-statistics/#one.
3. "Conflict Watchlist 2024," Armed Conflict Location and Event Data, https://acleddata.com/conflict-watchlist-2024/.

Appendix A

1. William G. Tierney, "Life History's History: Subjects Foretold," *Qualitative Inquiry* 4, no. 1 (1998): 49–70.
2. Michael Quinn Patton, *Qualitative Evaluation and Research Methods* (Newbury Park, CA: Sage, 1990), 169.
3. William D. Nowling and Matthew W. Seeger, "Sensemaking and Crisis Revisited: The Failure of Sensemaking During the Flint Water Crisis," *Journal of Applied Communication Research* 48, no. 2 (2020): 270–289.
4. Larry Smith and Dan Riley, "School Leadership in Times of Crisis," *School Leadership and Management* 32, no. 1 (2012): 57–71; Carol Mutch and Hannah McKnight, "'I Couldn't Do What I Needed to Do for My Own Family': Teacher-Parents During COVID-19 Lockdowns," *Social Sciences and Humanities Open* 7, no. 1 (2023): 100401; Patricia Virella and Casey Cobb, "Leveraging the Crisis for Equity and Access in the Long Term: A Brief Research Report," *Frontiers in Education* 6 (2021), https://doi.org/10.3389/feduc.2021.618051.
5. Kathy Charmaz and Robert Thornberg, "The Pursuit of Quality in Grounded Theory," *Qualitative Research in Psychology* 18, no. 3 (2021): 305–327.
6. Egon G. Guba and Yvonna S. Lincoln, "Competing Paradigms in Qualitative Research," in *Handbook of Qualitative Research*, ed. N. K. Denzin and Y. S. Lincoln (Thousand Oaks, CA: Sage, 1994); Matthew B. Miles and A. Michael Huberman, "Drawing Valid Meaning from Qualitative Data: Toward a Shared Craft," *Educational Researcher* 13, no. 5 (1984): 20–30; Juliet Corbin and Anselm Strauss, *Basics of Qualitative Research: Techniques and Procedures for Developing Grounded Theory* (Los Angeles: Sage, 2014).
7. Egon G. Guba and Yvonna S. Lincoln, "Competing Paradigms in Qualitative Research," in *Handbook of Qualitative Research*, ed. N. K. Denzin and Y. S. Lincoln (Thousand Oaks, CA: Sage, 1994); Matthew B. Miles and A. Michael Huberman, "Drawing Valid Meaning from Qualitative Data: Toward a Shared Craft," *Educational Researcher* 13, no. 5 (1984): 20–30; Juliet Corbin and Anselm Strauss, *Basics of Qualitative Research: Techniques and Procedures for Developing Grounded Theory* (Los Angeles: Sage, 2014).
8. Smith and Riley, "School Leadership in Times of Crisis."

9. Virella, and Cobb, "Leveraging the Crisis for Equity and Access."
10. Johnny Saldana, *Fundamentals of Qualitative Research* (Oxford: Oxford University Press, 2011).

Appendix B

1. Nick Davies, "Mindfulness Practices for Administrators," *Edutopia,* January 10, 2023, https://www.edutopia.org/article/mindfulness-practices-school-administrators/.
2. Anita Johnson, *Mindfulness Practices Used During Crisis Leadership Reported by Minnesota Secondary School Administrators* (EdD diss., St. Cloud State University, 2022).
3. Sharon D. Kruse, *Mindfulness and School Leadership: Contemplative, Cognitive, and Organizational Systems and Practices* (New York: Routledge, 2023).

Acknowledgments

Thank you to all who supported me on this journey to complete this book.

About the Author

Patricia M. Virella is an assistant professor of urban educational leadership at Montclair State University. Her research focuses on implementing equity-oriented leadership through leader responses, programmatic interventions, and preparation as well as on examining how school leaders can respond to crises without further harming marginalized communities. Virella is the founder of My Academic Writing Routine, an organization committed to demystifying academic writing for graduate students, focusing on graduate students of color. She began her career as an elementary school teacher in New York, later serving as an elementary school principal for an all-girls charter school in Manhattan.

INDEX